Peter Fenton describes himself as … rugby coach and writer who is a regi… … and corporate functions. He also writes for *Inside Rugby* magazine and is a regular contributor to Rugby Super 12 and Test Match programmes.

In his previous career he was chief sound mixer on 150 Australian feature films, including *Newsfront, Caddie, Sunday Too Far Away, Picnic At Hanging Rock, My Brilliant Career, The Devil's Playground, Gallipoli, Phar Lap, The Russia House* and *Paradise Road*. He also wrote and co-produced two documentary films on the Wallabies and a one hour documentary on Les Darcy for the ABC.

Peter has written six books on Australian sport, including biographies on boxer Les Darcy and jockey Wayne Harris and the story of the 1927/28 Waratahs rugby tour of the British Isles. His most recent book was a biography entitled *Olive Weston: The Heroic Life of a World War II Nurse*.

Peter has been a rugby coach for 20 years and has a Sydney 1st grade premiership under his belt, and was awarded the Australian Sports Medal 2000 for service to rugby.

They called him
BOY

PETER FENTON

WITH A FOREWORD BY GRANT HACKETT

RANDOM HOUSE AUSTRALIA

Random House Australia Pty Ltd
20 Alfred Street, Milsons Point, NSW 2061
http://www.randomhouse.com.au

Sydney   New York   Toronto
London   Auckland   Johannesburg

First published by Random House Australia 2006

National Library of Australia
Cataloguing-in-Publication Entry

Fenton, Peter.
  They called him boy.

  Bibliography.
  ISBN 1 7416 6558 2.

  1. Charlton, Andrew, 1908–1975. 2. Swimmers – Australia –
  Biography. I. Title.

797.21092

Cover and internal design by Darian Causby/www.highway51.com
Typeset by Midland Typesetters, Australia
Printed and bound by Griffin Press, Netley, South Australia

10 9 8 7 6 5 4 3 2 1

Dedicated to my daughter,
Amy Louise,
who taught me to swim

Contents

Foreword   ix

Prologue   I

1   Saltwater Prodigy   5

2   The Arne Borg Challenge   35

3   Paris 1924   69

4   The Escaped Torpedo   109

5   Seeing the World   129

6   The Jackeroo Meets Takaishi   148

7   Amsterdam 1928   167

8   Defying the Doctors   193

9   Los Angeles 1932   215

10 One More Swim   229

Acknowledgements   256

Bibliography   258

Foreword

What an extraordinary story about an extraordinary Australian. And what is even more amazing is that it has taken this long for the story of the life and times of the great Andrew 'Boy' Charlton to surface. He was the Phar Lap and the Don Bradman of the pool all rolled into one, in an era when Australians really idolised their sporting heroes.

I have always been a keen student of my sport and I have read much of the feats of the greats who have swum before me. But I have to say, so many young Australians probably have no real understanding of the man they called 'Boy' – Olympic 1500 metre freestyle gold medallist at the age of 16; champion Manly surfer; jackeroo cum successful farmer, husband and father, who, despite all his extraordinary performances in the pool, still couldn't believe what all the fuss was about.

It is the story of a true Australian champion – although believe it or not Boy never won an Australian swimming championship! His name is etched into the results pages of Australian surf-lifesaving, but the name A. Charlton cannot be found in the annals of Swimming Australia.

As author Peter Fenton uncovers, Boy made his name in races at the Domain Pool, now named the Andrew 'Boy' Charlton pool, and at the now defunct Manly Baths, where he learned to swim and loved to sit and sunbake with his mates.

It is not until you read Peter Fenton's book that you get a proper understanding of the life of an amateur sportsman of this era. It was a time when our Olympians would spend months on a boat travelling to the Games; a time when they would train in a canvas pool attached to a harness on the deck of the ocean liners. It was also a time when thousands of people would flock to the Domain and to Manly to watch the match races between Charlton, Borg, Frank Beaurepaire, Moss Christie and later Noel 'Tiger' Ryan and the Japanese swimmers.

The names that are scattered through the pages of this book read like a who's who of Olympic swimming – names like Johnny Weissmuller, Duke Kahanamoku and 'Buster' Crabb – all famous watermen and celebrities in their post-Olympic lives.

But Boy – although feted as a celebrity from the beach to the bush – always remained the same; still happy to return to The Corso in Manly and his favourite watering hole for a few quiet beers with his best mate, John Davies.

And isn't it amazing when you look back in history since 'Boy' won the 1500 metres in Paris and look at the dynasty he started? Swimmers such as Murray Rose, John Konrads, Rob Windle, Kieren Perkins and I have been lucky enough to carry on the tradition started by the barrel-chested boy from Manly, who trained for the 1928 Amsterdam Olympics by swimming in the Namoi River.

But the thing that touched me above all was his enjoyment of swimming, whether he was in his beloved Manly or in Gunnedah at an exhibition swim.

Boy was a fierce competitor, even at the age of 28 when he came back for his third Olympics, and despite his heart problems and rheumatic fever he never once complained or used his illnesses as an excuse. As Peter Fenton writes, Andrew 'Boy' Charlton was a player's-player – the only kind of player there is.

I'm sure you'll enjoy *They Called Him Boy* just as much as I have.

Grant Hackett

Come swim with me the water's clear
And later on we'll share a beer
Fear not defeat, fear not disgrace
The fun is there for all who race,
To win or lose is both a joy
The name is Andrew – call me Boy.

Author's Note

During the time of Charlton's career, America and British countries swam their races over imperial distances. European nations used metric distances. The Olympic events were always swum and run over metric distances. For the benefit of the younger reader the imperial yard is almost a tenth shorter than the metre, so for all intents and purposes 110 yards equals 100 metres, 220 yards equals 200 metres, 440 yards equals 400 metres and 880 yards equals 800 metres. Occasionally newspaper reports include the terms furlong, quarter mile and half mile. A furlong is exactly 220 yards, a quarter mile exactly 440 yards and a half mile is 880 yards. The mile is 1760 yards and is the only race that differed significantly from its metric equivalent, being 100 metres longer.

Prologue

WHEN GRANT HACKETT WON the 1500 metres freestyle at the Athens Games in 2004, his was the eighth Australian victory in the event in the past nineteen Olympics. This winning ratio of over 40 per cent is quite remarkable. Australia's post-war winners became household names – Murray Rose, John Konrads, Rob Windle, Kieren Perkins and now Hackett. Almost as remarkable is that on no fewer than four occasions Australians have placed first and second.

This dynasty of distance champions began at the Paris Olympics in 1924 when a sixteen year old Manly surfer and student of Hawkesbury Agricultural College, the youngest swimmer at the Games, produced one of the most remarkable swims in Olympic history when he broke the world record and left the world champion forty-five metres behind. His American and European adversaries were left in disbelief and though he had given indications that greatness was within his reach, not even his most ardent fans could have predicted such a result. His name was Andrew Murray Charlton, known simply to everyone as 'Boy'. Of the many champion Australian swimmers who followed none achieved greater popularity. Not only because of his extraordinary natural ability but because of the other qualities he possessed.

His is a story of a very different era, the time of 'the roaring twenties' and the worldwide economic depression that followed. A time when young Australians, like Americans, were dancing the Charleston and marvelling at the arrival of talking pictures. In the seaside village of Manly, where Boy grew up, there were no fewer than five cinemas. As America's disastrous experiment with the prohibition of alcohol was making multi-millionaires of small-time thugs, steam trams still operated throughout many parts of Sydney and punts carried picnickers from Mosman to Manly. Just as the city was separated from the north shore, so too was the north shore from Manly. As the motor vehicle began its inexorable journey that would replace the horse and cart, the latter means of transport still provided the modus operandi for most of the icemen, bakers, milkmen and vegetable sellers, who travelled daily from factory and market garden to the household.

It was also an era in which swimming clubs were springing up at an extraordinary rate right across Australia, and not only on the coast, but in country towns situated on a river. Australia's addiction to the sun and the water was expanding. It is just one life span from Charlton's swim to that of Hackett's but it might as well be an eternity. In sport, as in other areas, the differences are now difficult to comprehend. Even the very best amateur athletes had to find time to hone their skills while holding down full-time jobs. Employers who were able and willing to support them were scarce. Any suggestion of taking even the slightest mercenary advantage from their talents meant instant disqualification. Occasionally an outstanding athlete could use his or her prowess to forge a career after sport, but even the most gifted generally competed until they could no longer delay the need to earn a living. Champions who accepted official invitations to compete overseas and were paid legitimate, though meagre, expenses trod a very fine line. It was all right for the amateur associations to profit from their talents but not for the athlete.

Yet, paradoxically, there were advantages. Natural ability was never more important. All-rounders with exceptional skill proved they were able to participate in different sports. Reginald

'Snowy' Baker represented Australia at the 1908 Olympics in boxing, swimming and high diving. He had already played international football and water polo. Harold Hardwick, who won gold in the pool at the 1912 Games in Stockholm, would later become Australia's heavyweight boxing champion.

Athletes ran on well-prepared grass tracks, but which were subject to conditions of climate. To break ten seconds for 100 yards, not metres, was a notable achievement. But at least there were lanes. National and state swimming titles were conducted in tidal pools with no such luxury. Competitors drew for positions across the pool. No goggles were worn in water frequently too murky to see the bottom. Training facilities were often inadequate or non-existent, particularly aboard the ships that carried our athletes to the Games, making it difficult for them to hold their form in the six weeks it took to sail across the world to compete.

It follows that attitudes to sport were also vastly different. Winning was not everything. The sportsmanship shown in this era was a matter of due course and the respect and friendship between the fiercest of rivals was evident time and again. When Australia's main hope in the 100 metres freestyle at the 1912 Olympics, Cecil Healey, heard that the American contingent had arrived late and were being threatened with disqualification, he spoke on their behalf. Had Duke Kahanamoku, the fastest sprinter in the world, been disqualified it would have increased Healey's own chances of success immeasurably. But what satisfaction would there have been in winning without facing the best?

This attitude existed across the sporting spectrum. Cricket captains were accorded a round of applause from the fielding side after they had taken block and were about to begin their innings. Batsmen who refused to 'walk' after being caught were held in low esteem. Football teams lined up against their opponents to shake hands and wish each other good luck before kick-off. To boo a goal kicker in a rugby match, be it league or union, was considered extremely poor sportsmanship. Such courtesies were as natural as opening a car door for a female companion or doffing a hat at a passing hearse. Etiquette on the sporting field was considered as important as it was off the field.

Boy Charlton, like most of his peers, swam in the surf as well and as often as in the pool and took his turn patrolling the beach for his surf club. He rowed in the surfboat, sometimes in danger-ous seas, while waiting to go to the Olympics. Charlton was typical of his time. A magnificent, natural athlete, whose quiet charm, modesty and easy-going nature balanced the excitement of his many wonderful performances. Some of these efforts are still marvelled at today. After his swim in Paris he became the most admired person in Australian sport. As one team-mate recalled many years later: 'Everybody loved Boy, he was like a film star.' A most reluctant one nevertheless. Though he always shied away from publicity he was very moved by the nation's response to him. When it was suggested he might one day turn professional and set himself up for life he replied, 'Oh no, the public would never forgive me.' While his famous American contemporaries, Kahanamoku, Johnny Weissmuller and 'Buster' Crabbe went on to star in Hollywood movies, the strapping teenager prepared for a life on the land.

There is much to learn from the story of this young man who loved the surf even more than the pool, and who prepared for his second Olympics by swimming against the current in the Namoi River, in northern New South Wales, while employed as a jackeroo. Even then, the thought of spending two and a half years away from competition and then reappearing to compete against the world's best was hard to comprehend. As you appre-ciate the enormity of what Boy achieved, you will hopefully respond, as I did, to the admiration and affection even idolatry that he engendered, which has been enjoyed by just a small band of performers even to this day.

I

Saltwater Prodigy

ANDREW MURRAY CHARLTON WAS born on August 7, 1907, the third child and only son to Ada Maud and Oswald Murray Charlton. Delivered by a midwife, he was fair-skinned and chubby with bright blue eyes that did not change colour and became a feature of one of the most famous faces in Australia. His arrival took place in a private residence owned by the Bank of New South Wales, for whom his father worked as branch manager in the neighbouring suburb of Crows Nest, on the corner of West and Ernest Streets, North Sydney. Andrew had two sisters – three year old Ada, who carried her mum's name, and Enid, not yet two.

Family roots traced back to the Charltons of Hesleyside Bellingham, Northumberland, England, in the thirteenth century. They were a very prominent border family, the head of a clan, or grayne as it was then called, who received several mentions in ancient reference books including Burke's *Landed Gentry*. The founder of the Charlton clan in Australia, Thomas Apedaile Charlton, arrived in 1855. Andrew's father Oswald was one of eight children born to Thomas, a conveyancer, and his wife, Mary Matilda Farrell. Oswald married Ada Moore, only daughter of Andrew Howard Moore, a well-known auctioneer and wool broker, in Sydney in 1902. Though somewhat removed from the landed gentry, the Charlton family still had a strong affinity to the land and the Lord.

When Andrew was born, a mere six years had passed since politicians and public servants had posed in their finest clothes, chests expanded, smiles fixed, waiting for the magnesium flashlight to explode, lighting a photograph that would be sent across the continent and to many parts of the globe, announcing the federation of a nation. People born into a country of the harshest beginnings, as well as those who came to seek fortunes, had been granted a common bond. Though vast distances separated the collection of states those diverse provinces now constituted a nation.

Not surprisingly the challenge of eking out an existence where only the stoic survived went hand in hand with challenges of a strenuous sporting nature. Well before Federation tough men were vying for supremacy in all nature of sporting endeavours. Acceptance of a challenge in the sports arena, indoor or out, was a sign of strength and honour. The need to show each other, as well as the world, how healthy, courageous and proficient they were had already made such challenges extremely popular. A wager was often part of the equation, be it on a boxing match, a horse race, the felling of a tree or the swimming of a river.

The most basic of all sporting contests were running and swimming races, but in a climate the envy of its European origins all manner of games were played throughout the year.

Australia had inherited England's fascination with sport but would take it to a new level. Participants who excelled commanded respect and sports champions achieved a status few others could claim. When international challenges occurred, interest and excitement often knew no bounds. Antipodeans were highly parochial. Today, those who worry at the importance placed on the nation's sporting achievements, and the adulation saved for sports stars, need look back a long way to see just when this phenomenon began.

Australia was playing cricket against the mother country thirty-five years before Federation. Perhaps it was symbolic that Charles Bannerman, the very first man to face a ball in Anglo–Australian Test matches, hammered the English bowling to score a century in that first Test way back in 1877. The upstart had to show the parent, and so it did, winning handsomely. By the time of young Andrew Charlton's arrival, forty years later, cricketers like Fred Spofforth and Victor Trumper had made reputations that would last forever. But it was not just cricket that brought fame.

Famous international athletes, pugilists, cyclists and oarsmen regularly sailed to Australia to match their skill with local champions. Sculling races, which pitted overseas oarsmen against Australia's finest on Sydney Harbour, the Nepean and Parramatta rivers, were enormously popular. Crowds of up to 100,000 people watched Australia's first world champion, Edward Trickett, and his successor, blacksmith William Beach, match oars with foreign invaders well before the turn of the last century.

Sporting champions won a special place in people's hearts. When the boy wonder of sculling, Henry Searle, died of typhus after returning home from winning the world title in 1889, he was mourned right across Australia. Not that all contests needed an overseas challenger. In 1890 when the champion racehorse

Carbine, or Old Jack as he was affectionately known, defeated thirty-nine rivals to win the thirtieth Melbourne Cup, 85,000 people attended Flemington Racecourse to witness his stirring victory.

Team and individual sports brought equal pleasure. Three codes of football, including one that had evolved in Australia, vied for popularity during the winter months. As in cricket, Australians had a national football team before it had a nation, Australia defeating Great Britain by 13 points to 3 in their first rugby Test match in 1899. In 1908, our rugby team, for the first time called the Wallabies, sailed away to do battle with the British nations on a trip that would last several months and include a match against the champion English team Cornwall to decide the Olympic Games gold medal.

That very year the construction of the famous Sydney Stadium at Rushcutters Bay heralded visits by some of the world's most famous boxers. Originally an open-air arena, when roofed four years later it became the biggest indoor boxing stadium in the world. San Francisco was just three weeks away by ship and over the next decade many of America's most talented boxers traded blows with Australia's best, including Les Darcy, the greatest of them all.

Competitive swimming was destined to be a major part of Australia's sporting history. In an age where so many people across the world could not swim at all Australians took to the water like few others. Records show that by the 1880s people were competing in organised swimming races in Sydney at a location that was to become the famous Domain Baths. Across the world people had found breaststroke the fastest and most efficient stroke. The first English Channel crossing, made in 1875 by Englishman Captain Matthew Webb, was achieved using that stroke. When the sidestroke was introduced it was found to be much less exhausting. Both arms remained under the water and the swimmer used a wide leg scissor kick. The trudgen, which followed the sidestroke, was revolutionary, retaining the frog-like kick of breaststroke but using both arms alternately lifting out of the water as in modern freestyle. Australia was at the forefront of evolving styles, quick to seize on and experiment with new ideas.

Then came the crawl, introduced to Australia by two young Solomon Islanders in the 1890s, and so named because swimmers appeared to be 'crawling over the water'. The crawl also used the alternate, over arm stroke but with a flutter kick instead of the commonly used scissor kick. It changed freestyle swimming forever. The term freestyle was introduced by name to cater for all these styles of swimming, such as the sidestroke, trudgen, crawl, and their variations, then used in handicap races. The Australian crawl was introduced to America and with slight modification became the American crawl. With these changing styles came world records and excitement.

Pools were constructed in vast numbers in Australian harbours and rivers. Enthusiasm for a pastime that was at the same time relaxing, invigorating, exciting and, above all, challenging, knew no bounds.

The achievements of Australia's sporting heroes were always newsworthy. In Sydney alone, the *Herald, Sun, Evening News, Daily Mail* and *Daily Telegraph* each covered major sporting events while the *Sportsman, Referee* and *Arrow* were exclusively sporting publications. *The Referee*, a weekly publication of sixteen broadsheet pages, first published before the turn of the last century, brought news from all over the world on any number of sports and lasted well into the 1930s. Many other smaller, suburban papers also devoted a lot of space to sport. When the motion picture camera came into existence in the late 1800s, sporting events immediately became a popular subject. The Melbourne Cup was filmed for the first time in 1896 and film rights quickly became a major money earner for sports promoters, particularly in boxing matches. Soon a number of newsreel companies were sending images to silent picture theatres, with sport taking its place in the news stories of the day. The arrival of 'talkies' (films with soundtracks) in the late 1920s soon led to two large companies, Cinesound and Movietone, supplying weekly newsreels to cinemas all over Australia.

Oswald Charlton, though certainly not obsessive about sport, nevertheless enjoyed it. He saw it as a healthy diversion, particularly in one's youth, and had been a keen competitor with the Sydney Rowing Club and cricketer with the Old Belvedere Club. His brother, Percy Charlton, an ex-student of Sydney Grammar School, was an outstanding cricketer. Percy was captain of Manly and toured with the Australian team to England in 1890. His haul of 5 wickets for 37 runs against Essex prompted selection in the only two Test matches of the tour, where his best effort was 3 for 18. But sporting prowess in the Charlton family was not confined to the men. Two of Andrew's aunts were excellent swimmers and one was also Manly's tennis champion and a member of the New South Wales team that in 1922 went on to win the Australian championships. While sport would always be kept in perspective, the family had shown talent well above average.

During the latter part of the nineteenth century a group of European sporting men, headed by Frenchman Pierre de Coubertin, were working tirelessly to resurrect the ultimate sporting contest, the Olympic Games. The ancient Olympics had selfdestructed fifteen hundred years earlier due to scandals of political bias, professionalism and cheating, and those who worked so hard to have them resurrected were fanatical that lofty Olympic ideals must not be sullied again.

Australia's infatuation with sport made the concept of an

Olympic revival a most exciting one and it was quickly embraced by the nation. Competitors would have to travel vast distances and make great sacrifices to compete, but the chance to do so against the world's best was something to which most prospective champions aspired.

The modern Olympics began in Athens in 1896 and Australia was immediately involved. In fact, to date no Olympic Games has ever been staged without Australian representation. Fourteen countries were represented by a total of 245 athletes, two thirds of whom were from Greece, which, not surprisingly, was by far the most successful nation. Australia had just one representative, twenty-two year old accountant Edwin Flack, a product of Melbourne Grammar School who was working in London and running with the London Athletic Club. Flack was a wonderful runner who had won the Australasian mile championship as a seventeen year old and was thrilled that his being in England allowed him the chance to compete in Athens. He payed his own way, travelling by train from London to Dover, sailing across the English Channel to Calais, and then continuing by train through France, Switzerland and Italy before catching a steamer to Greece.

To his great credit Flack won both the 1500 metres and the 800 metres, so was not only Australia's first Olympic competitor but also its first champion. Obviously he was not a member of an official Australian team as there wasn't one. This was five years before Federation but he began a dynasty of Australian athletes who have represented at all the modern Olympics. Edwin Flack also competed, unsuccessfully, at tennis between his 1500 and 800 metre victories. With nothing to lose he also decided to run in the marathon, his first attempt at the distance, and led until collapsing with just four of the 42 kilometres left to run. Flack's letters home told of the marvellous time he had in Athens, where he became extremely popular.

Swimming races were held in the open sea amid huge waves in water temperatures at around 13° Celsius. There were just three races – 100, 400 and 1200 metres freestyle – and competitors were carried by boat to the starting point as spectators looked on from the shore. The Hungarian winner of the 1200 metre race admitted later his main concern was simply to survive the eighteen-and-a-half-minute ordeal. Australia had no swimming representatives but this would soon change.

The Athens Olympics had been very well run so it was not surprising that the 1900 Olympics in Paris attracted five times the number of participants from twice as many nations. Sadly they were a disaster. Run in conjunction with the Universal Paris Exposition of 1900, the Games started in May and continued until October, a period of some five months. Among the traditional contests, a hotch-potch of unusual events, including fishing in the Seine, underwater swimming, the tug of war and obstacle races. Disorganisation and confusion reigned, some competitors unaware of whether they were competing in the Olympics or special events staged as part of the Exposition. Arguments raged for years as to the legitimacy of certain competitors and events.

This time Australia had three representatives – swimmer Freddie Lane, track sprinter Stan Rowley and marksman David Mackintosh, about whom very little was known in Australia, though his record, particularly in Europe, was oustanding. Swimming races were held in the Seine where water temperatures were not much warmer than they had been in Athens, although at least the river was much smoother than the open sea. Contestants were pleased when races were swum with the tide. Freddie Lane, winner of several state and national championships at distances ranging from 100 to 440 yards, arrived to find his favourite event, the 100 metres freestyle, had been deleted from the programme. Nevertheless he won gold in the

200 metres freestyle and later that same day won a second gold in the obstacle race over the same distance. A series of boats moored in the river provided the obstacles as swimmers clambered over one set and swam under the next in the murky water of the Seine. This event was thankfully deleted from future Olympic competition. The novelty of the obstacle race, demanding though it was, tends to detract from Lane's effort but the Sydneysider was an outstanding swimmer who became the first man to break one minute for the 100 yards when he swam 59.6 seconds in Leicester, England, two years later. He will forever be remembered as Australia's first Olympic swimming champion. Freddie Lane showed the way for Australian swimmers who were to have much greater success than their team-mates on the track.

Stan Rowley won bronze medals in the 60 metres, 100 metres and 200 metres sprints and then created a remarkable record by accepting an invitation to compete with the Great Britain team in the four-man cross-country, an event he had never competed in. There were only two entries, France and Great Britain, who were one man short. Rather than give the French a walkover the British were granted permission to use Rowley. After all, he was from the colonies. As it happened Rowley only had to finish the event to give Great Britain the gold medal, a feat he achieved so far behind the others that officials had apparently left the course when he eventually arrived at the tape. He became the only athlete to ever win medals for two different countries in the one Olympics, including gold for his least successful effort, and would also be the last man to win a sprinting medal for Australia for the next half century.

The circumstances involving the shooter David Mackintosh were even more controversial. While touring Europe, shooting professionally, he entered the live game shoot and won gold by hitting twenty-two successive targets, all pigeons. He then won bronze in the pigeon shoot, adding eighteen more unfortunate birds to his total. It was the only time live birds were used in the Olympic Games. Just how Mackintosh qualified could only be attributed to the confusion as to whether events were part of the Olympics or the Paris Exposition. In fairness to Mackintosh, he was a magnificent marksman who believed the contests were simply a part of the Exposition and was happy to take the trophies and cash that accompanied his victory. The chaotic nature and duration of the Games had done little for the Olympic movement despite the fact that many great athletes had competed. Nevertheless, Australians were well pleased. The first two Olympics had seen the emergence of three champions in three different sports – running, swimming and shooting.

Intrepid officials, continuing to work towards establishing the Olympic tradition, hoped for an improvement in America in 1904, but were devastated by another fiasco. Despite the debacle in Paris, caused by tying the Games to the Paris Exposition, the same mistake was made in St Louis. The Games were again spread out over more than four months to coincide with another world fair, the Louisiana Purchase Exhibition. Half the number competed compared to Paris and 85 per cent of all participants were from the United States. A host of events featured Americans only. Neither Great Britain nor France sent a single athlete, which caused great resentment. It was America's whole-hearted support for the previous Olympics that had won St Louis the right to hold the Games.

Australia had just one representative, hurdler Corrie Gardner, a fine athlete who had won a premiership with Melbourne Australian Rules Football Club. Like Edwin Flack, Gardner was a product of Melbourne Grammar School. He was eliminated in his heat of the 120 yards hurdles and also competed in the long jump without success. Gardner was to have had a teammate, Leslie McPherson, another Melbourne Grammar student

(Flack's victory in Athens had been an inspiration to both), however, McPherson withdrew from the 400 metres hurdles when he discovered he had to live in a tent in a city park and that the hurdles which were supposed to be 3 feet 6 inches high were in fact a foot lower.

There were some unusual events, such as one-arm weight lifting, the standing high jump, the standing long jump, and the plunge for distance where contestants dived into a swimming pool and remained motionless until they came to the surface. The tug of war remained on the Olympic agenda until 1920. Yet it was not the occasional novel event that dragged the Games down, but rather the appalling conditions, the absurd time frame and a variety of tasteless events run at the end of the Games as part of the world fair, including women's boxing and a so called Anthropological Competition involving American Indians, African Pygmies and coloured people from remote lands, which had absolutely nothing to do with the Olympic ideals.

Following the debacles of Paris and, even worse, St Louis, the Games were in crisis. There was great concern among Olympic officials that they might be doomed. Certainly they would not stand another fiasco. With this in mind an interim event, called the Intercalated Games, was scheduled for Athens in 1906. The aim was to restore credibility. Almost nine hundred athletes from twenty nations competed in a greatly reduced programme.

Track and field events were held in the magnificent Athens Stadium. Australia sent five representatives, including two brothers, hurdler Harold Healy and swimmer Cecil Healy. Harold ran second in the 110 metres hurdles while Cecil finished third in the 100 metres freestyle. His effort was very meritorious as he was hampered by a late arrival after a long boat trip during which he could do no training. Nigel Barker, a New South Wales rugby representative, finished third in both the 100 and 400 metres track events. Though the Intercalated Games were not recognised as an official Olympic programme, Australia's strike rate of three medals from a team of five augured well for the Games of 1908. There was no doubt Australians relished the international competition and the desire to compete continued to grow.

The 1908 Olympics, originally scheduled for Rome but transferred to London, were the best organised modern Games to date. The new 68,000 seat White City Stadium specially built at Shepherd's Bush, accommodated swimming and cycling as well as track and field events. More than two thousand competitors from twenty-two countries participated in over one hundred events. Twelve Australians and two New Zealanders competed in the fourteen-man Australasian team.

It was at the 1908 Games that Australia unearthed a magnificent young distance swimmer from Victoria, Frank Beaurepaire, who finished second in the 400 metres and third in the 1500 metres freestyle. As he was only seventeen he was assured of a wonderful future. Australia narrowly missed a bronze medal in the 4×200 metres relay in which one of Beaurepaire's team-mates was the remarkable all-rounder Reginald 'Snowy' Baker, who stayed behind after the other athletes had gone home to compete in the boxing tournament. Despite having to fight three times on the one day, Baker was narrowly beaten in the middleweight final by Englishman J.W.H.T. Douglas. That it was the era of all-rounders was well illustrated when Douglas later captained England at cricket. Of the fifteen medals decided in the five weight divisions, Baker's was the only one not won by Great Britain. Douglas's father actually refereed the final but Baker made no complaint about the close decision.

Not all took their setbacks as well as Snowy Baker. Unfortunately the London Games were almost as notable for their controversies and protests as for their excellent organisation.

Though many nations were involved in protests, antagonism was most rife between the English and the Americans. The American tug of war team refused to compete when the British team arrived wearing boots with steel spikes. In another incident, officials ordered a re-run of the 400 metres final after the lone English runner had been run off the track by one of his three American rivals. The Americans, who had filled all three placings, refused to run again and so the British athlete won on a walkover. He was so disgusted he retired from athletics.

Australia's one gold medal came in rugby when the first touring Wallabies team defeated English champions Cornwall by 32 points to 3. It was the Wallabies' ninth of thirty matches played in Britain. Satisfying though it must have been, there were only two entrants as France, Scotland, Wales, New Zealand and South Africa decided not to compete. Australia beat England later in the tour by 9 points to 3 in their Test match at Blackheath. It was a much tougher encounter but players prized their Olympic medals nevertheless.

Not surprisingly these were the last Olympics in which the host nation supplied all the judges. Animosity between Britain and the United States would take some time to abate but officials were learning with each Games and several cities were already bidding for the right to host the 1912 Games. Wherever they were to be staged an Australian contingent was certain to compete. The nation's love affair with the Olympics had been well and truly established.

By the end of the first decade after Federation, Australia boasted a population approaching five million people and Sydney, by far the biggest and most crowded city, was showing signs of becoming too chaotic and hectic for some. Banjo Paterson, in his famous poem, 'Clancy of The Overflow', had written twenty years earlier of 'the foetid air and gritty of the dusty dirty city' and lamented how the city dwellers 'shoulder one another in their rush and nervous haste . . . for the townsfolk have no time to grow they have no time to waste'.

But the air was anything but foetid and there was time to grow, and even to waste, in the thriving, often exciting, yet always charming seaside suburb of Manly, where the Charlton family moved to when Andrew was a toddler after his father, Oswald was transferred by the Bank of New South Wales. The hub of the township was contained between Manly Wharf on the harbour side and a magnificent stretch of deep, unbroken ocean beachfront on the eastern seaboard. Locals referred to it as 'The Village'. The main road, The Corso, an attractive, wide thoroughfare named after a famous street in Rome, was only a few hundred metres in length and serviced by a steam tram, which connected the wharf and the beach. Towering Norfolk Island pines, growing in profusion throughout the township, stood proudly along The Corso and the beachfront.

The Corso's shops, which were many and varied, opened until 9 o'clock during the week and until lunchtime on Saturdays. The street was always busy and shop owners knew most of their customers personally. With a large number of expert anglers operating in and around The Village there was always fresh seafood available. So fresh, in fact, that at Sly's Fish Shop, by the wharf, the gum-booted proprietor would come up from his boat, which was tied to a pylon, to clean and gut the fish while his customers waited. Almost as fresh was the ham and beef in Mr McGowanlock's nearby establishment where he carved the meat with deft strokes of a long, narrow, well-worn, silver blade. The aroma of flowers from several stalls gave way to that of bread, baked fresh at the bakery and pie shop.

The long-established Adrian's shoe shop had its own particular smell of new leather as shoes were soled and heeled, tacked and glued. Around the corner in Belgrave Street was a shop specialising in homemade jams and conserves. With smoking a widely accepted habit, the cunning, portly tobacconist did a steady trade, even when forced to close on the weekends when he invariably stood outside his shop and patrons who were 'in the know' were still able to buy as he surreptitiously took tobacco and cigarette papers from his well-stocked pockets. Mr Morris's café and sweet shop tempted the youngsters as much as the tobacconist did the older customers. Situated near the Anglican Church, many a child on their way to Sunday school was tempted to take a penny or two from their plate collection money to trade for liquorice, toffee, boiled lollies or a sherbet cone. And, of course, neither the old nor young could resist the occasional penny ice cream. The Corso had something for everyone.

As well as the pines, Manly was famous for a variety of wild-flowers, including Waratahs, which grew in abundance, and the gas-lit promenades that followed the shorelines on both the harbour and seaside. Manly Oval, flanked by grass tennis courts, was a few hundred metres from the wharf. Here local cricket and rugby teams played in district competitions. Away from the town centre, particularly towards Queenscliff and Freshwater Beach to the north, an area serviced by infrequent private buses, stood holiday cottages and fishing shacks.

With The Village accessible to the city only by boat, workers commuted by ferry as they had done since the 1850s. Crossing the harbour at a leisurely pace, they read their papers, checked their investments or just took in the sights of the world's most beautiful harbour and the various craft busily plying their trade. To come home from a day's work in the city, change into casual clothes and simply take a walk along the beach was bliss. At the weekend much of the locals' leisure time was spent by, or in, the water. They swam in the sheltered harbour water adjacent the wharf or the surf beaches on the ocean side. Hundreds fished, sailed or enjoyed picnics in the many sheltered bays, such as Little Manly, and on the grass verge shaded by the Norfolk pines. The waterside was a way of life. Manly residents were decidedly parochial with a great love of outdoor activities and organised sport. The bicycle, athletic, swimming and rugby union clubs were incorporated in the Manly Sporting Union whose headquarters was on the Esplanade. Locals were adamant there was no place like The Village.

Manly vied with Bondi, in Sydney's east, as the city's most popular resort. In the holiday season and on summer weekends, the crowds at Manly were enormous. Many thousands of visitors were attracted to its features. There was non-stop entertainment, with pony and miniature train rides, shooting galleries and even a giant 15-metre high water chute that propelled a boatload of screaming passengers down a steep ramp at break-neck speed and into an artificial lake 50 metres in length. This chute ceased to operate soon after the Charlton family's arrival due to passenger fatalities but the excitement remained. Bathing in the surf, previously restricted to the hours between sunset and 7 am, had been legal throughout the day since 1903, and soon after volunteer surf patrols were in place.

Settling in to their new neighbourhood came easily to the Charlton family. They took up residence in Addison Road, a short walk to Manly's tidal baths on the eastern Esplanade, which were managed by Sid Eve whose son Richmond was destined to become a very good swimmer and a champion diver. It was not much further to the open beach and young Andrew was quickly introduced to its delights. With two older sisters to help him build sandcastles and doting parents to hold him in the water, life could hardly get much better. He could swim by the time he was three and was never happier than when in the water.

As Andrew approached the serious business of getting an education at Manly Public School, established in 1858, the world's best athletes were preparing for the 1912 Olympics in Stockholm. These were the games made famous by the outstanding American Indian athlete Jim Thorpe, who won the five-event pentathlon and the ten-event decathlon, laying claim to being the greatest ever Olympic performer. Later, when it was disclosed Thorpe had been paid to play college baseball, he was stripped of his medals. The Olympic ideals of strict amateurism were sacrosanct. (In 1982, almost thirty years after his death, his medals were reinstated.)

Australia sent twenty-six competitors to Stockholm, including its strongest ever swim team of eight. The notable omission was Frank Beaurepaire, also a victim of the strict laws of amateurship. Following the 1908 Olympics, Beaurepaire swam in Europe with considerable success, breaking several world freestyle records. There had been some controversy about the total expenses he was paid for those appearances, but he was cleared of any wrongdoing. However, in 1910 he accepted a paid job with the Victorian Education Department and part of his duties were to teach swimming. The New South Wales Amateur Swimming Association believed this infringed his amateur status and refused to allow their swimmers to compete against him. Eventually the International Swimming Federation barred him from competition. Despite the absence of Beaurepaire, Australasia won gold in the 4×200 metres freestyle relay, represented by Les Boardman, Harold Hardwick, Cecil Healey and New Zealand's Malcolm Champion. Hardwick also won bronze medals in the 400 and 1500 metres freestyle. He might well have been a medallist in boxing too as he went on to win the amateur and professional heavyweight championships of Australia, however Sweden did not allow boxing and the 1912 Games are still the only Games where the 'sweet science' was not included.

Manly's Cecil Healey finished second in the 100 metres freestyle final to the great Hawaiian swimmer Duke Kahanamoku. Healey's sportsmanship in that race became part of Olympic history after he argued that Duke, who was facing disqualification for failing to arrive for a semifinal, should be allowed to compete. Surely an Olympic first. These were also the first Games in which female swimmers were allowed to participate. Australia's only female competitors, Sarah 'Fanny' Durack and Wilhelmina 'Mina' Wylie, finished first and second in the 100 metres. With her win, Fanny Durack became Australia's first female gold medallist. This outstanding performance in the open pool in Stockholm Harbour set the tone for Australian swimming, which continued to be Australia's most successful sport.

The First World War, which began in 1914 and lasted four long years, claimed many thousands of young Australian lives, including that of Cecil Healey, swim hero of the 1912 Olympics. As the war came and went Andrew Charlton battled with the three 'Rs' (reading, 'riting and 'rithmetic) including endless repeats of mathematical tables. During the war the family moved around the corner to Stuart Street and into a substantial brick cottage called 'Ravenscroft'. A white magnolia tree adorned its entrance. Next door was another brick cottage, 'Kilrea', the home of Andrew's maternal grandparents, Andrew and Rachel Moore. It was a very happy and convenient arrangement for all concerned. While he was aware of the many uniformed men who strode The Corso, and the parades, pageants and other activities organised to support the patriotic fund, Charlton was at an age that did not allow him to fully understand the horror of those four years. By war's end he was eleven and had proven to be the best swimmer in his class, from the age of about eight when competitive races were first held in his age group.

Andrew enjoyed his schooling, more because of the mateship

than the desire to learn, for which there was no particular attraction and two great distractions – the roar of the ocean and the smell of the salt water. With each passing year the lure of the beach became that much stronger. Andrew, like many before him and so many more after him, was destined to be entranced by the seaside. He literally fell in love with the surf – the full two kilometres of waves that rolled in on golden sands all the way from Fairy Bower at the southern end, beyond South and North Steyne to Queenscliff and the rocky point that separated it from Freshwater. This uninterrupted stretch of ocean, as well as Freshwater hidden around the point, was a natural wonderland. There was nothing Charlton enjoyed more than to feel the sun on his back, the sand under his feet and the thrill of riding a wave amid the ever-changing vista of clouds and colour from sunrise to sunset. His circle of barefoot, suntanned friends felt just as he did. The closest of these were the Davies brothers, John, Bruce and Frank. The youngest, Frank, was two years older than Andrew and was his best mate. Their particular thrill was to jump from the rocks at Fairy Bower, swim out to catch the largest wave possible and ride it back to the beach. Even when the older boys thought the wave was too dangerous, young Charlton invariably took his chances with it, although he never forgot one wave that almost got the better of him, a story he told his son, Murray, many years later.

As he grew older, open-air change rooms became permanent dressing sheds extending along the seawall. Manly now had two surf clubs, at South and North Steyne, and were about to get a third at Queenscliff. In a few years they would have yet another, at Freshwater on the northern end of the shoreline. They were not only focal points for local youths but for many young men from other parts of Sydney who became club members and did surf patrol at weekends and swam in the carnivals. Clubhouses were simple wooden structures with the only luxury being a tub of water to wash the sand off your feet before entering. Rivalry between clubs was intense. Jamie Jenkins, a member of the North Steyne Surf Club as well as Manly Swimming Club for seventy years, and who still swims every day, recalls very clearly the early years of Freshwater Club, whose membership contained many Balmain rugby league players and whose wild surf club dances and parties caused considerable concern among the local community: 'They tried to change the name from Freshwater to Harbord at one stage to help with a new image. I don't know if it worked, from memory it remained a pretty wild old place. Not that the Balmain boys were the only ones who knew how to have a good time, the Manly rugby union boys did all right as well.' It would be a few years before young Andrew would join the strongest of the clubs, South Steyne, 300 metres south of The Corso.

Andrew was not yet in his teens when he was given his first serious swimming lessons by a well-known Manly swimmer and surfing identity, Fitz Lough, at the Manly Baths, home of the Manly Swimming Club. Built in 1905, the baths were 55 yards long and ran parallel to the shore. Manly had been recognised for some time as the strongest swimming club in Australia. It was also the second oldest swimming club, after Balmain. An indication of the strength of membership was the battle each year for selection in two relay teams – one from those swimmers who lived north of The Corso and one from those who lived to the south – where twenty competitors swam 50 yards each and the *Manly Daily* listed all forty swimmers in the 1000 yards swim. The swim season lasted for six months, from the beginning of October to the end of March, and attracted champions from all over Sydney who came to experience the toughest competition available. Having come to compete, more than a few stayed to join the club. Many stars of the surf were also stars of the pool. The Manly Club's reputation as Sydney's strongest lasted for at least forty years, by which time tidal pools had made way for more modern venues.

Andrew found the swimming lessons quite stimulating, although nothing would ever match his love of the surf and he soon found himself sharing his time between the beach and the baths. To Andrew the surf was exhilarating, the baths a place to see champion swimmers compete without the vagaries of the waves to alter a result. It was also a place for young friends to congregate, akin to a Police Boys' Club. Between the surf and the pool, Andrew spent every spare hour in the water.

It was at the Manly Baths that Andrew met a young returned serviceman named Tommy Adrian. It was a meeting that would have a profound effect on the youngster's life. Tommy was from an established Manly family whose grandfather, Robert Edward, had set up the shoe shop in The Corso many years earlier. The old man, invariably referred to as Colonel, was a Boer War veteran and the Adrian family still ran the shop. Tommy was a very good swimmer, good enough to win the New South Wales mile championship in 1915 and finish second in the half mile. He also defeated Hawaii's Duke Kahanamoku in a thrilling 440 yards swim at the Domain Baths in Wool-loomooloo, Sydney. Though Kahanamoku was essentially a sprinter, his fame was such that the victory earned Adrian great popularity in Manly.

In July of 1915, Adrian took himself off to Liverpool in Sydney's outer West and enlisted in the army to fight in the First World War. He was just twenty-two. When he returned to Australia, via Frankfurt, in August of 1919, he bought with him little more than three standard service medals and a host of horrific memories. As a gunner, and later a driver, with the Fifth Field Artillery Brigade, he was involved in the prolonged, debilitating and barbaric trench warfare in Europe that followed the Gallipoli campaign. During those three years, in which Australian troops made many more sacrifices than they had at Gallipoli, his only extended leave was when he had his appendix removed in London, after which he returned to the thick of the action in France. Physically exhausted by his own efforts, his mind tortured by the suffering he had seen and forever dismayed by the death of his Manly club mate Cecil Healey, he was officially discharged from the forces in January of 1920.

Tommy Adrian was a slightly built man, 5½ feet tall, with fair complexion, brown brushed back hair and blue eyes. He never got over the war and now spent his time pottering around the family shop but enjoyed, most of all, helping young swimmers improve their technique at the Manly Baths. Though not a professional coach, Adrian was a student of the sport and had a keen perception of styles that were constantly evolving. He had quite a few young swimmers under his guidance including Ernie Henry, only two years older than Charlton, who was already showing signs of becoming a champion.

Born in Grafton, Ernie Henry learned to swim in the Clarence River where he and his mates regularly swam out to an island and back, a distance of some 300 yards. His family moved to Manly when he was in his teens and he immediately joined the swimming club and surf club. He was also a very promising tennis player and it was Tommy Adrian who convinced him to concentrate his efforts in the pool, a decision for which Henry was later very thankful. He became a very close friend of young Charlton, the two boys often visiting each other at home.

Tommy Adrian was regarded as something of a loner, a trait put down to his horrendous experiences at the Western Front, but he took an immediate shine to Charlton, recognising in the twelve year old great flotation, a strong natural stroke and unusual stamina. Like most youngsters, Andrew had adapted the crawl stroke – head down, chest flat on the water. Though destined to be a tall man, he was still quite chubby and swam with a rather short splashy arm action. His right foot entered the water vertically in time with his right arm, the opposite to what Adrian wanted. Despite his rawness, Adrian realised the boy had genuine potential. He had good natural speed, and his buoyancy, strength and stamina convinced Adrian that he would develop into a distance swimmer rather than a sprinter.

Although very shy, Charlton was a quick learner and showed rapid improvement as Tommy Adrian set about refining his stroke, changing the timing of his kick and introducing a scissor kick as his right arm entered the water. When Adrian matched him with another promising youngster over 440 yards, Charlton won clearly and for his effort received a young swimmer's most prized possession – a silk costume. He was hooked. Each day after school Andrew swam laps at the Manly Baths under Tommy Adrian's watchful eye before going off to enjoy himself in the surf. If Adrian wasn't there he went directly to the surf, usually accompanied by his friend, Ernie Henry.

For much of 1920 Andrew's mother, Ada, was very ill. First stricken in January, she contracted influenza and suffered complications that led to neuritis as well as stomach ulcers. Her health slowly deteriorated and she died in early October, aged forty-one, and was buried in a private ceremony at Waverley's Church of England Cemetery. To watch their mother die was a terrible ordeal for Andrew and his sisters. He had just turned thirteen, Enid was fourteen and Ada sixteen. Even with the support of his family, including his doting grandparents who lived next door, it was natural that the swimming club became even more important to him. There, with Tommy Adrian by his side, he was master of his own destiny. There heartache gave way to joy. The clear salt water was the vehicle that carried him through that difficult time.

The year of his mother's death saw the resumption of the Olympics, which had been awarded to Antwerp, a tribute to Belgium's gallantry in the First World War. The aggressor, Germany, was not invited to compete and would be forced to wait until 1928 for an invitation to return. Again Australia's best performers were the swimmers who made up six of the thirteen representatives. The remarkable Victorian, Frank Beaurepaire, restored to the amateur ranks in 1919, eleven years after winning medals at London, again finished third in the 1500 metres in water so cold he was on the verge of collapse and had to be lifted from the pool suffering from hypothermia. He was also a member of the 4×200 metres freestyle relay team that finished second behind the Americans. Two Manly Club swimmers competed with him in the 4×200 metres relay team, Harry Hay and William (Billy) Herald. Despite the gap in his swimming career caused by his lengthy disqualification, Beaurepaire went on to win thirty-four national titles, a record only recently eclipsed by Susie O'Neill.

While Andrew's scholastic achievements were very modest (one report suggesting he had an apparent aversion to arithmetic) his swimming career was blossoming. At twelve years he was school champion of Manly, champion of Sydney's northern suburbs and New South Wales champion. He repeated these performances again at thirteen, adding the breaststroke title to his long list of freestyle victories. Andrew was now swimming very strongly over middle distances (440 and 880 yards), synchronising his breathing and newly fashioned kick with a longer, more powerful, fluent stroke. His photograph appeared in the *Manly Daily* for the first time when he amazed all by finishing a close second to the sixteen year old schoolboy champion, Owen Griffiths, in the 440 yards Barney Kieran

Memorial schoolboy scratch race. Charlton's time was less than a minute slower than that of Tommy Adrian when he won the state title six years earlier. The outstanding effort indicated Adrian was correct about his staying ability. It seemed certain the photographer would see a lot more of him. The combination of natural speed, stamina and courage was a rare gift.

In September of 1921, aged just thirteen, Charlton was enrolled at Sydney Grammar School in College Street, a ten minute walk from Circular Quay. Commencing in the third term he travelled across the harbour each day by ferry with his sisters, Ada and Enid, who attended SCEGGS, Darlinghurst. Sydney Grammar was typical of the Greater Public Schools, with a strong emphasis on sporting as well as academic success. It was Sydney's strongest rugby school, winning premierships in 1920, '21, '22 and '24, and would supply no fewer than six of the famous 1927/28 Waratahs including the captain–coach, A.C. 'Johnny' Wallace, vice-captain Charlie Fox, and the magnificent full back Alec Ross. In 1921 Grammar was also the premier school at cricket and athletics. A boatshed built on the Parramatta River gave rowing impetus and the eights won the Head of the River for the next two years. The school had already produced Olympic swimmers Freddie Lane, Bill Longworth and Billy Herald. Here at Sydney Grammar, Charlton again showed more aptitude for sport than study, excelling at swimming and displaying some promise as a rugby player.

As Andrew grew into a splendidly proportioned youth he surfed at the most inviting spot on his stretch of the Pacific, depending on the winds and therefore the waves. When the sou-easterly was blowing he would swim at Fairy Bower, when a nor-easterly blew up, making conditions choppy, he adjourned to the northern end or around the point to Freshwater. As soon as he turned fourteen, he was accepted as a junior member of the Manly Swimming Club and steady improvement saw him competing with the best open swimmers. He had already gained his bronze medallion at the Manly Surf Club. People really began to take notice when he swam eighteen seconds behind Frank Beaurepaire over 440 yards at the Domain Baths and a few weeks later cut his time by seven seconds to win the first grade scratch race against opponents of all ages. His time of 5 minutes 45 seconds was the fastest 440 swim ever recorded by a fourteen year old. In the junior events no one could come within cooee of him. Handwritten records, the proud possession of Jamie Jenkins, show that Charlton won the Manly junior 50 yards title in successive years – 1921/2 and 1922/3 – when he covered the course in 26.2 seconds.

Tommy Adrian kept working on Andrew's technique, refining his natural stroke and incorporating a shallow straight leg kick into what he described as a trudgen crawl. Young Charlton powered through the water with an extremely strong, always fluent, round-arm action that never seemed to tire him. His body rotation, stroke and breathing were so synchronised it seemed he could go on lapping indefinitely. It was during this time, when racing older men, that he earned the nickname 'Boy'. His swimming club mates never called him anything else. When he finished training he would invariably go for a surf. Any ambition in the pool would never get in the way of the enjoyment of the open sea.

After his second year at Sydney Grammar, where his master marked his performance as 'fair', Boy Charlton's family decided he should continue his schooling at Hawkesbury Agricultural College on the western outskirts of Sydney. This was not likely to assist his swimming but he and his family had always envisaged life on the land for him. His maternal grandfather, Andrew Howard Moore, a qualified auctioneer and wool broker, had been made chairman of the board of advice of Goldsbrough Mort, Australia's largest wool traders, when that company took over a stock and station agency for which he had worked since he was eleven years old. During the war he had been a member of the Central Wool Committee as well as the Necessary Commodities Commission and later became chairman of the Sydney Wool Selling Brokers Association. He was also chairman of directors of Alliance Insurance Company, president of the NSW Employers' Federation and a long-time member of the Australian Jockey Club. Andrew Moore promised to help set up his grandson on a property once he had gained adequate knowledge of agriculture. It seemed inevitable Boy Charlton, irrespective of his swimming prowess, was headed for the country. It was only a matter of when.

In the week before enrolling at Hawkesbury, Boy Charlton competed in his first NSW open state championship, contesting the 440 and 880 yards titles at the Domain Baths in Woolloomooloo. A promising youth racing against established, top-class senior swimmers always caused special interest and on Saturday, January 13, 1923, excited supporters travelled on the early ferries from Manly Wharf to Circular Quay, eager to ensure they gained entry to the baths to see their young champion. Special buses also ran from the Quay and other parts of the city. The talk was all about Boy Charlton. Johnny Weissmuller, America's sensational young champion, had been invited to compete but was unable to make the trip. In his place Hawaiian champion Bill Harris, though better suited to the 100 and particularly 220 yards events, was expected to be Charlton's main rival in the 440 yards, while Drummoyne's Maurice 'Moss' Christie, a first-rate middle distance man and a likely Olympic representative, as well as the previous year's winner, loomed as the likely danger in the 880 yards event.

Every vantage point was crammed with spectators when the field faced the water for the 880 yards championship. Eight laps of the 110-yard pool lay before them. Even members of the Manly Swimming Club, aware of his enormous potential, could scarcely believe what they saw. Charlton, showing not the slightest sign of nerves, stroked evenly from the start and led Christie by a body length at the end of the first lap. At each turn he increased his margin, leading by four body lengths after the second lap and by twenty yards at the halfway mark. Swimming with enormous power and stroking with the fluency of a much more experienced man, he left the field so far behind that second placegetter, Moss Christie, finished ninety yards behind him.

How had the youngster spreadeagled the field so dramatically? The megaphone announcement of his time soon answered the question and brought loud cheers from the crowd. He had swum the distance in 11 minutes 5.2 seconds, taking a full nineteen seconds off the world record set by America's Norman Ross in the same pool two years earlier. Ross won the 400 metres and 1500 metres events at the Antwerp Olympics in 1920 and was considered to be in a league of his own. The crowd realised that this was an achievement beyond anything they had seen before and to deafening applause the smiling youngster was rowed up and down the pool.

Bill Harris told reporters: 'It is the most wonderful swim I have ever seen. For a boy of fifteen to step out and crash the world record by nineteen seconds is a feat that will probably not be seen again. A race between Charlton and Weissmuller would be the best in the world's history.'

On Wednesday evening, Charlton and Bill Harris faced each other over 440 yards. If the 'quarter mile' was a fraction far for Harris it was probably a fraction short for Charlton whose training had ensured he would be ready for a solid 880 yards. Harris was able to stay in close contact for the first half of the race but Charlton, showing superb control for one so young, came away to win by fifteen yards with Harris hanging on grimly to touch Moss Christie out of second placing. Again Charlton's fans were ecstatic. The win was almost as pleasing for coach Tommy Adrian who had won the same race in 1915. Charlton's time was just under nine seconds faster than Frank Beaurepaire had swum to win the race the previous year and the fastest ever 440 yards swum at the Domain Baths. On the third day of the carnival Charlton swam for Manly in the 4×220 yards team's race and watched Bill Harris win the 220 yards title in Australian record time.

Not for many years had swimming so dominated the sporting news. Every newspaper carried articles about the swims and the future that lay ahead for the sensational youngster. Sports journalists were already speaking of him as the next Olympic 1500 metres champion. Some were worried he might be pushed too hard and his ability blunted. Others were concerned whether he would receive the coaching necessary to ensure his full potential was reached. Former champion Bill Longworth's appraisal of his performance, written in *The Referee*, was typical:

> *Charlton is a unique swimmer. He's such another as Trumper was in Cricket, as Messenger was in Football, as Searle was in Sculling.*
>
> *Barney Kieren, that wonderful boy of long ago might have done something unofficially stamped to equal it. But among the world's official swims the 880 yards by this fifteen year old boy goes into history as the absolute best.*
>
> *The long tireless, uniform and graceful stroke of the lithe youth from Manly won the plaudits of the packed thousands. His continuous speed, with a slower stroke, contrasted vividly with the quicker arm action and what seemed jerky efforts by his rivals — men matured and of superb physique, all struggling grimly far in the rear.*

The comparison with Victor Trumper, Herbert Henry 'Dally' Messenger and Henry Searle was highly significant. They were very special performers, the most famous and spectacular in their sports, who maintained a unique place in the hearts of Australian sports lovers. Charlton's performance caused as much disbelief outside Australia as it did excitement within. Here was a young marvel uniquely equipped to continue Australia's love affair with the Olympics. At fifteen years, surely the story had just begun. In recognition of his performance Boy was presented with a bronze statuette on which was inscribed, 'To Andrew Murray "Boy" Charlton to commemorate the establishment of a world's record for 880 yards of 11 mins 5⅕ secs; in his first state championship swim, at the age of 15 years, 5 months, Domain Baths Sydney, Jan 13, 1923'. Though thrilled with what had happened, the bemused, even embarrassed youngster was pleased to head for Hawkesbury Agricultural College to get away from the limelight.

Even his father, Oswald, proud as he was, found it difficult to understand the near hysteria his son's swims had created. He was often stopped in the street and was inundated with calls at his office. While Boy headed for Hawkesbury his father spoke at length to the *Sydney Sportsman*:

> *I'm coming in for so much congratulation and reflected glory from my son's record swims that I could almost think that I'd put up the times instead of Boy. All swimming enthusiasts, myself included, feel up in the air over this regaining of lost laurels but the one to feel least affected at all is Boy. He's naturally delighted, but all the admiration and praise will not change him. To Tommy Adrian for his great, unselfish help to my boy I am most thankful and all the congratulations received by me are his due by rights.*

2

The Arne Borg Challenge

In the summer of 1923, the *Sydney Mail* observed:

> *Sydney is the queen of Australia and Manly is the queen of Sydney.*
> *It has a careless, carefree atmosphere about it. Visitors from other*
> *climates are inoculated the moment they land. They arrest people in*
> *other parts of Australia dressed as they do in Manly. If anyone were*
> *to walk up King Street, Sydney, in bathing dress, with a transparent*
> *cloak or kimono that served only to reveal what it was supposed to*
> *cover, there would not be a policeman who would not immediately*
> *reach for his notebook.*

While this view of The Village was perhaps a little superficial, Manly was certainly a very special place. Boy Charlton was about to experience something completely different.

Hawkesbury Agricultural College, situated in Richmond, at

the foot of the Blue Mountains, was 60 kilometres to the north-west of Sydney and an hour and a half by train. It was established by the NSW Department of Agriculture in 1891, operating first from the township of Richmond, and within a few years, moved to nearby Ham Common. It was the first of such colleges in the state, dedicated to producing workers of the land. The Hawkesbury Valley's lush soil, with many areas prone to flooding, had proven perfect for wheat, vegetable and citrus farms, dairies and horse studs. Standing on 15 hectares, the school grounds contained some well-wooded areas and river land. In its first three decades the all-male boarding college had already earned a wonderful reputation. The diversity of studies and practical experience in all types of stock and produce farming had produced many leading pastoralists and graziers.

When Boy Charlton arrived at Hawkesbury he was, not surprisingly, the talk of the College. Fellow students wanted to meet the young man with the prodigious talent. At the very least, his presence on the swim team would greatly enhance their prospects in the keenly contested sports shield. He arrived on Monday, January 22, 1923, immediately after the state carnival, and sat for his entrance examination. Though he failed, just one week later Boy was admitted, on probation to begin a three-year agricultural diploma course. His enrolment at Hawkesbury brought with it an unexpected amount of publicity. The *Sunday Times* sent a reporter and photographer to do a special supplement on the College and their most recent acquisition. Charlton was photographed with brood mares, Jersey cows and a threshing machine. A glowing report on the 'largest such school in the world with students from all over the British Empire' must have pleased their very popular principal, Mr E.A. Southee, a Rhodes scholar, whose photo also appeared in the supplement.

Boy settled in quickly at Hawkesbury where all students were required to board, even if they lived locally. His precocious swimming talent meant he had been competing against much older men but at the College his peers were much the same age. As well as taking responsibility for their own discipline and punctuality, each student had his own modest room and was responsible for keeping it tidy. The day began at 7.30 am and ended mid to late afternoon, after which students were encouraged to play sport, where Boy found there was keen rivalry. When rostered to look after horses or cattle, students were woken by a staffer at around 4 am. Laundry was done in the township of Richmond and delivered back to the College on Monday mornings. Three meals a day were served in the mess hall and on weekends for those who remained. The College was self-sufficient providing its own meat, poultry and produce. Its aim was to produce graduates who were similarly self-sufficient.

At the end of most weeks, from January through to March, Boy took the steam train to Central, walked down to the Quay and breathed in the salt air on the ferry ride home to Manly. Over the weekend he would have a surf with his mates and continue his training with Tommy Adrian. In early March 1923, Boy added the state mile title to his list of victories, again defeating Moss Christie, which meant he now held the state titles at a quarter-mile, half-mile and mile, all at the age of fifteen.

Boy's time at the College preceded the building of the swimming pool by a year so the College's annual carnival was held in the nearby Nepean River, where Boy won all four freestyle events, from 50 to 440 yards, as well as the diving, just two months after enrolling. While Andrew was showing his prowess in the Nepean his sister Enid shared the spotlight after winning the Manly Ladies Club titles for 100 metres freestyle, 100 metres breaststroke and 50 metres backstroke.

For endurance training Charlton swam against the tide of the river, a common practice for distance swimmers at that time. He also participated in lifesaving activities that were organised by the College in conjunction with the Royal Life Saving Society. While the swim world waited for the 1923/24 summer and the return of their young marvel he was completely immersed in his studies of agricultural science.

After six months Boy had completed the first section of his diploma but was finding it very tough going. He resigned from the course and was transferred to the Experiment Plots section (later known as Agronomy). It was a change that suited him perfectly. Here he gained practical experience with farm implements, machinery and general agriculture. His commitment to farming was well tested during the icy cold mornings when frost turned the ground into a sheet of white, and stiff hands made it almost impossible to hold a plough shear. The College, at the foot of the mountain range, experienced temperatures below zero during the winter and in the high thirties, or even the forties, day after day during summer. Unlike Manly, Richmond provided no cooling sea breeze to counter the heat. A mosquito net in summer was as important as an extra blanket in winter.

Between the ages of fifteen and sixteen Boy Charlton grew very quickly. Evidence of this development is graphically shown in physical examinations published in the College *Journal*. When he enrolled in January 1923 he stood 5 feet 10½ inches high (179 centimetres) and weighed 11 stone (70 kilograms). By October, just nine months later, he had gained an inch in height (now 181 centimetres) and weighed just over 13 stone (83 kilograms). In that era, Boy was a big lad. With a neck measurement of 15 inches, a long reach of over 74 inches, a relaxed chest measurement of 39 inches and a waist of 32 inches, he was superbly built and already as tall and as heavy as most first grade rugby forwards. The world famous heavyweight boxing champion, Jack Dempsey, outweighed him by just three kilograms.

Dempsey was twenty-eight, Boy Charlton was sixteen.

The spring vacation preceded the start of the swimming season by just a week and all eyes were on the youngster when he returned to the Manly Baths. No matter when he appeared at the baths he was accompanied by a crowd of youngsters and well-wishers, the attention making it hard for him to concentrate on his training. When he lost to Moss Christie over 400 yards in an exhibition race at Manly on October 20, 1923, his first swim of the season, such were the expectations of his adoring public, and indeed the critics, there was immediate concern he might not regain his form of the previous year. Though he was well below peak fitness, any defeat was now seen as a portent of disaster. This one apparent failure was enough to prompt the following article by 'Trudgeon' in the *Daily Mail*:

CHARLTON SHOULD BE NURSED
Effects of Manual Labour
Will Australia Lose A World Beater?

The swimming season opened last Saturday, the majority of clubs holding 50-yards' dashes. The principal happening of the afternoon was Moss Christie's defeat of Andrew (Boy) Charlton in an exhibition swim over 400 yards at Manly Baths, where a big crowd assembled to see the prodigy in action. Christie led from start to finish, easily defeating Charlton by 18 yards in 5 minutes 12 seconds. Charlton's time was 5 minutes 28 seconds.

Boy Charlton's first performance this season was disappointing. Moss Christie, who, it will be remembered, swam a close race with him in the state mile championship in the same baths last season, defeated him easily. It has been stated that the time was slow and second rate. It must be considered that neither Christie nor Charlton had previously covered the distance this season.

Charlton was not anxious to swim against Christie, and did not hesitate in saying so, and it was solely due to his father's influence that he did. The lad was in no condition, two stone heavier than he was last season, and in the interim his muscles have been hardened by manual labour at the Hawkesbury College. It is being freely stated that Charlton did not over exert himself against Christie, but whether that is so is only known to Charlton.

In my opinion Charlton did try, but as previously stated he was not in a fit condition to do himself justice. His stroke was faulty and laboured. The long sweeping arm stroke and vigorous leg thrash of last season was not evident. His arm work lacked life, and his progress through the water was minus that 'non-stop' movement which aroused so much admiration, and was deemed the main factor in his amazing speed.

With the Olympic Games only a few months off Charlton should be given the opportunity of indulging in plenty of swimming under the eye of his mentor Tom Adrian. If he goes back to Hawkesbury College, where his muscles will be hardened by hard work, and with scant opportunity to swim under expert guidance, the possibilities are that he will deteriorate and Australia will lose a champion swimmer, the greatest she has ever bred.

Another journalist suggested that Tommy Adrian should be billeted at the College until the Christmas break so that he could supervise Boy's training in the Nepean River. This would avoid the problem of Boy being besieged by admirers whenever he trained at Manly and also give Adrian the chance to work with him more often. Despite their good intentions sports writers were now putting more pressure on their champion than anyone.

Boy was back at College when two important announcements were made concerning his swimming. The first was that his amazing 880 yards swim, which had taken nineteen seconds off the world record earlier in the year, would not be recognised by swimming's controlling body, FINA (Fédération Internationale de Natation Amateur), because it had been swum in a tidal pool. This caused considerable controversy worldwide and extreme anger in Australia, particularly as Norman Ross's previous record was set at the Domain Baths and had been recognised for two years. Logic said that even if there was an advantage swimming one way there must be a disadvantage swimming the other. Australia's representation to have times recognised in tidal pools, provided swimmers had travelled up the pool and back an equal number of laps, included a document from the government astrologer confirming that no advantage was available to the contestant. In fact, scientific studies indicated tidal pools, even in perfect weather, set the swimmer at a slight disadvantage compared to still water pools. Australian delegates would argue the case at the FINA meeting, set to coincide with the Olympics, where new times were to be ratified, armed with the letter from the astrologer confirming this view.

The whole system of recognising world records was quite unsatisfactory and led to much angst within the sport. In fairness to the international body they faced a difficult task. Races around the world were conducted under a variety of extremely different conditions and were swum over metric distances in Europe but imperial distances in the British Commonwealth countries and America. Pools were of different lengths (Sydney's Domain was 110 yards, others as short as 25 yards). Records were claimed over all sorts of unusual distances, 150 yards, 300 yards, 500 yards, 1000 metres and so on. Some pools were tidal, some salt water, others fresh water. Even when conditions met with official approval it was almost impossible to appraise different efforts. How do you compare a swim in a harbour pool in blustery winds with one made in the calm waters of an indoor pool? The fact that the international body met to approve records just once a year meant many records had again been broken before they were recognised. In the long term all distances would become standardised, as would conditions under which records could be set, but these were early days, for officials as well as swimmers. As arguments raged and official representation made in order to validate his record, Boy was much more interested in the second announcement that came on the November 1, 1923.

Sweden's Arne Borg, the world record holder at 400, 1000 and 1500 metres, had accepted an invitation to tour Australia in the New Year and would race Charlton at Sydney's Domain Baths in the state titles. Borg would also make appearances in Queensland, Tasmania, Victoria and Hobart. Tours by international champions were a regular and very popular occurrence. Associations agreed on a swimmer's itinerary and the proceeds from appearances made a vital contribution to the finances of the sport. When swimmers visited Australia several states invariably contributed to expenses. A full house of six thousand fans at the Domain had seen Duke Kahanamoku break the 100 yards world record in 1915. Five years later the American distance star Norman Ross thrilled crowds with a succession of wonderful performances and the next season Hawaiian sprinter Pua Kealoha was accompanied by another American world record holder, Ludy Langer.

It had been hoped the brilliant young American Johnny Weissmuller could be persuaded to tour but Borg was an even better catch as he swam sprint and distance events while Weissmuller restricted himself to the shorter races. He too would probably have proven unbeatable in the 100 and 200 yards events. Only at 400 yards and beyond would Charlton have been given any hope of beating him. When Weissmuller was unavailable Australian fans assumed that no overseas stars would tour that year due to the proximity of the Olympics. However, the Swedish and Australian swimming associations were able to arrange Borg's visit and the European champion spoke enthusiastically about the opportunity to race against Australia's new boy wonder early in the New Year. The announcement of his tour immediately caused tremendous interest.

While there had been excitement at Boy's appearance during the spring holidays it was a mere ripple compared to the reaction that greeted his return from College on December 20. The holiday season was on in earnest and Manly was inundated with visitors. Shopkeepers and those leasing out holiday cottages were enjoying their best season in a decade. The town clerk made the interesting observation to the *Daily Mail* that shopkeepers, who had been pressed for money, were paying their rates 'with a smile, and on the nail'. The surf beach changing sheds, which had been servicing one thousand patrons per day, were now catering for five and six times that number.

Boy immediately began his training in earnest for the races against Borg that would take place over the course of a week, commencing on January 12, 1924. This time there was no reluctance to compete and he quickly began to show signs of the effortless style that was his trademark. Swimming in Manly Club handicap events was an ideal preparation. Despite a heavy head cold he was soon approaching his best times. Not that they would necessarily be good enough to defeat Borg.

A few days before Borg's arrival in Australia, the Manly Swimming Club hosted the Melbourne Club in an annual interclub challenge. Boy Charlton and Frank Beaurepaire met over 440 yards in the most interesting event of the carnival. Though Beaurepaire was below top form, the effort of the young Manly swimmer, particularly the time he swam, would be a great indication of his chances against the Swedish champion. A field of six, including Ernie Henry, provided a keenly fought contest. Charlton and Beaurepaire swam alongside each other with nothing between them after 110 yards. Beaurepaire was still at Charlton's shoulder with half the course covered. At the three-quarter mark Charlton led narrowly and sprinted clear in the final lap to win by ten yards with Ernie Henry third, six yards behind Beaurepaire. The crowd was well pleased with their idol's effort, his time of 5 minutes 20.4 seconds only a few seconds outside his wonderful swim of the previous season.

Few knew that Frank Beaurepaire had swum an impressive trial at the Spit Baths prior to the event. He was extremely impressed with Charlton and made this clear in a comprehensive article he wrote for *The Referee* and published the following week:

In the Manly Swimming Club's yearly interclub contest, Boy Charlton put one across me, and despite the fact that I had very little training and was over to help the old Melbourne club in a sporting way (Melbourne's my native town) every credit must be given Charlton for his great effort. Beating me is nothing − others have done it before and will do it again. It is the time and conditions surrounding the making of that time that count.

When one looks back and finds that there have been just four swims over the quarter mile that are better than Charlton's quarter on Saturday, you gain a clear perspective of the merit of this phenomenal youth and can properly assess the position at the moment among contemporary and old time swimming stars.

Arguments have occurred and will occur again and again concerning the Manly boy's stroke. My own conviction may be interesting. Charlton was first brought to my notice as a boy of thirteen by Tommy Adrian. This boy was gifted with phenomenal staying powers. Tommy went to work with him straight away and has been guiding him ever since. To Adrian must be given credit of developing the latent powers that lay in that thirteen year old kid.

Adrian has no two minds about Charlton's stroke. He calls it trudgen crawl and would like to call it continuous trudgen. He reckons the stroke has been based on trudgen, and is trudgen, with the negative or retarding movements in the old trudgen scissors kick removed or eliminated, and crawl leg flutters added.

With Adrian's contention I agree completely. Charlton strokes with his arm very much in a manner common to all trudgen swimmers, and but seldom seen in crawl or American crawl swimmers. I am referring to the apparent unevenness of his arm placements. The right arm dips further ahead than the left, which is inclined to chop in a little short when compared to the reach of the right arm.

Some may call this a fault – I would not let him lose it. I am certain that it is a mannerism that is as necessary to Charlton's whole stroke and rhythm as water would be to a thirsty man.

Under water Charlton's forearms act correctly insofar that they pull into position and across the body with the elbows bent. That is to say the full arm reach is not made towards the bottom of the bath, but in relation to the body the arms pass beneath the trunk in boomerang shape until the arms (in rotating course) extend to the rear prior to lifting clear and coming forward again. It is here that any slight improvement might be made. Boy is inclined to sweep or swing one arm out of the water.

Charlton's sense of pace is superb and his evenness, lap after lap, almost a matter for wonderment. In fact he has the vital secret of long distance swimming. Coupled with his amazing stamina, these factors all make up a youth gifted with a knowledge of watermanship far beyond the average person interested in swimming. Fooling and swimming about the Manly baths since babyhood, in calm, delightful water, has taught a boy what possibly only a score of men have learned during the past thirty years.

Watching Charlton, one can readily detect a sturdiness of shoulder action that will stand him in good stead when he tackles fresh water and bumpy saltwater swimming. These he must carefully accomplish to put the hallmark of enduring fame to his name.

Paris Games, 1924, will be held in freshwater, and possibly a portion of this year's Australian championships. I am of the opinion that Boy Charlton can master the difficulties offered by fresh or bumpy salt water and I wish him luck in the doing.

His mentor will need to coach this lad carefully in these matters but I think Tom Adrian is old enough in the head to make the best of him in the new conditions that have yet to come to the Manly boy.

Charlton has rhythm – the co-ordination of leg and arm actions, together with trunk roll – in salt water almost to perfection. He almost hydroplanes, and, in fact, applies that principle to his swimming. His propulsion is continuous and ever forward, with a most marked absence of movements that might be considered a negative.

He is a phenomenal youth and we all, as good Australians, hope for a repetition of Sydney form under all conditions of interstate and international swimming.

Beaurepaire's observations were read with enormous interest. Students of the sport were taken with the views of Charlton's style. No two swimmers swam exactly the same and those aspiring to championship level, swimmers and coaches alike, were always keen to see the reason why one man suddenly stood out above the rest. Yet even those with no appreciation of the finer points of technique had to be aware of the impression Charlton had made on Beaurepaire, a man who had broken several world records and swum with success in many countries under all sorts of conditions. To them his appraisal merely confirmed what they already believed. Their young man was a world beater and Borg had better watch out!

On November 26, 1923, Arne Borg left London aboard the *Moldavia* bound for Australia. Sydney papers reported his departure and the progress of his journey. He had been offered a berth on another, larger vessel, on which a special training pool would be erected, but chose the *Moldavia* as it took shorter stopovers and therefore made a quicker trip. When he arrived in Perth he explained that he had been able to have training swims at Port Said and Colombo and would attain fitness very quickly.

Borg was a very experienced swimmer whose popularity had seen him invited to many countries. He had swum in the 1920 Olympics in Antwerp, Belgium, finishing fourth in a semifinal of the 1500 metres and fourth in the final of the 4×200 metres relay. Since the 1920 Olympics his times had continually improved. Swimming in Gothenburg, Sweden, in August of 1923, he recorded a time just over 21 minutes and 35 seconds for the 1500 metres, which took twenty-five seconds off the world record that had stood for eleven years.

A serious fire aboard the *Moldavia* in Perth, and an unscheduled appearance in Adelaide, financed by a local businessman, delayed Borg's arrival in Sydney until January 4, just eight days before the first of his clashes with Charlton. His arrival at Central Railway from Melbourne, aboard the Melbourne Express, caused tremendous excitement. Officials, pressmen and onlookers surged forward as the first two divisions of the long train rolled into the station twenty minutes after noon. Their apprehension when the visiting athlete did not emerge was quelled when he stepped from the first carriage of the third division, smiling broadly. As photographers jostled to get images of the champion, he was rushed to the Hotel Australia where a party of approximately two hundred 'prominent citizens' and sporting enthusiasts were joined by journalists and more photographers.

At twenty-two, exactly six years older than Charlton, Borg's physical appearance was interesting. Taller than Charlton, at over 6 feet, he was slightly built with nothing of the deep chest already apparent in the still developing youngster. His weight was almost a stone (6 kilograms) lighter than his rival. In Europe he was often called the Swedish Sturgeon, an apt nickname for a superb swimmer with long slender frame, modest chest and sloping shoulders. A pork pie hat, matching his light green suit, concealed much of his very blond hair and a constant smile revealed a full set of gapped teeth. W.F. (Bill) Corbett, of the Sydney *Sun*, described him as being 'as thin as a match, inclined to be knock-kneed, but as strong as a lion'. His times over long courses indicated Corbett was spot on about his strength.

After an official welcome by James Taylor, president of the NSW Swimming Association, Borg responded. All present were pleased to find his English was quite good. He thanked Mr Taylor for his welcome, predicted an exciting set of races and expressed his hope that the better man should win. He then asked the large gathering to drink a toast to the good health of his rival, a gesture that brought hearty applause. Borg proved only too willing to answer questions. Yes, he was well aware of Charlton's times, including his most recent, which were conveyed to him in Perth, and assured all present he looked forward to his races with Charlton whom he also referred to as 'Boy'. Many were surprised to hear he had broken 24 seconds for 50 yards and 54 seconds for 100 yards freestyle. Obviously he could sprint as well as stay. He was also Sweden's backstroke champion.

The following day, Saturday, January 5, there were several swimming carnivals across Sydney but Borg was interested in just one. He prompted great excitement by appearing as a spectator at Manly. Here he watched Charlton win the 220 yards championship of the Northern Suburbs, timing his rival on a clock the size of a man's hand. He was impressed with what he saw but undaunted by the task ahead of him. On Sunday he was the special guest at Cronulla's surf carnival and again impressed all with his friendliness and willingness to discuss his chances against Charlton. He happily entered the pillow fight but was soon knocked out of the event and finished last in the sack race. When offered a chance to swim with the surf belt, he picked it up, smiled and said, 'Too heavy, too heavy.' At the conclusion of the carnival he was presented with a club costume made of black wool with blue and white bands, which he subsequently wore at training sessions.

Both Borg and Charlton had entered the 440 yards, 220 yards and 880 yards championships in the state titles. Despite his lack of recent training Borg was supremely confident of winning all three races and believed he could also beat Charlton at a mile (1760 yards) though he had never actually swum that distance. He told Bill Corbett he expected to swim about 5 minutes 3 seconds for the 440 yards and if Charlton was close to him at the finish he would have enough in reserve to sprint away. His main threat would probably come on the last night of the carnival over 880 yards, which he recognised as Charlton's pet distance. Here he believed he would swim about 10 minutes 50 seconds. If his predictions proved accurate it would take tremendous swims to beat him. At a tick over 11 minutes, Charlton's best time for the 880 yards was ten seconds slower.

While Borg's records overseas had been made in fresh water, he saw no reason to believe he could not go as quickly in salt water. Others were not so sure. Riverina champion, Harold Roxborough, to swim in the country 100 yards title, said he had broken a minute for the distance in fresh water in Albury but could not go close to breaking the minute at the Domain Baths. Still, there was no sense of bravado in Borg's statements and local experts were as impressed with his genuine confidence as they were surprised at his easy attitude towards training. When former national champion and Olympic representative Bill Longworth told Borg he once swam 21 miles in a week preparing for a distance race, Borg exclaimed, 'Too much, too much!' He had no intention of a half-mile swim until the race itself.

The visitor was keen to get a feel for the water at the Domain, training twice on Tuesday, January 8. He swam a leisurely 330 yards alongside the 1920 Olympian, Keith Kirkland, with the Spit Club's champion sprinter, Charlie Stuart, joining them over the last 50 yards. That afternoon he returned to the pool and spent half an hour tossing a water polo ball about with members of the Sydney Club. He impressed with his dexterity, making some excellent catches and throwing the ball with plenty of power. Borg played water polo back home, a sport quickly increasing in popularity, and expressed a liking for the water at the Domain, which was much warmer than he was used to in Sweden. Like Charlton he enjoyed being in the water and not just the challenge of racing. When Moss Christie, Frank Carberry and Keith Kirkland stepped up to swim four laps Borg joined them and though not making fast time again demonstrated his quick stroking style. Christie later told reporters that Borg took three strokes to his two. George Barrell, proprietor of the gymnasium at the baths, rubbed Borg down and declared him in excellent condition.

Early in the week Charlton trained at Manly and later swam at the Domain. No matter the location both swimmers drew large crowds and each was closely watched by pressmen, keen to be successful in tipping the outcome of their races. Experts were quoted each day on their predictions. Charlton's fans were encouraged by a fine swim over 150 yards at Manly and by Tommy Adrian's declaration that his charge would be at his peak despite suffering a slight cold. Adrian was delighted with Boy's progress but made no prediction other than to say he was sure his swimmer would perform very well. Charlton seemed unconcerned at the excitement building around the contest and relaxed with a leisurely swim in the surf at Manly on Thursday afternoon.

Across the city at Coogee, Borg swam 400 yards in a manner that drew some doubts from Bill Corbett. He believed Borg had tired in the last 50 yards and seemed not to appreciate the heavy salt water. Borg admitted to feeling a bit stiff in the legs after the swim but was sure some Swedish massage would cure this. The bath's masseurs confirmed Borg was in excellent physical shape. Nevertheless his effort caused Corbett to write in *The Sun*:

> *If Charlton and Borg were racehorses the public would perhaps straight away fancy Charlton, after comparing Borg's gallops here with the Australian's. But a trainer is never too sure of what his horse will do until it is actually racing – despite the animal's fast or slow trials.*

Corbett went on to admire Charlton's quiet confidence.

> *He possesses a grand spirit, and Borg's sudden entry into the Domain baths gymnasium yesterday afternoon did not have any more effect upon Charlton than to make him turn his head for a moment and gaze at him. Boy laughed and chatted merrily, and didn't give the slightest indication he was going to take part in an important international contest.*

The pair were clearly on the best of terms. Boy passed a picture taken with his mentor, Tommy Adrian, and one of Borg himself, to be autographed by his rival. Borg then obtained a photo of Charlton to send home to Sweden. On the Charlton photograph Borg wrote: 'Boy Charlton. To Paris 1924.'

Borg's regular appearances at the Domain made him very popular with the local boys who treated him in a manner usually reserved for local heroes. One eight year old, Arthur O'Connor, had a reputation of being a fearless diver. Borg asked him if it were true he could dive from the top tower. The boy assured him that it was. Would he show him? Yes he would. And so he proceeded unflinchingly to the top of the platform, 60 feet above and plunged to the water below, to Arne Borg's loud applause. On request Arthur O'Connor did it a second time and Borg offered him two shillings for his bravery. Arthur explained he could not take the money as he aimed to be an Olympic diver and this might infringe his amateur status. So Borg gave the coin to the lady at the kiosk, putting young O'Connor twenty-four, one penny 'chester cakes' in credit. Chester cakes, made of a mixture of leftovers from a variety of cakes and topped with icing, were sold at kiosks at most baths, and were very popular with the youngsters. It took some weeks, but Arthur devoured his cakes and a firm friendship ensued. His worries about professionalism might have been unfounded but he did go on to be a champion diver and met Arne Borg on a subsequent trip.

Though Bill Corbett was a well-respected general sports writer it was thought the opinions of men who had swum at that level might be more incisive. In fact, Sydneysiders wanted to believe those who predicted success for their man. Freddie Lane, Australia's first gold medallist in swimming, had a good look at Borg in the water and predicted Charlton would win just one of the three races, probably the half mile.

Bill Longworth noted the difference in Borg's style in *The Referee*:

His stroke is unlike that of any other famous swimmer and can well be called one of his own. In my opinion it combines the Australian crawl and the American trudgen crawl action. Unlike present day swimmers Borg at times kicks out of the water and does similar timing to Australian crawl exponents. Borg's arm action is good and clean. Though swimming flat on his chest he rolls his shoulders slightly when reaching forward. His arms are placed in front of his head and pulled through in line with his chest. It is noticeable that he swims with great dash, and with his long reach he immediately takes the eye as a very speedy swimmer, rather than a distance performer.

Longworth, impressed with the times Borg had swum, from 100 yards to 880 yards, went on to say:

Borg has beaten every swimmer of note in Europe, and in England has outclassed such men as Hatfield so he comes with the highest credentials. Borg appears to be confident of carrying all before him here. If he does, he will find us good sportsmen in defeat, but I must warn him that he has a big contract in front of him, and I, for one, will be surprised if he can finish in front of Charlton in the half-mile [880 yards].

Longworth reserved judgement on the 440 yards after seeing Borg swim 220 yards in 2 minutes 21 seconds. Prior to that swim he believed his training might not have been sufficient to give him enough stamina to hold Charlton in the last hundred yards.

Bill Corbett was also swayed by Borg's effort. He had been concerned with Borg's battling 440 yards at Coogee Baths earlier in the week but this was enough to suggest that Borg was, in racing parlance, 'a good thing' to win the opening event of the series, over 440 yards. Harold Hardwick, gold medallist in London, favoured Charlton. The race was shaping up as one of the most exciting sporting contests for many years. Corbett wrote: 'On the eve of the great race, Sydney has reached a pitch of excitement over swimming never experienced before.' It was no exaggeration. In fact, not since the young middleweight boxing champion Les Darcy fought American Eddie McGoorty in July of 1915 had such interest been generated in any sporting challenge in Sydney. Spencer's newsreel company shot a sequence of Charlton in training which was snapped up by cinemas across the major cities.

* * *

Sydney's Domain Baths, 110 yards long and lit to accommodate evening carnivals, was situated in the sheltered Woolloomooloo Bay at the foot of spacious parkland and gardens. A huge Moreton Bay fig tree provided shade over a large rocky platform making it an idyllic spot. For centuries before European settlement the Cattigal tribe, who frequented the harbour foreshores, had used the area for bathing and swimming. Later, sailors from English sailing ships that moored in the Bay continued to use it for the same purpose. It played an important role in an era when there was a distinct difference between bathing as a part of cleanliness and swimming for relaxation. Primitive change room structures of some type have been noted at the baths as early as the 1820s. Despite disdain for the practice of open bathing, and attempts to ban it altogether, a government grant saw the building of substantial, separate men's and women's areas and pavilions, which were run by private enterprise – swimming had become Sydney's favourite pastime. The first Fig Tree Baths were built in 1858, by which time competitive swimming carnivals had been well established. When rebuilt in 1908 the baths took the name of The Domain.

The NSW Amateur Swimming Association was formed in 1892 and as competitive swimming grew in popularity around the world in the late nineteenth and early twentieth centuries, Australia became one of the leading swimming nations. Its champions had been at the forefront of the changing styles that saw the old sidestroke give way to the trudgen and later the crawl. Swimmers such as the famous Cavill brothers, whose family had arrived from England in 1879, Harry and Alick Wickham, who are credited with bringing the revolutionary crawl stroke to Australia from the Solomon Islands and the brilliant youngster Barney Kieran were outstanding athletes who broke many world records and achieved fame worldwide.

Numerous championship baths had been built all over the

city, the majority on the harbour foreshores. Strong swimming clubs existed in Rose Bay, Bondi, Drummoyne, Balmain, The Spit, Abbotsford, and many others suburbs. The Domain Baths, home of the Sydney Swimming Club, was the major venue for state and national championships. By 1924 the arena was capable of seating 3,500 spectators on the shore side, most in the two tiered, covered grandstand, and about twice that number over all. Dressing rooms existed at both ends and a gymnasium and massage rooms at the southern, or city end.

At the Domain Baths, fans turned up in their thousands to see local champions compete with visiting stars. The tragic death of the teenage prodigy Barney Kieran from appendicitis in 1906 had robbed Australia of a young champion, already a multiple world record holder, whose future had promised so much. Kieran had broken eight world records in England just a year before his death. Now Boy Charlton was poised to be the successor to his throne, a youngster who over the next few years could take Australian swimming to new heights. His admirers were about to discover whether he could overcome this first great challenge.

Saturday January 12, 1924, brought a typical, varied summer programme to entertain Sydney's sports lovers. There were two race meetings, thoroughbreds at Canterbury and a pony meeting at Victoria Park; Sheffield Shield Cricket at the Sydney Cricket Ground between New South Wales and South Australia; cycling and athletics at the Sports Ground, featuring a 100 kilometre team's race for wheelmen; the Country Lawn Tennis carnival at White City; several club sailing championships on the harbour; and boxing that evening at Rushcutters Bay Stadium featuring local and imported fighters.

Despite all the competing attractions, there was no doubt as to the main event. A huge crowd packed into the Domain Baths to witness the first of the three clashes featuring Arne Borg, Boy

Charlton and the pick of swimmers from New South Wales. Additional tiered seating had been added along the length of the harbour side of the pool to help accommodate the crowd. Patrons swarmed into the city by train, tram and ferry and special buses ran from Queen Square and Bent Street to the Domain. Though heavy advance bookings had been made, a large portion of the crowd always bought tickets on the day. Previous meetings at the Domain had sometimes been marred by disorganisation when the ticket office had not been opened early enough and confusion ensued. This time officials arrived early in the morning to control the large crowd that was anticipated. By 10 am, four hours before the carnival was due to begin, a long but patient queue was already awaiting entry. Boy Charlton button sellers were doing a roaring trade. By noon the baths were packed and the queue approaching the gate was met by one returning, disappointed that the full house sign had been shown. Patrons were packed like sardines into the grandstand and also the open enclosures.

The Referee described the scene:

Never before has such a tremendous crowd toppled and swayed over the water of the Domain Baths. Tier above tier of moving faces towered up into the pavilions, and the sides seemed like huge floating galleries, packed with swarming thousands. The very water seemed to shake, and the bath's beams creaked as if they were falling in. The official estimate of the attendance was 7,000, and if there were 7,000 in the baths there must have been at least 10,000 turned away at the gates. Most of them waited in an overflow pavilion of their own outside. They seethed over the hills and paths; they climbed trees and craned on tiptoe. Even the adjoining roofs were packed.

At 1 pm a police patrol arrived to ensure the crowd would not burst through the barricades. Some youths had already climbed the diving tower. With less than half the gathered crowd able to get in, those who had missed out had no option but to sit in the overflow pavilion or on the grass, and listen enviously to the roar of the spectators as there was no public address system to advise them as to what was happening. The large Moreton Bay figs provided vantage spots for adventurous youngsters, while boats of all sizes jammed into Woolloomooloo Bay, with one large ferry listing precariously towards the shore as passengers strained to get a look at proceedings at the baths. Sailors on the bigger yachts climbed masts to get a glimpse of the action as they cruised past.

The carnival opened with a performance by the state's military brass and a game of water polo followed by handicap club races, novelty races, including the popular musical buoy race, modelled on the old party game musical chairs, and diving. A superb diving troupe, comprising members from several clubs, entertained with a well-rehearsed routine, ending with a mass dive from different levels of the tower. The other feature event was the state 100 yards championship which was won narrowly by Athol Coppleson of Bondi, Charlton's Manly team-mate, Ernie Henry, also coached by Tommy Adrian coming in second. Henry was also to be a starter in the 440 yards event.

Though the crowd was predominantly male there were many women present, smartly dressed as befitted such an important occasion. Some sat alongside the men with their legs dangling over the edge of the pool, 6 feet above the water. All enjoyed the earlier distractions but were really there for one event – the 440 yards state title. When time came for the race, excitement was at fever pitch. A megaphone was used to introduce the starters, each announcement bringing generous applause. First Borg appeared, tall, slightly built, pale skinned, hair brushed back, a Swedish flag attached to the top of his costume. When Boy Charlton's turn came to be introduced there was a thunderous reception. He seemed unperturbed by the occasion, smiling and lifting his hand only briefly, his suntanned body in stark contrast to that of his main competitor. The swimmers drew for positions with Borg starting from number 1, nearest the grandstand, Moss Christie from 2, Owen Griffiths, the previous season's schoolboy champion, from 3, Charlton from 4 and Ernie Henry, on the harbour side, from 5. There were no lanes marked, but with only five competitors there was ample space between them. Swimmers who were able to keep a straight course, a much simpler task in daylight than at night, had a decided advantage in a close race.

The noise of the crowd abated as starter Percy Russell called the competitors to the blocks. His familiar call of 'Face the water . . . GO!' triggered a huge roar as spectators found a release for their nervousness. The five swimmers hit the surface together, churning up the water, immediately seeking a prominent position. Borg soon drew to the front and held a slight lead halfway down the first lap, with Charlton in second place and the others a yard behind him. Borg, as was his custom, swam the first lap at a blistering pace. At the first turn he led by three yards from Charlton, with a similar distance to Christie in third place, covering the distance in just under 1 minute 7 seconds. Borg's tactics were apparently to make Charlton swim faster than he had planned, so upsetting his rhythm. However, the youngster was swimming smoothly, his long strokes in contrast to his quick-stroking opponent.

Down the second lap they came with Borg holding his lead over Charlton and the pair gradually pulling away from the others. At the end of the second lap Borg maintained his three-yard lead in a time of 2 minutes 22 seconds. Into the third lap the crowd urged Charlton along with cries of 'Boy, Boy, Boy'. With long powerful strokes he responded and gradually gained on Borg. The huge crowd were now all standing and cheering wildly, the cacophony echoing across the harbour. Twenty yards before the final turn Charlton had almost drawn level. As he came out of the 330 yard turn, Charlton was slightly ahead for the first time. Borg was now feeling the pinch as Charlton led by three yards halfway down the last lap. Borg rallied momentarily as Charlton supporters wondered just how much the visitor had saved for the sprint to the finish. Apprehension soon abated as Charlton pulled away to win by twenty yards, with Moss Christie ten yards further adrift narrowly beating Ernie Henry for third place.

The whole arena was in uproar. No one could have wished for a more exciting race. Borg had laid down the gauntlet to Charlton and the youngster responded magnificently. Pool announcer Joe Morgan, in knickerbockers, open neck shirt and bare feet, walked to the end of the springboard and raised the large brass megaphone to his lips and announced that Charlton had equalled Borg's world record of 5 minutes 11.8 seconds. Further cheering broke out. Borg had swum 5 minutes 28.4 seconds. Then, in a tremendous display of sportsmanship, Borg hustled Charlton into an official's boat and rowed him up and down the pool shouting, 'Charlton is champion, Charlton is champion!', as Boy, showing obvious embarrassment, huddled in the back of the boat. Arne Borg stood in the boat, balanced himself, put his hand on Boy's head and called for three cheers for his vanquisher.

When the swimmers made their way to the dressing rooms they were besieged by excited well-wishers and autograph hunters. The good news quickly spread across the harbour and ferries and tugs began a chorus of horns and whistles that echoed over the water and lasted for minutes. The noise from the arena gave no cause for speculation among those who had been excluded from the pool and they too were shouting 'Charlton, Charlton'. The vociferous cheering from the crowd as their hero touched the wall had been heard at the Town Hall, over 2 miles away. At the Cricket Ground, New South Wales' century makers, Warren Bardsley and Alan Kippax, had put on a huge partnership against South Australia. Suddenly, sustained cheering broke out and Kippax, who was on strike, looked at the scoreboard to see they were momentarily sharing the spotlight with the young swimmer as a hastily painted sign appeared announcing: 'CHARLTON WINS'.

Borg's time was well outside what he had predicted but he made no excuses for his defeat, declaring Charlton the best swimmer he had met and a true champion. While he had little time to prepare since his arrival, and he was certainly unused to the salt water, he refused to offer any excuse, stating that he had simply been beaten by a better man. Charlton admitted to reporters that he was superbly confident after the first lap and felt very comfortable throughout the entire race. Thinking Borg might finish strongly, he even had a little in reserve after the final sprint.

Immediately after Boy won, his father, Oswald, was asked for a comment for *The Sun* newspaper:

I don't think there is any danger of the boy being spoiled. He takes it very well. He knows that there are other things in the world than swimming. But after all, he is only sixteen and it is a fine thing so long as he doesn't overdo it.

So after he has swum in the 220 yards on Wednesday and the half-mile on Saturday he will take a spell from swimming and stick to work for a time. He will not compete in the championships in Melbourne. But he will be available to represent Australia in the Olympic Games in Paris. A trip like that would be an education in itself.

And after that? Well, I hope to see him do some more good swims. He is so young that it will be some years before he can launch out for himself, and he can well spare the time to do some racing. He is going to the land, more or less mixed farming. He will have sheep as well as cultivation. His grandfather is looking after him and he will be able to make a good start.

He would never do any good in any sort of office life. He is too big for one thing and has been too used to the open-air life. But farming will suit him in every way.

When Boy Charlton returned to Manly on the 5 o'clock ferry, which was bedecked with bunting and streamers, the wharf was crowded with people who had come down to welcome him home. They joined with those who had returned from the carnival with their hero on the *Balgowlah* to give three cheers and sing 'For he's a jolly good fellow', and then cheered him all the way down the wharf and along the roadway. Flanked by his father and Tommy Adrian, the weary young warrior made his way home to Stuart Street and a much-needed rest, not so much with the effort of the swim, but with the drama of the day.

If the occasion had exhausted the swimmers, it would also exhaust reporters' superlatives, which were lavished on both swimmers in the next couple of days – Borg for his sportsmanship and Charlton for his achievement. Bill Longworth's summary of the event in *The Referee* was perhaps the best:

Swimming has always been a leading Australian sport, and for a great period of years Australians were noted especially for their wonderful ability as champion swimmers. Of late years we have, unfortunately, lost prestige, because we have not produced outstanding champions, and made improvement that other nations, such as America and Sweden, have done.

With the advent of Andrew Charlton, the wonderful Manly boy, every enthusiast hoped we had found a swimmer to win back our lost laurels. By his great swimming last year he carried the confidence of the populace, and now that he has defeated the great Swede, Arne Borg, champion of Europe, he can well be called champion of the world. He will surely win the title at the forthcoming Olympic Games.

Sydney's Domain baths have been the deciding place of some great contests. All of our best swimmers of late years have competed here. Duke Pao Kahanamoku, the wonderful sprinter from Honolulu, was the first International performer to compete, then followed Norman Ross, Olympic champion of 1920, Ludy Langer, Pua Kealoha, George Cunha and W.W. Harris last year.

On Saturday 7,000 people witnessed the greatest event in swimming history. The famous bath was never so packed, and those lucky enough to get in experienced a scene of wild enthusiasm. It is safe to assume that not one person who witnessed Charlton catching Borg in the third lap will ever forget the thrilling scene.

I had witnessed many great swimming races, but never one like this. The huge crowd began to cheer as soon as the competitors in the great International event lined up on the bath sides. They swam to the accompaniment of applause, and this became almost hysterical when Charlton, who had been hitherto behind the Swede, forged ahead with 280 yards of the journey covered. He had timed his effort wonderfully well for one of his years. Like one man, the crowd urged Charlton along. Borg wouldn't give in, and swam on very gamely, but 50 yards further on the Australian has a lead of three yards. Down the last lap his wonderful stroke and stamina told the tale. Without any apparent effort he drew right away from Borg and finished like a motorboat, his head and shoulders cleaving through the water and his feet churning it up as if equipped with a screw propeller. Charlton sprang onto the pontoon showing no signs of fatigue. Borg finished very badly.

Charlton's time – 5.11.8 – equalled the world's record, established by Arne Borg at Stockholm, and which now is awaiting recognition, but Charlton has covered the distance over long laps and in *actual competition. This denotes that his swim is the best yet accomplished over the distance. Borg took 5.28.4, which is nowhere near the figures he had put up in shorter baths.*

Though there was a risk the remaining events might prove to be something of an anticlimax after Saturday's sensation, this certainly was not how the contestants, nor the public, viewed them. The 220 yards, to be swum on Wednesday night, was generally considered to be ideal for Borg whose first two laps in the 440 had been very fast, but others gave themselves a real chance of causing an upset. Who was to know just how fast Charlton could go over two laps? He relished the long stretch of the Domain Baths and had swum a controlled race in the 440 yards. Billy Herald had won the 100 and 220 yards the previous year. Ernie Henry had swum a fine 440 after contesting the 100 that same day, and Moss Christie was considered a dark horse who might be better suited over 220 yards.

On Monday afternoon three heats of the 220 yards were swum, the first two placegetters in each race going into the final. Though times were irrelevant they would still give an indication of the likely result on Wednesday evening. Borg won the first heat by a very comfortable five yards from Keith Kirkland of The Spit Club in a time of 2 minutes 30.6 seconds. Charlton won the second heat, also by five yards, from Frank Carberry of the Sydney Club. Boy's time of 2 minutes 34.4 seconds was almost four seconds slower than Borg but he had plenty in reserve. The most exciting race of the afternoon was the third heat, Moss Christie beating Ernie Henry in a time of 2 minutes 32.2 seconds – two seconds faster than Charlton but two seconds slower than Borg. Having trained specifically for the event, Christie was extremely confident he could cause an upset. An outsider had sprung many a surprise when the favourites had concentrated on each other. Perhaps this would not be a 'two-horse race'. None of the champions was fully extended, satisfied simply to qualify. Nevertheless Borg, who was a firm favourite before the heats, was now being tipped by most to win and win well. Again Bill Longworth's article was read with interest:

Although Charlton's admirers again think he will defeat Borg I believe that at this distance the Swede will regain some of his prestige. Charlton is a wonderful swimmer who displayed surprising pace during the first 220 yards on Saturday but I expect Borg to prove too speedy. On Friday Borg covered 220 yards in the wonderful time of 2.21.4. If he repeats this swim, and I think he can, he should win. By coming all the way from Sweden to meet our champions on their home ground Borg has shown most generous sportsmanship. While here he has proved himself a great loser, and I feel sure that if he is able to defeat our champion tomorrow night he will receive a reception that will surprise him.

Despite general opinion among experts that this would be Borg's race there was no lack of confidence among Charlton fans. He had gained a place in their hearts, where logic gave way to emotion. This was no ordinary swimmer. He had shown surprising pace in the first two laps of the 440 yards and if close enough to Borg with fifty yards to go might well overtake him with his superb finishing burst. Tommy Adrian was making no prediction but Boy's father told Bill Corbett of *The Sun*: 'I believe that my boy would win if the race was swum in daylight, but he does not steer very well by the artificial light. But I have no doubt about the half-mile. Andrew will win and he will break 11 minutes if all goes well.'

A crowd of five thousand turned up to see the Wednesday night clash on a programme that also featured the final of the 220 yards breaststroke. When the field of six emerged from the dressing rooms to take their places for the 220 yards freestyle final there was spontaneous applause. The introduction of Charlton brought such prolonged cheering it seemed it might not end. While the experts had declared a win for Borg, the public was not so sure. The Australian record had been set in the corresponding race the previous year by Hawaiian champion Bill Harris at 2 minutes 26.2 seconds and Borg was very confident he would beat that time. If Charlton were to win he would almost certainly have to break the national record. Over the shorter course this was a difficult task.

A mighty cheer went up as the race commenced. Borg was not first to hit the water but was soon in front. Setting a sizzling pace he led Charlton by two yards halfway down the first lap and continued to pull further ahead. When he reached the turn there was a gap of five yards to Charlton with Ernie Henry in third place. Charlton made up some leeway by virtue of a strong turn but was still at least four yards from the quick-stroking leader. Soon after the swimmers turned the crowd noticed Borg swimming erratically. Their cheering reached new levels as Charlton began to haul in his rival. With fifty yards to go he was within two yards of Borg and still gaining steadily. Charlton drew level with thirty yards to swim. Borg rallied momentarily but to the delight of his supporters Charlton fairly lifted his body out of the water and came away to win by a full three yards, with Ernie Henry another three yards behind Borg and Moss Christie close up in fourth place.

Those who had watched the first clash of the two great swimmers on Saturday afternoon would never have believed they could relive such excitement. Charlton had swum 2 minutes 23.8 seconds, almost two and a half seconds inside Harris's national record. Considering he was better suited to longer distances, Charlton's achievement was even more remarkable than his sensational victory in the 440 yards title. Again Borg showed his sportsmanship by congratulating his victor and telling the press what a great swimmer he was. There was no disagreement from any quarter.

Having beaten the 'Swedish Sturgeon' at 440 yards and again at the seemingly unsuitable 220 yards, everyone was sure Charlton would inflict an even more comprehensive defeat on his rival in the 880 yards championship on the last day of the carnival. Some even doubted Borg would finish the race if he again attempted to outspeed Charlton from the start. But to doubt Borg's ability over the distance was to ignore his wonderful record, which included his holding the world record for 1000 metres. Clearly he had underestimated the difficulty of adapting to Australian conditions but he was a great competitor whose fitness was actually improving all the time. It was now Charlton who felt the pressure of favouritism. The unknown factor was whether the earlier swims had taken the edge off either man.

Once again a huge crowd, estimated at six thousand, arrived at the Domain Baths to witness the final meeting of the pair. The crowd roared their approval as the starters made their way to the platform for their introductions. Eight laps and eleven minutes of sustained effort awaited them. Both would feel the pressure in the last few laps and tactics could play a big part. What if Borg changed his pattern and allowed Charlton to lead? How well would the youngster pace himself? There were just four starters, Borg, Charlton, Moss Christie and Owen Griffiths.

'Face the water . . . Go!' The favourites were in front immediately. Down the first lap they went side by side, turning together on even terms, both stroking fluently. At the second turn they were still level, already some yards ahead of Christie and Griffiths. At the end of the third lap Borg was slightly ahead, swimming as fast as ever. Down the fourth lap Charlton lost some ground with erratic swimming. The crowd was suddenly worried. Perhaps their man could not triumph a third time. It was here that Charlton's fans had expected him to go to the front but Borg was going just as well. Charlton was again level at the end of 500 yards but not able to pull away. The huge crowd was calling frantically for their idol, as the pair were now twenty yards ahead of Christie and Griffiths. Screams of delight rang out when Charlton turned slightly in front at the end of the sixth lap. The bell signalled two laps to go and Borg again drew level as they approached the 770 yards mark. Charlton could not shake off his rival. This was Borg's best effort by far. Down the final thrilling lap the Manly boy slowly forged to the front. One yard became two, then three. Borg was all in with fifty yards to race but Charlton began to surge away. He was going to do it. It had been a magnificent race, a much tougher task than anticipated, but he would not be denied. The crowd had seen him put to test. His courage had matched his skill.

The official margin was fifteen yards with fifty yards to Moss Christie in third place. The semaphoring of the time sent the crowd into more rapturous applause. At 10 minutes 51.8 seconds, Charlton had taken more than thirteen seconds off his own world record of 11 minutes 5.2 seconds. Borg had also broken the previous record by swimming 10 minutes 59.4 seconds. Both swimmers paid tribute to the other's effort with Charlton saying: 'I thought all the way that I would win. I expected Borg to stick, but I was not nearly all out at the finish. I thought Borg would sprint at the finish. I will not swim again until the Olympic Games and I intend to return to Hawkesbury Agricultural College about Monday week.'

The most extraordinary week in Australia's swimming history had seen the sixteen year old champion defeat his famous adversary over 220, 440 and 880 yards, setting two world records and an Australian record. Each race had provided its own special drama. The first because no one really knew what to expect, the second because Charlton, the underdog had proven the experts wrong, and the third because Borg had shown his true colours and taken Charlton right to the wire.

As had been the case with Boy's first state tiles, Oswald Charlton was besieged by well-wishers congratulating him on his son's triumphs. During the week he had shed his conservative banker image, attending all three races dressed immaculately in blazer, slacks and cravat, smoking from a long cigarette holder and being photographed with Boy, Arne Borg and other competitors. The heights that his son had reached obviously brought him tremendous satisfaction.

3

Paris 1924

WHILE *THE REFEREE* URGED THEIR READERS to be early in ordering a special supplement featuring an exclusive picture, on art paper, of 'Andrew Charlton, the Australian Swimming Marvel', Arne Borg's form continued to improve and impress. Ten days after his gallant second place behind Charlton over 880 yards he dead-heated with Billy Herald over 100 yards and then produced a magnificent swim in the state one-mile title at the Domain. In the mile he beat Moss Christie by 125 yards. On the way to victory he broke his own world record for 1000 metres by almost twelve seconds and his 1500 metres world record by almost twenty seconds. His finishing burst was described by Bill Longworth as 'the finest sprint I have ever seen under such circumstances'. Borg was now swimming as quickly at the Domain as he had in his home country. Victory for Boy Charlton in the 1500 metres at the Olympics was not a foregone conclusion after all.

Though Tommy Adrian had determined Charlton would not compete in any more championship races before the Olympics, he would retain his fitness by competing in lesser events, such as club races and exhibitions. On the eve of Borg's wonderful mile swim, Charlton competed for Manly in the 4×220 yards club team's race, helping them to a clear victory before watching Borg's impressive performance. The continuing good form of his Manly team-mate Ernie Henry was a pointer to Australia sending a very competitive relay team to Paris, provided funds were available. *The Sun* had reported, with some alarm, during the carnival:

> One of the things made clear at last week's meeting of the Olympic Federation Council was the backwardness of N.S.W. in regard to the funds necessary to ensure a good representation of Australia. While little South Australia has 750 pounds in cash in hand, or very nearly her quota of the 10,000 pounds required from the whole of Australia, N.S.W. is on the 250 pounds mark with Queensland.
>
> This apathy is the more remarkable since on the figures many, if not most, of the athletes who will represent Australia (if there is money enough to send them) will come from N.S.W. In swimming this state has Charlton, Herald and Christie and other fine performers; in running and athletics 'Slip', Carr, Bailey, Winter and other top-notchers; in cycling Coppins, and front-rank men in other branches of sport.
>
> So enthusiastic is South Australia that it feels that if the Murray Bridge eight is chosen to represent Australia the money to send the crew can be raised in that state. New South Wales has a fine eight in the Mosman crew but it is hard to be so optimistic about raising the money in N.S.W. if their eight is chosen.
>
> However a determined effort is to be made to end the apathy shown so far. A meeting of representatives of all sporting bodies, of members of the citizens' representation fund committee and other

associations or bodies interested, has been called for Monday at the Sports' Club.

Definite proposals for raising New South Wales's quota of the Olympic funds will be put before this meeting. Among them is the proposal of a fortnight's 'drive', with the appointment of a paid organiser, who will be able to devote his whole time to the campaign.

It will be put up to New South Wales sports and sport supporters that if they do as well as South Australia they will be all right. N.S.W. has the men and she ought to have the money.

The clashes of Charlton and Borg had drawn record crowds and not only produced a wonderful profit for the NSW Swimming Association but also gave a tremendous boost to the public's interest in Olympic funding. Swimming fans were now contributing generously and proceeds from other swimming carnivals were also adding to the coffers.

Boy Charlton was back at Hawkesbury Agricultural College by February and Arne Borg continued his tour. In Queensland Borg swam a spectacular time in the freshwater Brisbane Baths, an indoor pool where water was pumped from the Brisbane River and which reminded him of those in Europe. Though not considered a venue to make fast times, even though laps were 33⅓ yards long, Borg covered 880 yards more than half a minute faster than Frank Beaurepaire's best time there two years earlier. Two days later at Toowoomba he beat Keith Kirkland in the 100 yards and then swam just four seconds outside Charlton's world record for 440 yards.

The Swedish champion defeated Frank Beaurepaire in the Australian championships at Hobart's Sandy Bay Baths but the Victorian veteran turned the tables over three quarters of a mile (1320 yards) in the choppy waters of St Kilda where he was a specialist. Bill Longworth, well aware of Beaurepaire's ability in such conditions, had predicted the result. It showed

Beaurepaire was anything but a spent force and increased his chances of going to his third Olympics, sixteen years after his first.

After a farewell dinner at the New South Wales Sports Club, at which he expressed the view that Australia had a host of talented young swimmers whose greatest need was a well-organised coaching system, Borg sailed the next day, March 19, aboard the *Niagra* for the Territory of Hawaii via New Zealand. En route he was to make several appearances before going on to Europe via the United States. Naturally impressed with Charlton, Borg had also become close friends with Keith Kirkland and Moss Christie and vowed to return after the Paris Olympics. A farewell message to the people of Australia was published in *The Referee*:

> *On the eve of leaving Australia, I wish to convey to you all a hearty and sincere thanks. My whole tour through your beautiful country has not only been to me a pleasure trip, but it has given me knowledge of your great prosperity and the kindness of your people. I shall always look forward to coming back here and spending the rest of my life in Australia and becoming one of yourselves.*
>
> *From the first day of my arrival here I loved the country on account of the way you wished me welcome. I do not think any continent in the world has better sportsmen than yours. Once more, thanking you for all your kindness to me.*
>
> *Yours sincerely,*
> *Arne Borg.*

Upon his return to college, Boy's course took him to 'Shops', where he learned the rudiments of carpentry, saddlery and blacksmith's work. Just as his father had predicted, practical, outdoor work suited him perfectly. Stitching a saddle, making a horse rug, cutting fence posts, pumping the bellows and striking hot iron on the anvil was very much to his liking. So too was competing in the College's annual swimming carnival where he again won all four freestyle events, from 50 yards to 440 yards. He would have just over two months schooling before leaving for Paris. Irrespective of his swimming results at the Olympics he was due back in the blacksmith's shop in September. His experience at practical farming was punctated by weekend trips to Sydney where he was about to embark on another journey – that of a competitive surfer.

By the early 1920s, well before the advent of radio or television, Saturday surf carnivals had become a major sporting attraction, luring crowds of many thousands to the beach to witness a series of exciting events. In excess of twenty local clubs regularly competed at Sydney beaches. Some carnivals were held in the afternoon, others ran all day and club members would begin preparing the beach area as early as Wednesday evening, erecting heavy tiered seating. Early on carnival day, comfortable deck chairs – some reserved for special guests, others for those who booked early – were placed in prime position and marker buoys rowed out beyond the breakers and their heavy anchors lowered into the water. Hessian enclosures were also erected for those spectators prepared to pay a little extra to get a clear view. Money from admission prices was vital to help buy and maintain lifesaving equipment.

Carnivals began with a spectacular march past of all club teams, each comprising twenty members. The blue-riband event, from a surfer's point of view, was the open surf race. Depending on the seas, swimmers would negotiate distances from 200 to 400 metres to the buoys and a further 100 metres parallel with the shore before turning to come back to the beach. Natural buoyancy, speed and strength were just as important in this race as in still water distance swimming. The first to turn for home had first crack at the waves on the long journey back. Many a surfer with the race apparently in his keeping was relegated back in the field after missing a wave that others had caught. The top four swimmers from each club also competed in a team's race with all swimmers starting simultaneously and each man's finishing position added together so the lowest score won. This was a very exciting event where a poor performance by one swimmer could cost a team the race.

The belt race saw three linesmen and a reelman deployed as each beltman swam to his designated buoy. Co-ordination was important as pulling too quickly or too slowly on the surf-line negated the beltman's efforts. When seas were big buoys would be anchored well past the breakers and the reelman had to keep a close eye to see if he was running out of line. When this occurred a knot had to be tied on to a second line and a silent prayer said that it did not come undone.

In the R and R (rescue and resuscitation) exercise, each member in a crew of six drew marbles to determine which part they played, meaning all had to be proficient at each station. The patient swam out, signalled he was in difficulties and the rescuer donned the belt and made for the sea. The linesmen, standing about 15 metres apart, fed the line above their heads as he made his way to the patient then helped bring the pair back to shore by pulling the line underhand to the reelman. Judges kept a close eye on the resuscitation drill. Time and technique were important in scoring. This event was extremely popular with clubmen. Manly entered its first R and R team in carnivals in 1912. By 1930 there would be twenty-one teams competing in their own inter-patrol competitions.

For the public there was nothing as thrilling as the surfboat race, where open wooden boats with six oarsmen and a sweep battled breakers and swells on their way out to the buoys and fought to catch waves on the way back. Cinema patrons around the world watched in amazement at this unique Australian contest. Collisions and upturned boats were a regular occurrence in big seas. The constant risk of serious injury was ignored as in few other sporting adventures.

Carnival action was non-stop with beach sprinting, flag races and novelty events – such as the pillow fight where combatants balanced on poles 10 feet above the ground and flailed at each until one was unseated – adding to the fun. The top surfers were very popular with the locals and quickly recognised as they made their way down The Corso to participate. When carnivals were held at other clubs, forty or fifty Manly surfers, steak sandwiches and soft drink in hand, crowded onto the tabletop of a large truck, along with the surfboat and reel. A mighty cheer would follow them as the truck thundered down The Corso, headed for glory, on a distant Sydney beach. Little wonder they, and their rivals, were often referred to as the epitome of Australian manhood.

Charlton's swimming ability made the surf race and belt race natural events for him though the thrills and spills of surfboat racing also appealed. Now a junior member of the Manly Surf Club, Boy began his surfing career by taking his share of patrols, invariably surrounded by admiring youngsters. His first swim in the junior surf race at Manly, resulted in victory and drew this report from *The Arrow*:

> Great interest was shown in the novice surf relay race in which Boy Charlton made his initial appearance as a surf racer. His partner J. Davis swam first and finished 12th leaving Charlton to concede about 40 yards to [Ken] Foster. He gained ground quickly and when rounding the buoys was lying fifth. He continued to make up ground and passed Foster about forty yards from the beach. Charlton sprinted to the rope forty yards ahead. He was 'all out,' but recovered quickly and a few moments later rowed in the junior boat race.

Tommy Adrian was naturally keeping a close eye on his protégé and was not too happy about his surfboat escapades as an injury could put his fitness at risk, but Boy continued nevertheless. Many experts were of the opinion that surfing was not helpful to still water swimming but in Australia it was a way of life. Boy's last swim of the season was an exhibition race at Clifton Gardens at the Commonwealth Bank's annual carnival, where he did excellent time over 440 yards. On that same evening the crowd was thrilled by another wonderful exhibition by the state diving troupe. Manly's last carnival of the season featured past and present champions in exhibition swims showing how styles had changed. The side and single overarm action was followed by the Australian crawl, then the trudgen crawl demonstrated by Tommy Adrian and finally the six-beat trudgen crawl by Ernie Henry.

Despite earlier concerns, all states fulfilled their financial requirements for the Olympics by various fundraising methods. The Manly Swimming Club's 'All-white Ball', where ladies were required to wear light coloured evening gowns and gentlemen all white, priced at three shillings and sixpence for dancers and one and six to sit in the gallery, was typical of fundraising functions conducted throughout Sydney. In Murray Bridge, South Australia, a rather different approach to raising money saw a prize bull, donated by cattle baron Sir Stanley Kidman, go to auction.

With the federal government honouring a promise to contribute generously to the fund, provided the sporting associations of each state reached their goals, Australia was able to announce its largest Olympic team to date of thirty-seven athletes, a rowing coach and four officials. Naturally Boy Charlton was selected.

The team manager, O.G.H. 'Ossie' Merrett, was a fine sports-man who had been a national surf champion as well as a first grade rugby player. Merrett had pioneered many of the sporting clubs in Manly and his commitment to amateur sport was immense. Not only was he the first president of the Manly Sporting Union he also served as president of the Manly Rugby Union Club, Manly Amateur Athletic Club and Manly Amateur Swimming Club. Merrett was also a foundation and life member of the North Steyne Surf Club, chairman of the NSW Amateur Swimming Association and honorary secretary of the Australian Olympic Federation. The fact that the forty year old had run his own successful millinery business since he was twenty-four was an indication of his energy and zest for work as well as sport. Merrett's Hats, situated in the centre of Sydney, was the largest manufacturer of men's boater hats in Australia. Ossie Merrett would need all his business acumen and enthusiasm over the coming months.

Although he was without doubt Australia's most likely gold medallist, Boy's selection to the Olympic team did not please everyone. There were some who had taken exception to his missing the national championships and arguments ensued among reporters and correspondents to the press, particularly in Hobart and Melbourne, as to whether he should be allowed to go to Paris. Interstate rivalry played its part, Victorians still rankled over the part New South Wales played in banning Frank Beaurepaire when he took the job of teaching swimming. Boy had been invited to attend the championships but not compete unless he wished. The Australian Swimming Union's annual meeting in Melbourne that followed the national championships was a fiery affair with acrimonious debate on the issue of Charlton's decision not to swim there. The criticism upset the Charlton family and Tommy Adrian.

Announcement of the team was followed by another sensation.

Rumours began to surface, almost immediately, that Boy Charlton might miss the Games, causing great concern among officials and fans alike. With Charlton unavailable for comment until he returned from College, the rumours became stronger. Central to these rumours was the belief that Charlton was nervous about making the trip without Tommy Adrian. Already there was a groundswell of opinion that Adrian should accompany the team to take particular care of him. There was a special bond between them. Charlton had actually worn the same costume in his swims against Borg that Tommy Adrian had used when he beat Duke Kahanamoku. If Adrian were to go, money would have to be found from outside the team's budget and offers soon came to organise a fund to send him. Though not wanting to believe their champion might miss the Games, the public began to understand the situation following this article in *The Sun*, which appeared under the headline, 'Grandfather's Objection'.

Boy Charlton's grandfather, Mr A.H. Moore, chairman of the Advisory Board at Goldsbrough Mort and Company, says that he has not attempted to prevent the champion from accepting the invitation for Paris, but is convinced that the lad is too young to go abroad and fears that it would be 'morally unsafe'. He has promised to set Boy up in the farming business. If he goes to Paris he will still have that chance, but the grandfather stipulates that he must 'return the same lad as he went'.

'He is too young. You know what it is like when a young man gets away with grown men. I don't know any of the men he would go with. I don't know Adrian or anybody else. All I know is that they are men and Andrew is only a youngster. If Boy had been going away with a batch of other boys, like the crowd of Young Australian League lads that left recently, in the charge of an officer to look after them and keep them from danger, there could not possibly be an objection. But for a boy to go away, undisciplined, as it is proposed

Andrew should go, is very different. You know, as well as I do, it is much easier to do the wrong thing than the right thing in the world.'

Some time ago Mr Moore said he had made certain promises to his grandson.

'I have not withdrawn those promises,' he declared, 'and I have not bound him in any way. If he decides to go, the opportunities I have offered will still be open. What I said to him a fortnight ago was this. "I think you're too young to go abroad but if you make up your mind to go I'll not stand in your way."

'If he returns the same boy as he went, the promises will be honoured and I'll think more of him for it. It rests with himself. I can't stop him and his father can't stop him. If he wants to go it would be foolish to attempt to stop him, but still – I think it is inadvisable. When he beat Harris I said he was too young to go abroad and I still think so now. However I hope that it will be settled somehow in a sportsmanlike and honourable way. It has not been all sportsmanship up to date. I don't know who started that demand for Adrian to accompany Andrew but I think it's not quite the thing. If the controlling body of any sport is to be dictated to every time it selects a representative we'll get nowhere.'

Boy was suddenly in a no-win situation. His grandfather, who obviously had a lot to say in the decision, did not want him to go to Paris unchaperoned, but on the other hand declared no knowledge of Tommy Adrian's character despite the praise previously accorded the coach by Boy's father. So strong was the feeling in Manly that Adrian should go that Billy Herald, fourth in the 100 metres final in the previous Games and again chosen for the swim team, offered to stand down if it meant Adrian could accompany his young charge. His offer was repeated in the *Manly Daily*: 'There is no doubt,' said Herald, 'that the Australian public is looking towards Charlton to create a new standard for Australian swimming. I say again that I did make that statement and I certainly hope that Adrian will go to the games.'

Tommy Adrian refused to consider the magnanimous offer but was now in a very tenuous position with the issue causing so much controversy. Some were not in favour of sending people from outside the selected team. Others saw Boy's young age as presenting unusual circumstances and thought Adrian should definitely go. In any case no fund to send him could be conducted until it was known that Boy was a certain starter. Manager Ossie Merrett was quoted as saying that Frank Beau-repaire, with his vast experience, and Merrett himself would be well suited to look after the lad. After personal criticism by a journalist, Tommy Adrian found fit to defend himself publicly in the Sydney press:

> Boy Charlton expressed his wish, publicly, some months ago that if he went to the games I should accompany him so why should the realisation of his desire come as a surprise at 'the eleventh hour' as one writer termed. As far as I know no demand that the money to send me should come from the Olympic fund. A couple of months ago a fund was started by Manly sportsmen to furnish my expenses. It was stopped by Mr. Merrett and other workers for the Olympic fund and I was given to understand that it would be revived when the Olympic fund quota was reached. However no attempt to revive it has been made. On the contrary I think it has been retarded by the circulation of rumours that I could afford to pay my own fare. Another rumour was that my people were averse to the idea of my being sent by public subscription. These rumours did not emanate from me.
>
> When Mr. Merrett returned from Melbourne after the selection of the Olympic team he informed me that no provision had been made for the inclusion of coaches or trainers. I asked him if the money could be raised to send me and whether he had any objection to make being

included in the team as mentor to Charlton as well as Ernie Henry and Herald. He said he did not have any objections and would be pleased if I accompanied the team. The following day I asked him the approximate cost of the trip in that capacity and he replied it would be 350 pounds. He added that the council was not bothering about coaches and that I would be more useful as a masseur. As a masseur it would cost me considerably less. Obviously he valued my services as a masseur, which I know nothing about, more than as a coach.

Mr. Merrett said that Frank Beaurepaire has had more experience than I have and that he (Mr. Merrett) has had thirty years experience and that they are well able to look after Charlton. My opinion is that it does not matter how much experience Beaurepaire or others may have had they do not understand him as I do. The fact that Boy is unwilling to go without me is only a minor obstacle.

And so the arguments continued until Charlton, under extreme pressure, wrote to Ossie Merrett declining the invitation to compete in Paris. Though his letter was never published the reasons seemed clear enough: his family's concern at his being on the far side of the world with grown men, the controversy surrounding his mentor Tommy Adrian and the fear that swimming, a pastime, might infringe on the more important aspects of his life. The public was shocked. They hoped fervently he might be persuaded to change his mind. It was a hope given little encouragement when his father was quoted as being unwilling to give his consent even if he wished to go. Furthermore his father added that he might not even swim again competitively.

These comments were in direct contrast to those quoted after Boy's first victory over Arne Borg. With all that had been said and written there was tremendous relief when a letter from Charlton to Ossie Merrett was published in *The Referee* a little over three weeks before the team was due to depart.

Ravenscroft
Stuart St
Manly
March 16 1924.

O.G.H. Merrett, Esq.,
Manager
Olympic Team

Dear Sir,

I have reconsidered my decision not to join the Olympic team, and I have decided, if your kind invitation still holds good, I will accept same. I wish to express my regret that I have stated that I would not go except under certain conditions. My inexperience in these matters must be my excuse, and after I had the position fully explained to me I must admit that it was not the correct thing for me to have stated that I would not accept your invitation excepting under certain conditions.

Needless to say I am still in hopes that arrangements will be made for Adrian to accompany the team as I feel that under his direction it would inspire me with more confidence. Should I again be selected, I hope to bring back fresh laurels to Australia and I shall take such pains that my conduct will be a credit to my connections as well as myself.

I intend to play the game and to show by my actions my sincere appreciation of the many kindnesses that I have received from my friends during my career, and trust on my return to find the same warm little corner in the hearts of those who have shown me such kindness and consideration,

Yours sincerely,
Andrew. M. Charlton.

The Referee was adamant rival newspapers had contributed to the controversy and declared so in no uncertain terms:

A section of the daily newspapers in Sydney appear to have unwittingly conduced to the yes-no attitude of the young champion to accept the invitation. They have day by day served up sensations to their readers, and created an unsettled and artificial atmosphere not good for amateur sport.

Considerable controversy took place last week owing to reports that Andrew Charlton was not going to the Olympic Games. Several reasons were advanced, until after a great deal of publicity, Charlton wrote to the secretary, Mr Oswald Merrett, declining the invitation.

This created consternation in swimming circles but after further consideration the youth has accepted the invitation unconditionally. One of Charlton's reasons for refusing was that his fidus achates, Tommy Adrian, was not selected to accompany him. Now that Charlton has decided to go Adrian is likely to be sent by public subscription. Without Charlton the team would not be worth sending. No doubt Charlton has been worried by what has lately been said in certain quarters but he will never regret going to the games.

Only members of the family, or perhaps Boy himself, would ever know exactly what prompted him to change his mind. Bill Corbett in *The Sun* spoke for most when he wrote: 'Australia is delighted although it cannot fully understand the boy's uncertainty.' Frank Beaurepaire echoed his sentiments in Melbourne's *Evening Sun*: 'Whatever was behind it all, Boy Charlton did the logical thing when he finally accepted the invitation to the Olympic Games.'

The publishing of Boy's letter was accompanied by statements from his father and grandfather confirming their approval of his decision. Boy's grandfather declared he was 'full up of the whole business' and expressed the hope that he would return to Australia 'retaining the respect and esteem which he appears to enjoy on leaving. Anything further becomes a family matter, and cannot be of any interest to the public.' Arthur Henry Moore might well have been a most astute businessman but he was underestimating his grandson's influence on people generally. Boy Charlton had assumed a position where everything he did was of interest to the public. In any event, Boy's grandfather took him to the finest clothing store in Sydney and fitted him with a complete wardrobe for the trip. Not only was he going to the Games, he would look 'a million dollars' while he was there.

Once it became clear that Charlton was a certain starter a public subscription was organised through the *Sunday Mail* to pay Tommy Adrian's way to Paris. Hugh. D. McIntosh, former boxing promoter and builder of Sydney Stadium, now proprietor of the *Sunday Mail* as well as *The Referee*, began proceedings with a donation of thirty pounds, which was matched by a prominent Manly businessman. The fund quickly gained momentum with donations ranging from a few shillings to several pounds, each being acknowledged in the press. On April 2, the paper happily reported an anonymous donor had arrived at the newspaper office and asked the sum still needed. When advised of the amount he wrote a cheque for 174 pounds. Three hundred and fifty pounds had been raised. Tommy Adrian would accompany his young champion to Paris.

The 1924 Olympic team had a very strong Manly connection. Apart from Charlton and Ernie Henry, diver Dick Eve, close friends with both, was also a member of the Manly Club and athlete Nick Winter was a local fireman. Billy Herald, who was chosen to be part of the five-man swim team, withdrew for personal reasons, not associated with the Adrian controversy, and was replaced by Moss Christie. Frank Beaurepaire had also won selection in his third games. The fifth member was Ivan Stedman, who would swim the 100 metres freestyle and backstroke, and probably heats of the relay to rest Charlton. With

Charlton and Ernie Henry, Australia would field a strong 4×200 metres relay team, though America had announced twelve swimmers all of whom had better times over 220 metres than the Australian swimmers except for Charlton.

The team was due to sail on the Orient liner *Omar* on April 12, 1924, but when the ship was found to be in need of dry dock repairs departure was delayed until April 30 when the 15,000-ton, twin-propeller, RMS *Ormonde*, flagship of the famous Orient Line, sailed for London. There were misgivings about the delay, particularly in relation to Charlton, who would need longer to prepare for the 1500 metres than the sprinters for their events. The team would not arrive in Paris until June 7, a month before the commencement of the Games. Nevertheless they would enjoy the very best sailing conditions possible on the largest, most luxurious ocean liner servicing Australia.

On April 28, Boy was given a rousing send-off at Hawkesbury Agricultural College and presented with an Old Boys' gold badge. Edwin 'Slip' Carr, Australia's finest track sprinter, was another student at the College on his way to Paris so the school was rightly proud to have two representatives. Slip Carr had also gone to Hawkesbury from Sydney Grammar School. The New South Wales and Queensland team members enjoyed a public send off at the Theatre Royal and were on board, ready for departure, the next day.

A huge crowd had assembled on Wednesday, April 30, to farewell the team. By midday visitors had been sent ashore and the team lined up on deck, dressed in green blazers and caps, to participate in an exciting farewell. Thousands of streamers broke as the giant liner slowly pulled from the dock and the vast crowd of well- wishers sang 'Auld Lang Syne'. The harbour was awash with small craft, laden with people keen to get a glimpse of the athletes who stood waving on deck. As the *Ormonde* moved proudly down the harbour the crew of HMAS

Melbourne lined the deck to give three cheers. Ferries and tugboats sounded cock-a-doodle-doos, one after the other. The crowd stayed on the wharf for almost an hour until the liner disappeared from view.

By 1 pm the *Ormonde* had cleared the Heads, dropped her pilot, and was underway. At four that afternoon, manager Ossie Merrett issued team jumpers – cream with a green and gold V neck trim – not all of which fitted too well and some judicious swaps were made. The sea was calm and remained so all day. Not one team member suffered the slightest seasickness. The departure had gone off smoothly.

The *Ormonde* was to follow the traditional route to London, sailing via Melbourne and Adelaide, across the Great Australian Bight to Perth then northwest, across the Indian Ocean to Ceylon's capital, Colombo. The ship would then make its way through the Arabian and Red Seas, the Suez Canal, across the Mediterranean to Toulon in the south of France and on to England. In all, the journey would take about six weeks. The athletes would not be without strong Australian support. A large contingent of fans had booked passages including a group from Manly organised by Fitz Lough who had given Boy his first swimming instruction at Manly Baths and who had taken a keen interest in his career ever since.

Tommy Adrian had not been well for a fortnight before departure and was too ill to sail on the *Ormonde*, but it was hoped he would be able to leave soon after on the *Levuka* and join the team at its first port of call, Melbourne, where the Victorian contingent were waiting. Adrian was to share a cabin, at manager Ossie Merrett's discretion, with the two Manly teenagers, Charlton and Ernie Henry.

The weather remained calm and by the time the ship arrived in Melbourne on Friday morning the team was already getting used to the shipboard routine, enjoying some traditional games of quoits and deck tennis and doing fitness work with medicine balls and skipping ropes.

The *Ormonde* berthed in Melbourne for five days, during which the Olympians enjoyed a variety of official and private functions. Friday morning was taken up with photo sessions, followed by lunch as guests of the Victorian Olympic Council, and a trip to the Princess Theatre that night to see *The O'Brien Girl*. On Saturday several members attended the Carlton and Essendon Australian rules fixture, which ended in a draw. When news came through that Sydney Grammar had won the GPS Head of the River, Boy Charlton, Moss Christie and Slip Carr gave Ossie Merrett quite a chiacking as his boys were attending Shore. On Sunday the entire company went on an all-day motor trip to Healesville, about 75 kilometres from the capital, lunched at a popular hotel, continued over Black Spur Mountain and returned to the *Ormonde* for dinner at 7 pm.

On Monday, May 5, a public holiday, Tommy Adrian joined the team much to the relief of the swimmers, particularly Boy and Ernie Henry. Moss Christie noted in his diary that Adrian 'looked far from a fit man'. All hoped a relaxing sea journey would help his recovery. The only Victorian who did not join the team was Frank Beaurepaire who was travelling via the United States on the *Aquitania* and would meet up with his team-mates in London.

By the time the *Ormonde* left Melbourne on Tuesday evening the whole team had been feted and looked after in a way usually reserved for visiting dignitaries. The weather was a little less kind after Melbourne and Boy Charlton was one of quite a few who did not make it for breakfast on the morning they reached Adelaide. Here the Murray Bridge boat crew boarded and immediately made an impression on Moss Christie who noted in his diary: 'If mere brute strength will win the 8-oar crews' race we have one on the slate already!'

The journey continued from Adelaide after just one day's rest, but not without incident. Soon after three sharp whistles signalled the *Ormonde*'s departure on Thursday, May 8, Ivan Stedman arrived at the wharf. Fortunately Moss Christie spotted him, advised the captain and the *Ormonde* stopped. Stedman paid three pounds to have a launch take him 300 yards to the liner, much to the amusement of passengers all round. He felt the embarrassment much more than the expense.

Continuing its journey across the Bight, the weather, often very wild on this section of the trip, remained very kind. Even the most apprehensive sailors were finding their sea legs and holding their balance at the nightly dances.

The *Ormonde* had been fitted out with special equipment to facilitate training for the athletes and a committee was elected to supervise each day's proceedings. After a session of callisthenics they followed routines to prepare for their different sports. A square canvas pool, 12 feet by 12 feet and containing about 3 feet of water, was now erected on deck and swimmers were able to assimilate racing, in a fashion, by swimming in the one spot, pulling against a rope harness fixed above them. It was very primitive, but better than nothing. Once they became used to it, swimmers were able to practise their technique while retaining reasonable fitness. Charlton and Christie were first to try it. Unfortunately Dick Eve caught a toenail in the canvas causing a tear, so the boatswain was summoned to repair it before the next day. Eve was duly admonished for not cutting his nails. The pool was drained and disassembled each night and reassembled the next morning if weather permitted.

Members of the four-man cycling team would be the least disadvantaged by the long trip, pedalling for hours on rollers as they did on land. Oarsmen 'rowed' by sitting opposite each other in pairs and alternately pulling on a heavy rope loop or using a rowing machine fixed to the deck. These sessions proved quite an attraction to other passengers and crewmen alike.

Once the liner left Sydney, sports lovers received only occasional reports about the team. However, in one issue *The Sun* was able to show a series of excellent photographs of the swimmers and rowers training on deck as fascinated crewmen looked on.

When the ship docked at Fremantle team members were pleased to be able to spend a relaxing day in Perth. After lunch the Western Australian swim champion, Brusher Jones, drove Christie, Eve, Charlton and Henry to Crawley Baths, a tidal pool over 300 yards in length, where they had their last good swim before leaving Australia. The *Ormonde* left Fremantle at six that evening and at 8 pm passengers took their last look at Australia's coastline. The uninterrupted voyage from Fremantle to Ceylon's capital, Colombo, was by far the longest of the entire journey. Barring accident the trip would take eight and a half days and cover almost 7,000 kilometres, in ever increasing heat. As if to announce the trip was on in earnest, a storm that lasted six hours hit the ship the next morning, their first in the Indian Ocean.

Each day, except Sunday, weather permitting, the swimmers did a session in the canvas pool lasting from fifteen minutes to an hour. They were the envy of other passengers as the weather continued to get hotter. Despite the daytime training sessions, the cinema and the nightly dance, an amount of boredom was inevitable. On one occasion the Sydney press published a letter from a team member describing conditions on board and how the team was reacting to the tedium of a long sea trip and the heat as they approached the tropics. Ossie Merrett did all he could to counter the monotony, he and as his committee organising sports' carnivals that involved other passengers as well as the Olympians.

There was plenty of time for letter writing and Boy, like most, prepared letters filled with shipboard news for posting at each

port of call. A few days after leaving Perth the team was introduced to the father of the former English cricket captain,
J.W.H.T. Douglas, who had been holidaying in Australia with
his wife. They had plenty to talk about as Douglas senior had
refereed the boxing match in which his son had beaten
Australia's Snowy Baker for the Olympic middleweight title in
London in 1908. The following day an elderly passenger died
and was buried at sea. None had seen a sea burial, conducted by
the captain in an area near the swimmers' cabins. The body was
sewn in a canvas bag and cast into the ocean. On a lighter note
the swimmers were first to realise that having had supper in the
music room a short walk aft to the smoking room meant you
could have another. The same ruse proved just as successful with
ice cream at morning tea.

Tommy Adrian was known to have suffered depression when he
returned from the war but seemed to have been able to put this
behind him in the years that followed. His involvement with Boy
Charlton and other young swimmers had given him a real
purpose and his coaching had been a tremendous help in
Charlton's rise to fame. His articles on swimming were expertly
written and his interviews before and after Charlton's swims
were those of an articulate and focussed man. He was extremely
grateful at having been sent to Paris but upset at the furore
concerning his departure as well as personal criticism and had
been ill and in poor spirits since before the trip began.

As the ship neared Colombo, Tommy Adrian became increas-
ingly moody and elected not to sit with Charlton and Ernie
Henry at meals or when resting on deck. By the time the
Ormonde reached Colombo, on the morning of May 21, she
had been at sea three weeks and the tropical heat was oppressive
to the point of almost unbearable.

The entry to Colombo Harbour was made more exciting than usual when the *Ormonde* struck the 300-ton SS *Pacific*, but remarkably the lighter vessel sustained no apparent damage, though the incident terrified native sailors aboard her. The team had a rest day in Colombo and many sporting personalities were among the large crowd that came out to welcome the visitors. Mr Foender, a well-known sports' journalist who seemed to be in charge of proceedings, presented Ossie Merrett with several huge pineapples, which were placed in the ship's refrigerator.

Local sporting authorities had arranged an athletics carnival where the team could compete but unfortunately rain prevented any outdoor events. Ivan Stedman, Moss Christie and sculler Arthur Bull were able to arrange a pleasant swim in a private pool. Charlton and Ernie Henry elected to stay with Tommy Adrian and went on a tour of the very pretty city. It rained for several hours so overcoats were the order of the day. A photograph taken by Henry shows his two companions posing by a rickshaw in a very serious mood. That afternoon the entire team attended the YMCA to see their boxers fight exhibitions against local champions. A request to interview Charlton in the ring was knocked back by the shy youngster, but he was cajoled into walking down ringside and to wave at the crowd when introduced. He was so embarrassed by the reception he quickly hurried back to his seat.

The *Ormonde* left Colombo in the early hours of the next morning. Before breakfast, Adrian produced a cutthroat razor, dragged the blunt side across his throat and said to Charlton and Henry: 'That'll be the end of me.' Greatly concerned about this extraordinary behaviour the youngsters reported the incident to Ossie Merrret who was faced with a very difficult problem. If he approached Adrian it might exacerbate his depression. Hopefully his mood would brighten as the tropical heat abated and the ship got closer to its destination and the excitement of competition. Merrett decided not to speak to Adrian but asked that the boys keep a close eye on him and not leave him alone on deck. Now the chaperone was being chaperoned. These incidents were generally not known until some years later, when Ernie Henry confided in historian Harry Gordon.

On the afternoon of Friday, May 23, two days after leaving Colombo, with the *Ormonde* steaming towards the Arabian Sea, Tommy Adrian was quietly watching passengers playing games on the top deck. Suddenly he got up, made his way quickly to the ship's railing and flung himself from the ship, fully clothed, into shark infested waters below. There was mayhem on deck as the call of 'Man overboard!' was heard above the screams of horrified passengers. The captain was at lunch and the officer on watch immediately ordered the ship to go about. Boy Charlton and Ernie Henry had just walked upstairs to the deck and ran to the rail in time to see Adrian hit the water. Henry and others had to restrain Charlton from diving in to save him. All they could do was watch as the drama unfolded.

Crewmen threw lifebelts towards Adrian as the captain was advised of the misadventure. Four loud blasts came from the funnel and the *Ormonde* began a wide arc to attempt a rescue. The sea was relatively calm and Adrian trod water, shedding his coat and shoes. Some half hour later the *Ormonde* was within a hundred yards of the hapless Adrian and two lifeboats were lowered over the side and rowed towards him. Adrian, who had continued to tread water, clapped his hands, swam towards one of the boats and was helped aboard by the seamen.

When it was ascertained that Adrian had jumped from the ship and not fallen, the captain ordered that he be locked in the brig, below decks, for his own safety. There he would stay for the rest of the journey – he was allowed no visitors. It seemed Tommy Adrian had suffered a panic attack, part of extreme post-traumatic stress, brought on by the confinement of the ship's long journey, his first since travelling home from the war four years earlier. Boy Charlton had lost his coach and mentor. As it transpired, neither Charlton nor Henry, his two young friends, would see Tommy Adrian again until they returned to Manly well after the Olympics. Few of Charlton's friends in Australia were aware of the extra burden now placed on the youngster's shoulders.

It is impossible to imagine exactly what effect this bizarre incident had on Charlton. Certainly it must have had some impact. Adrian was to supervise Boy's training and plan his race tactics. But he was more than just his coach. Charlton would have felt extremely sorry for his mentor and could not have had any real understanding of his condition. Even medical experts knew little about post-traumatic stress, or shellshock as it was then known. Adrian's incarceration in the bowels of the ship, necessary though it was, would do nothing to help his problems.

The captain was naturally distraught about the incident. He questioned Charlton and Henry as to whether Adrian had given any indication that all was not well. They had no choice but to plead ignorance. The captain's concern was to become much greater. In order to quickly go about, one of the *Ormonde*'s huge propellers had been shut down, putting enormous strain on the other. The tail shaft of the operating propeller was badly damaged. Already slightly behind schedule, the *Ormonde* was now travelling well below her normal speed of 15 knots. In the early hours of Sunday morning the ship's engines stopped altogether for a short period. The silence was eerie. When the big liner got going again it crawled along at about 9 knots. Only one of the turbines was now operating. The next port of call, Aden, on the Arabian peninsular, where repairs would be attempted, was several hundred miles away.

The lost time was a worry for manager Ossie Merrett but the team members took it in their stride, exercising conscientiously and enjoying the evenings' festivities including a fancy dress ball in which several of the group won prizes for their creativity. Merrett's deputy manager Cam West won first prize for his witch's costume. On the following night the regular dance was replaced with a concert in which the Olympians again participated. The crew did everything to ensure that, despite the mishap and subsequent slow progress, all one hundred and fifty passengers were given every chance to enjoy themselves. Certainly Boy Charlton had experienced nothing like it before.

When the *Ormonde* limped into Aden on Thursday, May 29, the ship's clock showed 7 am. Having moored just inside the harbour entrance the ship was besieged by peddlers in small boats who had come to sell all manner of knick-knacks and souvenirs. The bargaining was fun but when allowed to go ashore immediately after lunch passengers who walked about the town found it very dirty and uninviting. There were many beggars and lepers and the Australians were glad to rejoin the ship, where engineers were still working on the damaged motor, reminded of how lucky they were to live where they did.

The repairs, carried out that day and the following morning, were successful to the point that the *Ormonde* was now capable of reaching speeds of about 12 knots. It was fortunate that the seas were calm and there was a following breeze. She was now two full days behind schedule. By 11 pm the *Ormonde* had passed Perim at the entrance to the Red Sea. Throughout Saturday, Sunday and Monday passengers experienced perfect weather, hot by day but cooler at night. Having reached Suez at 2 pm on Tuesday afternoon, the *Ormonde* had to wait seven hours to start the journey through the Suez Canal. No one was allowed ashore and the team was ushered onto the top deck to get a good look at the entrance to the canal. Having taken in the spectacular view Boy and Ernie Henry followed the others' lead and went to bed early then rose at 4 am to see the marvellous man-made canal at sunrise.

Travelling the length of the canal took twelve hours. Lunch in Port Said, Egypt, was followed by a tour of the city and a return to the *Ormonde* for an early evening departure. A statue of its French designer, De Lesseps, which stood at the far end of the canal, and the modern signal station buildings indicated they were about to enter the dark blue waters of the Mediterranean Sea. Excitement was growing among the team. The major part of the trip over, they now looked forward to cruising the Mediterranean and enjoying cooler weather. With a dance on Thursday, the sighting of the island of Crete and a masked ball on Friday, somehow the pace of the trip seemed to be speeding up. The *Ormonde* reached the Italian coast mid-morning on Saturday, June 7, the day they had originally expected to arrive in London. There was tremendous excitement at the sight of the green coastline with yellow beaches close together. Boy had not seen anything more spectacular than the black volcano Mt Etna standing high on the port side as the *Ormonde* entered the Straits of Medina. Next came the sight of another active volcano, Mount Stromboli, continually belching white smoke, and intermittently brown, so high into the air passengers could see it for several hours. They were amazed to see a village, well inhabited, on the coast of the small island on which the volcano stood.

When the *Ormonde* reached the picturesque Bay of Naples, Boy Charlton, Moss Christie and Dick Eve, their bodies well greased with oil, swam alongside the ship, collecting shillings thrown from passengers on deck. It was their third last day on board and all were in lively spirits. After a hot bath and some vigorous scrubbing the trio joined the rest of the party on a tour of the city followed by a train trip through several beautiful vineyards to the ruins of Pompeii, returning to the ship for dinner. They were a tired but happy bunch when they departed Naples for Toulon, over thirty hours away.

Ossie Merrett had decided earlier in the trip to leave the

Ormonde at Toulon and travel to Paris by train, rather than completing the boat trip to England, where he had originally planned several days of serious competition for the team prior to the Games. When the ship finally reached Toulon it was 3.30 am on June 10. They had been at sea for forty-two days. It had been a wonderful trip aboard a magnificent liner. The Olympians had been treated like royalty and had made many friends, some of whom they would see again in Paris. Their only regret was the tragic incident with Tommy Adrian. One press report stated that three doctors had advised manager Ossie Merrett to leave Adrian at Colombo but this would have been an extremely difficult decision to take, particularly in view of the furore his addition to the party had caused. *The Brisbane Courier* published Merrett's account of the incident and now *The Referee* reported that Merrett was about to take a flight from Toulon to England to supervise Tommy Adrian's transferral from the *Ormonde* to a London hospital. He cabled authorities in Australia to assure them that Adrian would have the very best treatment there before being shipped back to Australia.

The team travelled to Paris by train via the seaside port of Marseilles. Unfortunately the delay from damage to the ship's engine caused the team to miss a special train with sleeping compartments so they got little rest but instead saw some beautiful French countryside and views of the River Seine as they approached the capital.

By the time the Australian team got to Paris they were well behind the original schedule, made when it was assumed they could sail on the *Omar* on April 12. They had less than four weeks of preparation time before the Games commenced. The swimming events began in the second week so the men in the pool were marginally better off than those on the track. Training in harness in the canvas pool and the occasional swim in foreign ports meant the swimmers, particularly Charlton, had a lot of work to do.

Though Boy Charlton's training had been curtailed en route, his appetite had not suffered at all. A photograph in Fitz Lough's tour scrapbook shows Boy standing at the baths in Paris soon after arriving, his stomach protruding noticeably. Fritz's hand written caption reads: 'Boy at Tourelles, 14½ stone'. One press report actually put his weight at over 15 stone and went on to say he expected to lose 2 stone in the next few weeks, a very difficult task for a growing lad. The weather was extremely hot which was fortunate as he set about reaching peak form while paying for his extra suppers on board the *Ormonde*. Ossie Merrett's cables, sent home each day, were eagerly transposed into newsprint so readers were able to keep abreast of the team's progress. Some lucky fans were also able to get occasional news reports of their heroes from a new and revolutionary medium, the wireless radio. Country folk now got their news at the same time as those in the cities.

Though the French had built an Olympic village not too far from the new stadium at Colombes, 18 kilometres from the city centre, Ossie Merrett elected to have his team stay at the Hotel Normandie, located in the heart of Paris. This meant the boxers, athletes, cyclists and swimmers trained in different parts of the city. It was an inexpensive hotel and accordingly had no special qualities but being right in the centre of town meant the Australians quickly got a feeling for the foreign and fascinating metropolis. The swim team was immediately invited to train at the Sporting Club de France and were soon to have the Olympic pool available to them as well. The Sporting Club pool contained fresh water, was 25 metres long and made of marble with a large glass panel down one side. Swimmers could walk down stairs and check the technique of their team-mates under water. Tommy Adrian would have loved it. They were amazed to find female attendants walking around the dressing rooms, picking up towels, while swimmers were dressing. Every bather went through a scented shower before entering the pool.

There was much to like about Paris, particularly near the Seine with its cobblestone streets and succession of bridges. The Hotel Normandie was a five minute walk to the Opera House and a similar distance to the Plaza de Concorde. But there was also plenty to get used to. Ossie Merrett had determined the team should retire at 9.30 pm, but it was still light and the streets were always busy with people. Breakfast, which consisted entirely of croissants and coffee, was another surprise, as was the difficulty of organising regular baths at the hotel.

The apparent immodesty of the French was also a topic of conversation when roadside urinals were found. The Australians could not get used to the idea of standing in the toilet between two partitions at chest height, visible to passers-by. Moss Christie's diary entry summed it up: 'Rather embarrassing if your girl friend walked past'. They also had difficulty adjusting to extremely heavy traffic travelling on the right-hand side of the road. One of the rowing crew stepped out into oncoming traffic and was knocked down. Fortunately he only suffered a minor cut, which athlete Doctor Richard Honner fixed up with two stitches. The Australians were amused to be told that a pedestrian who walked into a car could be fined for obstructing traffic! It certainly was a different place.

Charlton and Ernie Henry, already good mates, had become even closer after the Tommy Adrian affair. Henry admired his younger friend's modesty and quiet nature and was in awe of his ability, a feeling that inspired him and lifted his own efforts, something for which he remained thankful all his life. The boys were given free passes on the underground railway and buses and were virtually inseparable as they took advantage of their travel passes and took in the sights of Paris. They had seen nothing like the underground rail system and after morning training sessions spent each day visiting popular attractions, such as the Left Bank, the Latin Quarter, the Louvre, the Opera House and the Follies Brasserie, where they were regularly invited. As one of the Games' youngest competitors, whose record-breaking efforts against Arne Borg had made a big impression in Europe, Boy was an immediate attraction and often recognised from photos in the press. On July 14, Bastille Day, they joined in the celebrations with thousands of locals dressed in brightly coloured costumes who danced in the streets.

Boy continued to write home, giving few details of his training but much of the time spent touring Paris. Harry Hay, yet another member of the Manly Swimming Club and a 1920 Olympic representative, was one of four volunteer team masseurs, all of whom paid their own fare to Paris. He now assumed the role of Charlton's unofficial coach, wearing his 1920 blazer to training sessions and functions with great pride. Ernie Henry thought he was a bit 'pushy', but Boy was happy enough with his new coach and Hay was to remain a great supporter of Charlton throughout his career.

Following a swim at the Sporting Club the French swimming committee took the team to see the Colombes Stadium. They travelled in two large motor-driven charabancs. Though not yet finished the complex was very modern and most impressive with dressing rooms under the grandstands and a series of tunnels to take the athletes onto the track.

Meanwhile, Frank Beaurepaire had arrived in London from America on the *Aquitania* and spoke in glowing terms of what he had seen of the American swimmers and their preparation for Paris. Beaurepaire had visited all the prominent swimming clubs from San Francisco to New York and declared their swim team, led by the remarkable Johnny Weissmuller, was all but invincible. With their indoor facilities the Americans were able to train all year round with expert coaches and a support staff of doctors, fitness trainers and masseurs all on hand. Beaurepaire had travelled across California with Arne Borg who he described as 'twice the swimmer he was in Australia'. The Americans intended doing most of their training at home but even on the SS *America*, on which they were to travel to France, there was a 200 metre circular training track and a 100 metre straight track laid on the promenade deck, as well a pool. The budget for the 350-strong team was believed to be US$350,000.

Beaurepaire sounded a warning to all sporting nations when he said: 'Until Australia is willing to spend money similarly she cannot hope to reach the American's perfection.' His point was well taken. Among the US Olympic party were professional coaches, many from leading universities, including nine for various track and field disciplines, as well as others for swimming, boxing, wrestling, rowing, cycling, shooting, fencing and water polo. The Victorian veteran had enjoyed much better training facilities on the *Aquitania* than the rest of the team. He also had several swims in America and was in excellent condition and looking forward to his final Olympics.

The strong, though relatively small, Australian swim team was set to oppose an elite band of competitors. First was the wonderful, dual Olympic champion from Hawaii, Duke Paoa Kahinu Mokoe Hulikohola Kahanamoku. He had won the 100 metres in 1912 and 1920. Only the abandonment of the 1916 Games had prevented him from already being a three-time champion. Duke Kahanamoku (Duke was his Christian name, not a royal title) was a full-blood Hawaiian who had first come to prominence in 1911 through his world swimming records in the harbour at Honolulu. His truly amazing times in the salt water were often disbelieved and sometimes disallowed. However, his prowess was proven when he won the 1912 Olympic 100 metres in Stockholm, and broke the world record in a heat of the 200 metres relay. Denied the chance to repeat his victory in 1916 he returned to Europe to win the 1920 Olympic 100 metres in Antwerp, swimming the distance in 1 minute 4 seconds, another world record.

The Australian team were aware of Kahanamoku's athletic brilliance and also of the standing he enjoyed worldwide. The tall, charismatic, yet very modest athlete was famous not only for his still water swimming, but also for his reputation as the father of the new exciting sport of surfboard riding. Between Olympics he travelled to many countries, including Australia and the American mainland, demonstrating the art that had originated in his native country. When Andrew Charlton was a boy of seven, Duke Kahanamoku had come to Manly's Fresh-water Beach to demonstrate his board riding skills to Australia. The walls of the famous surf club are still adorned with the newspaper clippings of the day, telling how he paddled his solid, hardwood long board through the breakers and rode the waves back to the beach, to the applause of hundreds of onlookers. When Duke took a young local teenager, Isabel Letham, out on the board with him he provided her with a story she would tell until her death some eighty years later. A 16 foot (4.8 metre) board, weighing 114 pounds (52 kilograms) still stands in the Freshwater Club, a testimony to the significance of that famous day in the summer of 1915.

The thirty-four year old Kahanamoku's clash with his unbeaten American team-mate, Johnny Weissmuller, would be a highlight of the Games. It seemed certain the winner would break the one-minute barrier for the first time in Olympic competition as Weissmuller had already done so on several occasions. Even though it would be many years before Hawaii officially became the 50th state, Duke and his younger brother Samuel swam for the US. Although Charlton would not oppose Duke Kahanamoku in an individual race, there was every chance he would do so in the 4×200 metres relay.

Johnny Weissmuller, a product of Chicago's Illinois Athletic Club, coached by America's best-known mentor, William Bachrach, was unbeaten at 100, 200 and 400 metres. There was no doubt he was the heir apparent to Kahanamoku's Olympic crown having swum the first sub-minute 100 metres in 1922 recording 58.6 seconds, a time he lowered to 57.4 early in 1924. Weissmuller's eligibility to swim for the US had been the subject of serious debate when he was unable to produce a birth certificate verifying that he was born in America after the *New York Times* ran a story doubting that he had. Eventually a birth certificate was produced and Weissmuller was allowed to represent his country, however doubts lingered among many as to the certificate's authenticity. Weissmuller was tall, handsome and well built, all traits he would exploit when his Olympic career was over. He had once shown enough stamina to win a 3-mile surf marathon, but it was as a sprinter that he excelled, America proclaiming him as their greatest ever short distance swimmer. With no individual 200 metres event on the Olympic schedule he would contest the 100, 400 and 4×200 metres relay, as well as compete in water polo. At twenty years of age, and still improving, he had a definite advantage over the veteran Kahanamoku but would certainly strike keen competition from Arne Borg and Charlton in the 400 metres.

Although defeated by Charlton in the Domain Baths some months earlier, Sweden's world champion Arne Borg was favoured by many European judges to have his revenge over the young Australian. As holder of many world and European records over various distances he was one of Europe's most popular sportsmen. The vastly experienced twenty-three year old had trained specifically to win an Olympic title. He seemed equally suited to the 400 and 1500 events. His knowledge of Charlton's ability and racing style would stand him in good stead. It was generally conceded they would fight out the classic distance event.

Despite Boy Charlton's wins against Borg, there was still lingering scepticism in Europe about the times generally recorded by Australians in Australia. This was because after the long trip to Europe on boats with no training facilities on board and then having to swim soon after arriving, usually in extremely cold water compared to that back home, Australian swimmers' times often fell short of their best causing European fans to doubt the conditions under which they were achieved at home.

It wasn't until Frank Beaurepaire had run out of money on a European trip in 1910 and had to stay for some months that his times got down to his best. He won races in Britain, France, Belgium and Germany, breaking four world records, but still there were sceptics in Europe. Theories that tidal pools gave swimmers an advantage against the clock in distance races seemed absurd but were still accepted by many critics. The Australian Olympic delegates were about to argue that case. Arne Borg was not among the doubters. He stated that Boy Charlton was the logical favourite for the 1500 metres but he and Weissmuller would be too fast for him in the 400 metres.

The 1500 metres event was to be swum before the 400 metres and though there were only nineteen competitors they had to negotiate heats and a semi-final. That meant Charlton and Borg would have to swim three 1500s before contesting the 400 metres. It would be an awesome task for either to defeat Weissmuller in the shorter event, his first swim of the carnival. Not that Charlton was the least bit worried by what lay ahead. To compete with such illustrious swimmers was a thrill. Notwithstanding that the 1924 Olympics would feature one of the greatest distance runners of all time, the 'Flying Finn', Paavo Nurmi, it is fair to say the array of champions in the pool was absolutely outstanding; collectively, probably above that of any other sport.

With just five swimmers making up the Australian swim team, Charlton would be rested from the heats and perhaps the semi-final of the relay. Stedman was to swim the 200 metres breaststroke as well as the 100 metres freestyle. Who would make way for Charlton, should they make the final, was to be decided shortly before the swimming commenced. Despite the size and strength of the American team there was genuine confidence in the Australian camp and excitement at the prospect of facing such famous opposition. All that needed to be done was to ensure swimmers reached their peak by the time the Games began.

The group had their first solid training in the Olympic pool at Tourelles in the heart of the city just two days after arrival and were impressed. The pool, built especially for the Olympics, was 50 metres in length and 18 metres in width, and surrounded by an impressive grandstand capable of holding 10,000 spectators. It was the finest pool in Paris with forty cloakrooms and 750 cabins provided for swimmers. The nearby railway station had been extended to facilitate the large crowds certain to attend one of the most anticipated series of events at the Games. The water was extremely cold, however swimmers were assured it would be heated for the Games. They returned to their hotel by underground railway and trained again that afternoon at the Sporting Club. All swam at Tourelles on Saturday and Sunday morning before going to the cycling on Sunday afternoon. It seemed half of Paris was at the cycling to see many of the world's best competitors who would perform at the Olympics.

Despite the short time allowed for preparation there was growing confidence they would be ready to show their best. Though Moss Christie admitted he did not find the fresh water to his liking, Charlton adapted very quickly. He began his preparation quietly enough with leisurely swims over 500 and 800 metres and stated he did not find the water at all heavy.

Frank Beaurepaire arrived in Paris on Wednesday, June 18, looking very fit. As the most experienced swimmer he quickly began working with Moss Christie, Ivan Stedman and Ernie Henry. He was an extremely good team man but Charlton preferred to train separately from the others. Without Tommy Adrian, Boy might well have been under pressure to properly time his preparation. Some early press reports gave fans at home some cause for worry but Charlton had proven before he did not take a long time to come to peak. Harry Hay was working with him but Charlton was happy to take full responsibility for his own preparation. Though reserved by nature he was extremely confident of knowing just what he had to do. Still a boy out of the water, he was a man in it.

New Zealand swimmer Gwyther Shand arrived on Friday and French swimming authorities asked if she and Boy Charlton would give exhibition swims at the conclusion of the French trials on Sunday afternoon. They were only too happy to do so. After morning and afternoon sessions at the Sporting Club on Saturday all five swimmers and Dick Eve attended the French trials. Boy received a wonderful ovation when he waved to the crowd and willingly posed for photographs after his swim. The trials revealed that the French were not strong and the diving standard was very poor. The carnival, however, was extremely well run and an excellent French army band was much appreciated by the Australian contingent

As athletes continued to arrive from all parts of the world, the excitement increased each day. The Japanese swimmers arrived at Tourelles but found the water too cold for them. The weather continued to get hotter and the Australians loved to sunbake after training stints. Local newspapers invariably commented on their fine physiques and bronzed bodies. While Beaurepaire and Christie concentrated on distance training, Boy interspersed his longer swims with sprints over 200 metres.

The Americans arrived mid-week and went immediately to Tourelles. Their sessions were far more regimented than those of other teams. Onlookers were amazed at the organisation and precision of their workouts. Swimmers reacted to professional coaches who barked instructions to them across the water. Press reports stated the Americans were on special diets and some were being billeted in private homes owned, or leased, by wealthy countrymen. A matron and a committee of ladies were caring for the team. Frank Beaurepaire was right about the thoroughness of America's preparation. Johnny Weissmuller sprinted across the pool, covering its 18-metre width in 8.2 seconds. At the end of the session the Australians were introduced to Weissmuller, Duke and Sam Kahanamoku, Pau Kealoha, who had visited Australia in 1921, and many others. Arne Borg also arrived with his brother Ake, whom he insisted on introducing as 'my twin brother who is twenty minutes younger than I'.

On the same afternoon he had seen the Americans train, Charlton beat Frank Beaurepaire easily over 1000 metres, and in a time ten seconds faster than Arne Borg's world record. Boy was rapidly getting into shape and was now only half a stone over his normal swimming weight. On the strength of this swim and an allowance for further improvement, Bill Longworth, covering the Games for *The Referee*, predicted victory for him in the 1500 metres event.

Ossie Merrett, always immaculately attired and in good spirits, was proving a resourceful manager. With so many different teams looking for accommodation and training facilities throughout the city, Merrett was able to arrange for the rowing contingent to move into a large chateau at Nogent on the Marne River, 20 kilometres out of Paris and just a few hundred metres from their training course. Its rural atmosphere suited the Murray Bridge boys perfectly.

Paris was now in the grip of Olympic fever. Shops were decorated with national colours, newspapers carried special Olympic editions almost every day with stories of the overseas champions. Tourists appeared everywhere, doing their best to find their way around the city, reading timetables for the underground and trying to make themselves understood in restaurants and shops. The Australians were easy to pick out as they wandered the streets, taking in the attractions of Paris. One London press report said:

What with the players and supporters, Paris seems to be full of Australians, all easily detected either by their carriage or their hats or their idioms, of which 'too right' or 'dinkum' are the most noticeable, or by some peculiarity which indelibly marks an Australian in any part of the world.

On Saturday, June 28, just one week before the opening ceremony, the Australian, American, Japanese and Swedish swim teams put on an exhibition at the Sporting Club where all spectators in the gallery wore dinner suits. It was something the Australians had never seen before. After their swims they changed and were introduced to a number of the Paris society set. The evening finished after midnight and was the only late night so far. On Sunday the swimmers spent one of their most enjoyable days in the company of the Australian oarsmen at Nogent. They found them in good spirits and Moss Christie was given a chance to try out Arthur Bull's single scull.

All five swimmers were happy with their fitness, having rarely, if ever, been able to train so regularly. During the final week one swim session per day was generally considered sufficient. Having spent so much time on the *Ormonde* worrying about getting ready they were now concerned with not leaving their best efforts at training. Still, with two weeks to go before the swimming carnival commenced their confidence was on a high.

The Games had made steady progress since London in 1908, with each new Olympiad bringing innovations that became standard practice. Advances in technology produced a public address system as well as some experimental electronic timing at Stockholm in 1912. The doves of peace were released for the first time in the post-war Games in Antwerp in 1920, which also saw the introduction of the Olympic flag and the reading of the athletes' oath. The 1924 Paris Games also brought its innovations. One was the Olympic motto, *citius, altius, fortius* – swifter, higher, stronger. The other was one that was of special interest to Charlton and the Australian swimmers. For the first time, lanes, suspended in the water by cork, were to be used in the pool. How this would affect him or other competitors remained to be seen. He had a tendency to pull slightly to his right when at full pace. If the lanes corrected this it might well be to his advantage. If he got fouled in them the very opposite would apply. With the confidence typical of youth he had no doubt that everything would be fine.

4

The Escaped Torpedo

THE 1924 OLYMPICS BEGAN on Saturday, July 5 with an impressive opening ceremony on a typically warm day. Over three thousand athletes from forty-four nations marched into the magnificent, new, open-air Colombes Stadium, which was painted predominantly blue and gold and packed with over fifty thousand people. The Australians were third to appear, marching behind South Africa and Argentina. They were dressed in green blazers, cream slacks and green caps. A.V. Scott of the Murray Bridge rowing eight held the standard aloft as Edwin 'Slip' Carr carried the national flag and later took the athletes' oath on behalf of Australia.

America fielded the largest team with 365 representatives, dressed in blue blazers with stars and stripes on the pocket and white flannels. They were led into the arena by naval and military officers. France was next in size, having almost three hundred athletes and officials, all dressed in white. The Great Britain team was led in by the Cameron Pipers and they too wore blue blazers and white flannels. Ireland competed for the first time as a separate nation.

The proclamation was read by President Gaston Doumergue, in the presence of the Prince of Wales, then flag bearers formed a semi-circle and read the Olympic oath of amateurism. Thousands of pigeons were released and guns fired a military salute as the Olympic flag was hoisted on the main flagpole. Out of the blue sky came a squadron of military aircraft followed by a light plane that drew a loud gasp from the crowd when it flew low over the presidential stand and a cameraman could be seen leaning from it. The Games of the seventh Olympiad were about to begin.

The first week of the Games featured track and field events, giving the swimmers a chance to savour the atmosphere of the competition and round off their own preparations, which had gone without mishap. Frank Beaurepaire, discussing Charlton's chances before leaving Australia, was adamant that they depended greatly on his ability to adapt to fresh water swimming, enabling him to repeat the marvellous times made in salt water. So far Boy felt confident he could do so but only the actual races would tell the tale.

The swim team trained at Tourelles on Sunday morning and then hurried out to watch the first day of track events. This would be their routine for the next few days. They found it extremely exciting to be sitting alongside famous athletes, such as Paarvo Nurmi, who had won three gold medals in 1920 and was in the process of winning five more, Britain's Harold Abrahams and the American sprinter Charley Paddock, in the area reserved for those who were not competing that day. They got another insight into American thoroughness when each runner carried a small spade to the starting point and dug foot holes to eliminate any chance of slipping. On the track Australia's outstanding representative was Slip Carr. Some were even predicting a gold medal for him in the blue-riband event, the 100 metres. Carr was in excellent form and began with a very good second place to Harold Abrahams in his heat followed by a second in the quarterfinal to Jackson Scholz of America.

That evening the British team held a dance at the Hotel Continental. The Australians were invited and had the pleasure of meeting the Prince of Wales and Prince Henry. Monday was a quiet day for the swimmers who were to trial over 200 metres to determine their relay team on Tuesday morning. They again went to the track to cheer on Slip Carr who finished fourth in his 100 metres semifinal, missing out on a place in the final which was won by Abrahams from Scholz.

The next morning Boy Charlton won the 200 metres trial clearly from Ernie Henry, with Frank Beaurepaire third. Moss Christie finished ahead of Ivan Stedman so won fourth spot. Again they went out to cheer for Slip Carr who, over the next two days, competed in the 200 metres. He won his heat in a time that equalled the best of the day and also won his quarterfinal, but, hampered by a calf muscle injury, finished fourth in the semifinal and failed to qualify for the final.

No such bad luck was to beset Manly's Anthony 'Nick' Winter. The son of the local snooker room proprietor, Winter could well have made a living with a cue and invariably entertained team-mates with trick shots whenever a billiard table was available. He was one of six permanent firemen employed at Manly's modern fire station which boasted a 1921, Dennis 60 horsepower fire engine, a bicycle, a curricle ladder, which could be pulled by motor vehicle or horse, and 3,700 feet of hose.

Winter was born in the country and had worked as a shearer before moving to Manly. By 1924 he had been a fireman for five years. The Fire Brigade gave him six months paid leave to attend the Olympics and the tall, lean, laconic twenty-nine year old was determined to repay such generosity. He was one of the last selected for Paris, despite being a likely medallist. His event, the hop, step and jump (now called the triple jump) was contested in club meetings in Australia but was not included in national championships. Nevertheless he was very proficient at the discipline, which was held on the last day of the athletics programme, and was in excellent form at training. On his first jump, Argentinean Luis Brunetto broke the Olympic record, which would be hard to beat. Then, in the final round, Winter, who had overstepped the foul line three times in four attempts, sailed through the air in his final leap breaking the new world record and winning the gold medal. His victory gave the team an enormous thrill and a real confidence boost prior to the swimming, which started the next day.

Heats of the 1500 metres, a race that had created more interest than any other, were held in stifling heat on Sunday, July 13, the first morning of the swimming programme. The first two placegetters in each of five heats would advance to the semi-finals. They set the scene for an exciting week with a large crowd on hand to get their first glimpse of the Australian teenage sensation. The hot weather was to continue for the entire carnival. This, and the water, now warmed by Bunsen burners operating below the pool, suited the Australians. The suntanned boys were about to strut their stuff in the white-tiled pool in Paris.

Among spectators was a large contingent of Australians, including a group of medical students studying in London, many Manly sporting enthusiasts who had travelled across to Europe on the Australian Commonwealth Line's *Jervis Bay*, a teenage surfer from Narrabeen and a member of the Pyrmont Club who had paid his way by working his passage to Europe aboard a merchant ship 'to see Boy win the 1500 and learn to play water polo'.

Moss Christie was eliminated when he finished third in heat one to Harold Annison of Great Britain and Lester Smith of America in a time of 22 minutes 38.4 seconds. Annison won by five metres with Christie just a metre behind second place. In the second heat, Ake Borg, Arne's twin brother, easily defeated the British veteran Henry Taylor in 22 minutes 45 seconds. The next heat saw Charlton come to the pool for his long-awaited European debut. His main opposition seemed likely to come from another British veteran, John Hatfield, though he was expected to win. By what margin and in what time was eagerly anticipated. Arne Borg held the 1500 metres world record, 21 minutes 35.3 seconds, set in Gothenburg twelve months earlier.

Charlton hit the water first and immediately went to the lead, swimming well within himself. His style was relaxed and fluent. He led by five metres after four laps and increased that to almost twenty after 400 metres, his nearest competitor the American Richard Howell. Charlton continued to extend his lead in a manner that Australian crowds had become used to as Hatfield challenged Howell for second place. Sprinting in the final lap, Charlton won by eighty metres from Hatfield in 21 minutes 20.3 seconds, fifteen seconds inside Borg's world record. The applause, which had started midway through the race and increased during the last lap, became almost deafening when the time was announced. The youngster had lived up to all that had been expected of him. After the race he expressed surprise at his time as he had swum easily. The lanes had caused him no problem. In fact if anything they kept his line straighter. Johnny Weissmuller, an interested spectator, declared it a 'dandy per-formance' adding that Charlton was 'some swimmer'.

The fourth heat matched Arne Borg, the 'Swedish Sturgeon', with Katsuo Takaishi, a seventeen year old Japanese boy begin-ning to make his mark in distance swimming. Employing a much faster stroke than Charlton, but lapping just as easily, Borg was every bit as impressive. He too led from the start and made a one act affair of the race, easily beating Takaishi and breaking Charlton's world record, set just half an hour earlier, by almost nine seconds. Again the crowd was ecstatic. Which was the more impressive swim? Opinions varied, but Borg was pleased his faster time might have given him a psychological edge over his young rival. As if to emphasise the point, Borg told press-men, 'Boy hasn't seen me swim yet.'

The fifth and final heat was won by the remarkable, thirty-four year old Frank Beaurepaire who beat Canadian George Vernot in 22 minutes 17 seconds. It was a pleasing result for Beaurepaire who was beaten by Vernot for the silver medal in 1920. While Beaurepaire's time was well outside the amazing performances of Charlton and Borg it was the next fastest and he too had swum within himself and now fancied his chances of making the final. If he did so a bronze medal might be within his grasp, which would make a fitting finale to a magnificent career. The semifinals, to be swum the following day, would feature the two Borg brothers from Sweden, Charlton and Beaurepaire from Australia, Annison, Hatfield and Taylor from Great Britain, Takaishi from Japan, Vernot from Canada and Smith from the USA. The first two in each semifinal together with the next fastest would contest the five-man final.

On Monday night the first semifinal pitted Borg against Charlton. This was the perfect opportunity for the crowd to determine who deserved the title of favourite for the final. The cooee call of the Australian spectators had already become well known and many Europeans joined in as Charlton took his place at the start. It was expected that Borg would lead from lane 2, but Charlton, in lane 6, went to the front and led by two metres after four laps. At 400 metres Frank Beaurepaire ran to poolside and yelled the time to Charlton who was now four metres in front and stroking smoothly. The pair kept a keen eye on each other as the race proceeded with Charlton never looking likely to surrender the lead. He came away from Borg over the final two laps to win by almost twenty metres in 21 minutes 28.4 seconds. It was slower than he and Borg had swum in their heats, but still a very fast time. Britain's John Hatfield was third. As Borg congratulated Charlton enthusiastically, he gave an exaggerated wink and a wide smile. The Swedish fans were sure this meant he had plenty in reserve for the final.

In the second semifinal Katsuo Takaishi led for the first 600 metres but Beaurepaire slowly overtook him, taking a narrow lead in the thirteenth lap. Responding to the cooee calls of the Australian supporters he swam strongly over the second half of the event, prevailing by five metres in an exciting race and finishing in 21 minutes 41.4 seconds. Ake Borg finished a close third but his time was outside that of Hatfield. The scene was set for a gripping final with experts still divided as to the likely winner. The American camp favoured Charlton because of his tremendous strength. Borg fans were confident their man had been foxing in the semifinal. Among Australian fans there was no doubt whatsoever. Their boy had won today and would win again tomorrow or any other time they met.

At 3 on Tuesday afternoon the field of five lined up for their third 1500 metres in three days in what had been described as the race of the Games. The arena was packed. The draw for lanes put Beaurepaire in lane 1, Hatfield in 2, Charlton in 3, Takaishi in 4 and Borg in 5. With just one lane separating them the two favourites were set for a mighty duel. Borg smiled confidently as he took his position while Charlton showed no sign of nerves. The young Australian, reacting instantly to the starter's gun, was first to hit the water, but this time Borg was keen to lead, a sign that pleased his supporters. He was a natural front-runner. Charlton was three metres behind the Swede at the 100 metres mark with both having settled into a good rhythm.

There was a cheer from the Australian supporters as Charlton drew level at the 300 metres mark and the pair came down the seventh lap together. Twenty-three laps to go. Should Charlton have let Borg carry him along for a few more laps before applying the pressure? The next few minutes would tell.

The Olympic 400 metres record was broken as Charlton turned narrowly ahead of Borg who responded to the challenge and at 500 metres the pair were almost level. Then without apparently lifting his pace Charlton slowly moved ahead. At 600 metres he led by a body length. The cheers of the Australian contingent that began as soon as Charlton had taken the lead, continued to build over the next ten laps as he ever so slowly increased his margin. With twenty-four of the thirty laps completed, Charlton led Borg by fifteen metres, with a lap to the other swimmers. Now the huge crowd joined in the cheering as the young Australian continued his remarkable performance. They could scarcely believe what they were seeing. His faultless stroking never wavered as Borg was left far behind. The teenager sprinted in the final lap to beat his famous rival by over forty metres in a time of 20 minutes 6.6 seconds, lowering the world record, set by Borg in his heat, by almost sixty-five seconds. On the way he had swum an Olympic record for the 400 metres and a world record for the 1000 metres. It was the finest distance swim ever seen. As the crowd roared their approval, Frank Beaurepaire battled gamely all the way down the last lap to edge Hatfield out of third place. His third bronze medal in the 1500 metres had come sixteen years after his first.

Boy admitted he had surprised himself with the time, having felt very comfortable throughout. Johnny Weissmuller was astounded at the effort, as was his coach Bill Bachrach who called it the greatest swim he had ever seen, describing Charlton as 'an escaped torpedo'. Bachrach said: 'I wish he was in my team. He is a knockout to the last word. We probably will not

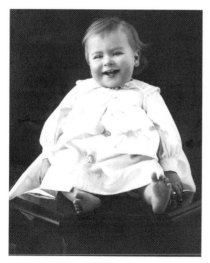

A champion in the making. Andrew Murray Charlton at 12 months.

Boy's maternal grandfather, Andrew Howard Moore, who argued Charlton was too young to compete at the 1924 Paris Olympics.

Boy with his father, Oswald (centre), and coach Tommy Adrian prior to the Borg challenge in January 1924. (Photos courtesy Murray Charlton)

Joe Morgan announcing Boy Charlton's 440 yards world record at the Domain Baths on January 12, 1924.

World champion Arne Borg congratulates Charlton after his win in the 440 yards.

(Photos courtesy Murray Charlton)

Above: The capacity crowd at the Domain Baths, there to watch Charlton race Borg.

Left: Arne Borg rows the embarrassed victor around the Domain pool.

Part of the crowd that rushed to Manly Wharf to welcome Charlton as he returned from defeating Arne Borg. (Photos courtesy Murray Charlton)

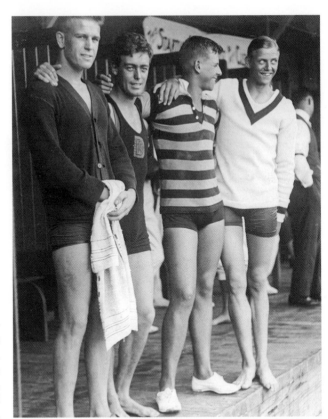

Starters in the New South Wales 880 yards final, January 19, 1924. From left to right: Owen Griffiths, Moss Christie, Boy Charlton and Arne Borg.

Charlton with his 1924 Olympic team-mates, Frank Beaurepaire (left) and Ernie Henry, at the Domain Baths. (Photos courtesy Murray Charlton)

The 1924 Olympic team on the deck of the *Ormonde* as it leaves Sydney for Paris on April 30, 1924.

A day in Colombo en route to the Olympics. Charlton kept a close eye on Tommy Adrian.

The Olympians going ashore in Aden after four weeks at sea.

(Photos courtesy Murray Charlton)

Charlton, among the group who called themselves 'The Hoboes', exploring Aden. (Photos courtesy Murray Charlton)

Right: A welcome cool dip in Aden.

Below: Charlton flanked by tourist Tom Gunning (left) and team-mate Ernie Henry amid the ruins of Pompeii.

Below right: Boy with Australia's best sprinter, Edwin 'Slip' Carr, at the Olympic pool in Paris, 1924.

Boy Charlton coming in to touch for the 1500 metres Olympic gold medal at the 1924 Games in Paris, while rival Arne Borg (not in picture) pushes off from the other end.

A relieved Johnny Weissmuller (centre), an exhausted Arne Borg and a smiling Boy Charlton after his close third place in the 400 metres in Paris, 1924.

(Photos courtesy Murray Charlton)

Sixteen-year-old Boy featured on a postcard of Olympic champions printed in Paris, 1924. (Photo: Popperfoto)

Droving at Kurrumbede, a far cry from the Manly surf and the Paris Olympics.
(Photo courtesy Shirley Coote, Gunnedah & District Historical Society)

Charlton, second from right, with workmates at Kurrumbede.
(Photo courtesy Shirley Coote, Gunnedah & District Historical Society)

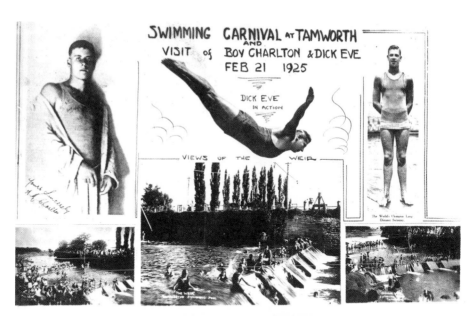

Above: A programme featuring Charlton and Dick Eve on one of the few occasions Boy was tempted back to the water while a jackeroo.
(Photo courtesy Murray Charlton)

A carnival at Cohen's Bridge on the Namoi River where Charlton swam when he had the chance while working as a jackeroo at Kurrumbede.
(Photo courtesy Shirley Coote, Gunnedah & District Historical Society)

'Apple Charlotte' with the glamorous Jantzen girls at Manly Beach. On Boy's immediate right is Marie Gelling. (Photo courtesy Christine Gelling)

Boy Charlton towers over rivals and team-mates at a surf carnival at Manly Beach. (Photo courtesy Murray Charlton)

Boy poses with Japan's Katsuo Takaishi after defeating him at the Domain Baths in 1927.

Charlton with Arne Borg after their surprise defeat by Argentina's Alberto Zorilla in the 400 metres Olympic final in Amsterdam, 1928. (Photos courtesy Murray Charlton)

A spar in the cockloft at the Manly Surf Club with 'Kewpie' White, inter-services boxing champion. Note Charlton's second has a reviver ready.
(Photo courtesy Manly Surf Club)

Relaxing with Harry Hay (far left) and Frank Beaurepaire (centre) at the house of the famous comedian Harold Lloyd (back left) in Los Angeles, 1932.
(Photo courtesy Murray Charlton)

The most successful team and the most photographed. From left, Bobby Pearce, Boy Charlton, Manager Jim Eve and 400 metres runner George Golding with Hollywood stars Ruth Selwyn and Anita Page at the Olympic Stadium in 1932.

Boy Charlton and Noel Ryan 'teaching' Ruth Selwyn the Australian Crawl in Los Angeles, 1932. (Photos courtesy Murray Charlton)

An out of form Boy with
muscular Buster Crabbe
at the Olympic pool in
Los Angeles, 1932. (Photo:
Australian Picture Library)

Charlton with Duke
Kahanamoku in Hawaii
after the 1932 Olympics.
(Photo courtesy
Murray Charlton)

Jessie Hyles on her engagement day, Canberra 1937.

Left: Boy and Jessie at St Mark's Church of England, Darling Point, Sydney, on their wedding day in 1937.

Bottom: Kilrea, the 12,000-acre property near Goulburn, where Boy and Jessie settled after they were married.

(Photos courtesy Murray Charlton)

The 7th Regiment Bungendore Light Horse, a reservist unit with which Boy served between 1940 and 1943.

Charlton and Sam Herford with John and Lisa Konrads in Townsville, 1960.
(Photos courtesy Murray Charlton)

see another like him for half a century. When I saw him in his heat I thought he was trying to frighten Borg. Then when Borg beat his time I thought the Swede had a shade on Boy. The result staggered us all. We have never seen a distance swimmer use so little effort, use his legs less and float so well.' Weissmuller simply said: 'It was too much for me.'

The good-natured, sportsmanlike Borg offered no excuse for defeat, declaring his conqueror 'a world wonder' but still believed he and Weissmuller would be too brilliant for Charlton in the 400 metres. When asked if he had deliberately set out to beat the world record Boy answered with youthful honesty, 'No, I just went.' Fitz Lough later told his close surfing mate George Max Riddington that Boy had assured him he was 'going half pace'.

Several thousand kilometres away Oswald Murray Charlton's phone rang. It was at 2 o'clock, Wednesday morning. Normally he would have been most annoyed. But this was different. The news of Boy's victory, though no surprise, was still music to his ears. There was now no consternation that his son had made the trip.

Manly council had met on Tuesday evening and so confident were they of Charlton's success that they made arrangements for celebrations the next day. One councillor suggested the meeting should continue into the early hours of the morning until the result was known but this suggestion was vetoed. One motion that was carried approved the expenditure of five thousand pounds to rebuild the Manly Baths with room for several thousand spectators.

Early on Wednesday morning, Sydneysiders were woken by the sounds of steamers, tugs and ferries blasting away on sirens, horns and whistles. There could only be one reason for the cacophony echoing across the harbour. Flags flown from business and private dwellings now complemented bunting and streamers, that decorated The Village. It seemed no motorist passed another without blowing the horn. Tributes were paid at assembly at Manly Primary School and Sydney Grammar. Flags were raised and three cheers called for. Though many students were on holiday from Hawkesbury Agricultural College, farming students, attending the Winter School, shared in the celebrations and helped produce a school newspaper lauding Boy's victory. Staff of the Hawkesbury College and Victoria's Dookie Agricultural College, which was visiting for a sporting challenge, sent cables of congratulations.

More cheers were also called for that afternoon before a midweek crowd of five thousand rugby fans at the Sydney Show Ground. The tribute was given by the New Zealand captain, Richardson, before the kick off against the Waratahs who, fittingly enough, were led by Ted Thorn of Manly. By lunchtime Manly's Corso was crowded with people. The Manly Municipal Band and the Fire Brigade Band performed throughout the afternoon and into the evening. Members of the Manly Surf Club marched up The Corso to the cheers of the large crowd, still very much in carnival mood. A march past by other sporting bodies took place at 8 pm.

The *Manly Daily* carried large photos of Boy's father and grandfather, who naturally expressed delight at Boy's victory. Both were adamant he had done his country proud. His grandfather's words shifted continually from euphoria to caution, one moment sounding ecstatic as he thought of the swim, the next emphasising the importance of business as opposed to sport:

I didn't think it was morally right for him to go but now he's there I'm happy and proud. He's putting Australia on the map. Mind you I've always been closely interested in the lad. I've been watching him since he was a youngster. He's done something for Australia, and I won't forget him. If he comes back the same boy I'm going to do all

I promised him and more. I'm going to egg him on. My word I'm delighted with him. But he's not going to be a swimmer pure and simple. I mean he's not going to go through life as a swimmer. There's something better than that ahead of him. When he comes back he's going to have to knuckle down and show his grit on the land. But my word it must have been a wonderful swim. Over a minute off the record!

The acting state premier released a statement applauding Charlton's effort, making particular reference to his fine physique and outstanding personal characteristics, attributes that had already made him a hero in Paris. The Manly District Sports Union sent a cable to Ossie Merrett:

Merrett,
Hotel Picardy, Paris.
Heartiest congratulations splendid victories Manly representatives.

Printing presses ran hot as news of Charlton's sensational performance made headlines in every daily paper. Journalists struggled to find words to adequately describe the swim. Perhaps Bill Longworth summed it up best when he preceded his detailed description of the race with the following:

By his achievements in Paris, Charlton has placed his name among the immortals in sport. His feats have set the imagination of the people aglow, because a boy of sixteen has eclipsed, by a big margin, anything ever done in the water by any other living being. Australia has had its heroes in sport, such as Trumper in cricket, Messenger in Rugby football, Searle and Beach in sculling, Darcy in boxing, but none has excited with his deeds wider interest than Andrew Charlton has done. As with our other heroes the latest is a modest young athlete.

Physiologists had taken a keen interest in the Olympics endurance swimmers for some time and did tests on them for the first time. After the 1500 metres they tested Boy Charlton's lung capacity with a manometer, a machine used to measure the strength of gases and vapours. Boy took a deep breath and blew mercury through a set of tubes. They reported they had never seen such capacity in any human being. Later, when George Riddington retold this story, the mercury had been blown out of the top of the manometer and across the room!

If the young man was likely to be affected by praise then he was certainly being given his chance. But it was not going to happen. In fact, Boy had little time to dwell on his victory. The next day he was scheduled to meet Johnny Weissmuller in a heat of the 400 metres. Charlton's effortless 1500 metres win added considerable spice to the event. Though the American's best times were much quicker than Charlton's, they had often been swum in short pools, conditions conducive to flattering times. Charlton would presumably have had the edge taken off his early speed by the three successive 1500 metres swims. A straight 100 metres course, such as that at the Domain, would have suited him better but his win in the 1500 was so outstanding, who was to say he could not cause an upset. Boy only needed to finish second in the heat to advance to the semifinals. He would no doubt have to give the brilliant Weissmuller a start over the last couple of laps, but he would be coming home strongly. Of that there was little doubt.

Despite Weissmuller's sensational times, and the advantage of his being fresh, there were many who believed Charlton would beat him. The Australian fans had no doubt, but their confidence was based as much on parochialism as logic. Bill Longworth, however, was also confident of a victory for the Manly boy, citing the amazing speed shown in the early stages of the 1500 metres, speed that saw him break the world 400 metres record.

There had been several false starts during the early swimming events. Too many, in fact, for the rather volatile starter who stunned the competitors as well as the crowd by firing all six blanks towards the competitors after one swimmer hit the water early. This brought a protest from several team managers and a special meeting was called. It was too late to save Moss Christie, however, who was disqualified after finishing third in his 400 metres heat for beating the gun. Ossie Merrett's protest was dismissed but Christie was not a likely finalist and was able to be kept fresh for the 4×200 metres relay.

The first heat of the 400 metres was won by Ralph Breyer of America, the second by Ake Borg from another American Lester Smith. The third heat brought Weissmuller and Charlton to poolside. Here fans would get their first indication of things to come. The heat was an anti-climax. Weissmuller went to the lead immediately and was never challenged. Weissmuller, quickly realising Charlton was saving himself, tended to play up to the crowd on the turns. He won by ten metres from Charlton but swam in a time many seconds slower than Boy had swum in the 1500. Both advanced to the semifinal to be contested the following morning.

The fourth heat was won by Arne Borg from Frank Beaurepaire, who was not originally to swim in that event but after the disqualification of Moss Christie that decision was reversed. During the heat Arne Borg caused considerable anger when he dog paddled the last few metres to the finish. Fans were incensed that he had shown apparent disrespect for a great competitor, Beaurepaire, and for the Games. It was an error of judgment by Borg who apologised to the Australian camp the next day. The Americans were upset when he likened his actions to those of Weissmuller, who had also shown off, though to a lesser extent, during his heat. The Americans didn't understand Borg's extroverted personality.

The anticipation of Weissmuller, Borg and Charlton clashing in the metric quarter mile final was causing enormous interest. Yet some were concerned about Charlton's workload. On the eve of the semifinals Bill Corbett made the following interesting observations in *The Sun*:

> *Years ago Australia reeled at the death of a swimmer idolised just as much as Charlton. Barney Kieran made Australia's name in the swimming world but he paid for it with his life. Charlton was sent to Paris to win the 1500 metres. He has fulfilled his duty. Those who have the Manly youngster's interest at heart should be contented.*
>
> *Australians are expecting too much from Charlton. I believe he has an excellent chance in the 400 metres and perhaps would be one of the least surprised if he defeated Weissmuller. If Charlton continues to exhibit such amazing progress, one has no fear in predicting that he will be the greatest swimmer from 200 metres to a mile the world has ever known.*
>
> *In the excitement of the moment it is not realised what a tremendous week this has been for the champion. In the 1500 metres heat, semi-final and final he swam 1500 metres in competition which is vastly different from training swims. Added to that he has covered 400 metres in his heat of that race. He will swim 400 metres more today and probably in the final tomorrow. Therefore the actual distance he will have swum this week will be 3700 metres.*
>
> *It is not so much the great distance as the continuous mental strain and certain amount of anxiety that affects the swimmer in such important contests as the Olympic Games. Agreed that Charlton is practically a super-man there must be a breaking strain. There is nothing in creation able forever to withstand continuous test.*

In the meantime the Australians had the thrill of seeing Richmond 'Dick' Eve perform in the plain high board diving. In that event, one of three diving competitions, all divers executed the same series of graceful dives from the 10-metre tower. With a perfect swallow dive as his final attempt Dick Eve overtook his Swedish and British rivals to take victory. Yet another Manly boy had struck gold. A magnificent photograph of the winning dive soon featured in major Australian newspapers.

Charlton again raced Johnny Weissmuller in the first semifinal of the 400 metres, a race that proved to be a replica of the heat. This time Weissmuller won by almost twenty metres with Charlton content to finish five metres ahead of the other American, Lester Smith. Weissmuller's time was several seconds faster than that in the heat but still well outside either swimmer's best. The second semifinal was won just as easily by Arne Borg from Hatfield. Frank Beaurepaire withdrew from the race to concentrate on the relay. The five finalists, made up of the two winners of the semifinals and the next three fastest placegetters, were Weissmuller, Charlton, Hatfield and the Borg twins, Arne and Ake.

After the 400 metres semifinals, victory ceremonies were held for Charlton and Dick Eve. As Charlton came down from the top of the stand he said, 'I am just as proud of Australia's good wishes as I am of my championship. When I see the Australian flag hoisted I will thrill with pride as much for the sake of Australia as myself.' The pair stood proudly as the Australian flag was raised to the sounds of 'God Save the King'. Heavyweight boxer Charlie Jardine was so impressed with their performances he bought them both a pair of expensive leather slippers, which he presented to them on their return from the pool that evening.

Another capacity crowd of ten thousand filled the arena for the showdown between the three outstanding swimmers in the 400 metres final at 3 o'clock the following day. There was not a sound as the contestants waited, poised for the showdown. As the starter's gun echoed across the pool a huge roar went up and

Arne Borg immediately challenged Weissmuller for the lead. The American responded and the pair swam side by side, turning together at 50 metres with Charlton, in a green cap, a body length away. After 100 metres Weissmuller and Borg were level with Charlton two body lengths back. The crowd cheered on the two leaders who maintained their positions, at no stage either swimmer getting more than half a stroke ahead. Charlton, though swimming fluently, slowly drifted further behind. Moss Christie estimated Charlton was giving the leaders seven metres start at the halfway point. His plan had been to swim the first 200 metres fast enough to stay within touch of the speedsters and then go all out in the second half of the race.

With three laps to go Weissmuller and Borg were so close the crowd was not sure who was in front. Charlton had made up some ground but it seemed doubtful he was close enough to throw down a challenge in the last 100 metres. At the final turn Charlton had reduced the lead to four metres and Borg was within a stroke of Weissmuller. The two leaders were now sprinting at full pace. Borg tried desperately to draw level as Charlton continued to take ground from them both. With the huge crowd urging them on the three champions drove for the wall, giving their all in the final lap.

Despite a superb finish, Boy Charlton came in a body length behind Weissmuller with Borg splitting the pair in second place. Weissmuller's time of 5 minutes 4.2 seconds set a new Olympic record, beating that established by Charlton during the 1500 metres by almost six seconds. He was quite distressed, hanging on to the cork lane for some time before getting out of the pool. Borg too seemed close to exhaustion. Both were completely spent. Charlton was clearly the fresher of the trio, smiling broadly as he stood on the half-submerged steps. It was a close contest that had been as exciting as the 1500 metres and would be talked about for years.

The Australian team was disappointed for Charlton, believing that if he had started his sprint earlier he could have won. Certainly this was the view of Frank Beaurepaire and Bill Longworth. Beaurepaire said, 'Charlton is as happy as if he had won because of his wonderful time. I believe he would have won in another ten or twenty yards or if he had started his final spurt twenty yards sooner.' However, Boy showed no sign of disappointment. He had swum 5 minutes 6.6 seconds, many seconds inside his best time, and was narrowly beaten by the two fastest 400 metres swimmers the world had seen. His comment was typical of him: 'The best man won but I was quite fresh and could have continued at the same speed for twice the distance. I am as happy as if I won because I cut four seconds off my previous best time.' Weissmuller, having regained his breath, said, 'I wouldn't like to race that guy over a half mile.'

Bill Bachrach described the race as the finest 400 metres event he had ever seen or expected to see. He expressed amazement at the speed Charlton was able to generate with what he described as a distance swimmer's stroke. Bachrach said: 'When I first saw him I believed he could not develop pace as the term is applied to sprinters, and I could not have believed it possible that he could get so close to five minutes if I had not seen him in his phenomenal 1500 metres swim. Maybe the day will come when Charlton will change his stroke and favour one giving him speed. If he does he will lick creation.'

There was much speculation that Boy might have won with Tommy Adrian's help in planning the race. Sadly, however, Adrian was in not in a good state. Shortly after the Games commenced *The Referee* quoted Ossie Merrett lamenting that Tommy Adrian's health had deteriorated and that he was in a 'very low condition'. The tragedy surrounding Boy Charlton's marvellous performances was that the man who had done so much to help him was not there to share in his triumph. Instead he languished in a London hospital, his nerves so broken no one could guess when he might be allowed to return home.

Charlton had one more race to swim, the 4×200 metres team race, a contest Australia won over the USA in 1912 and the USA won over Australia in 1920. Ivan Stedman, who had reached the semifinals of the 100 metres freestyle but was eliminated in the heats of the 200 metres breaststroke, had proven an excellent substitute for Charlton in the heat and semifinal. The Australians were easy heat and semifinal winners but almost half a minute slower than the Americans who easily won their semifinal. The Americans, who replaced three of their four swimmers for the final, were considered certainties and Sweden, bolstered by the inclusion of the Borg brothers, were considered by many to be Australia's equal.

Australia decided Charlton should swim second in the relay, contrary to the usual ploy of using the fastest man first or last. Such was the strength of the Americans that neither Duke Kahanamoku nor his brother Sam, who placed second and third behind Weissmuller in the 100 metres, made the team. Frank Beaurepaire swam first for Australia. Charlton hit the water next, four metres behind American Ralph Breyer who went out very hard in the first two laps. Charlton was giving Breyer the best part of eight metres start at the 100 metre turn but powered home so strongly he was within a metre of him at the end of his swim. His popularity was such that the French crowd joined the Australians, many echoing the cooee call, others shouting, 'Allez Sharlton! Allez Sharlton!'. Wallace O'Connor, swimming against Moss Christie, added to America's lead and with Weissmuller to finish they led by five metres from Australia, with Japan third and Sweden well back in fourth.

Ernie Henry had no chance of catching America's anchorman but was determined to hold off Takaishi of Japan and Sweden's trump card, Arne Borg. Henry was tired, having swum a heat and semifinal of the 100 metres, as well as a heat and semifinal of the team's race. To the amazement of all, Weissmuller eased up in the final leg and let Henry get on terms with him. He then paced the Australian until the last lap before pulling away to win convincingly. With Weissmuller's help Henry was able to hold off Borg who had passed Takaishi, making up a full twelve seconds with a wonderful swim. The official result showed America had beaten Australia by almost nine seconds with Sweden more than four seconds away in third placing. Henry stated some years later that Weissmuller had assisted him because of some ill feeling between the USA and Sweden, particularly against Arne Borg, and the strong affinity between the USA and Australia.

There had been no surprise results in the swimming carnival but the quality of the performances made it a remarkable meeting. As expected, the highly proficient American men carried virtually all before them, winning five of the six events, losing only in the 1500 metres. They took out all three places in the 100 metres freestyle, won the 400 metres, were first and second in the 100 metres backstroke, first and third in the 200 metres breaststroke and won the team's race. They also won four of the five women's events showing just how far ahead of the world their coaching had taken them. Nevertheless Australia's five swimmers and diver Dick Eve had achieved all that could have been expected of them. They had won two golds, in the 1500 metres and the diving, a silver in the 4×200 metres relay and two bronze medals in the 400 and 1500. The great competitor Arne Borg had not been able to win gold but had performed marvellously. Placing in the 1500 metres and 400 metres, he had also managed fourth in the 100 metres and third in the 4×200 metres relay.

Boy Charlton's youth, modesty and enormous natural talent had made him extremely popular with the crowds at the pool. The Parisian newspapers had been particularly taken with him.

His demeanour and physique were favourite talking points. Veteran English swimming authority, Willam Henry, founder of the Royal Life Saving Society, said of him after his 1500 metres victory:

> *Charlton outdoes everything I have seen from other Australian champions. Surely he must have been taken from the cradle and placed in the water instead of a perambulator otherwise he would not have developed, at the age of sixteen, such remarkable speed. He is a veritable turbine. The best swimmers are like the best-built ships. They cause a minimum displacement of the water and the least resistance. Charlton is symmetrically proportioned; broad shouldered and deepchested. It is absurd to say his record will never be broken. Such prophecies are always falsified. Looking forward I can see Charlton smashing many records.*

Frank Beaurepaire's summation was somewhat less flowery and very much to the point: 'Charlton is a wonder. I consider it an honour to swim behind him.'

The French had put on a wonderful Olympics. Though their runners and swimmers had no success, their ability in other sports saw them the third most successful of all nations. On the tennis court, where they won silver in the men's singles and doubles, they produced outstanding young players who were to become among the most famous French sportsmen ever, and who were destined to thrill Australian audiences just as Boy Charlton had thrilled theirs.

5

Seeing the World

WHEN OSWALD CHARLTON SAID that for his son to experience Paris 'would be an education in itself', how right he was. Boy had been excited by Paris, but resisted, to his father's and grandfather's great relief, the temptations of the exotic and wonderful city. A city of artists, writers and thespians, where Bohemians, painters, poets and pretty girls paraded each day by the banks of the Seine. Where people embraced the new jazz music, with French devotees performing alongside black Americans who came to play and remained for long periods, enjoying their acceptance by the liberal thinking French. Nor was it just the artistic who were different. As Boy observed in one of his letters, even 'normal' folk came home from work, had a rest after lunch, then went back to work and out to dinner at ten o'clock. This *was* a different place, even to Manly.

In March that year, when Boy was contemplating whether to

go to Paris or miss the Games, Bill Corbett wrote in *The Sun*: 'The revelations of the marvels of other countries may make him restless when he returns. Having seen the great cities of the world, there is often a longing to see them again.' Boy had not seen London, where the team were invited to compete as part of the British Empire against America, nor other great European and American cities. The adventure was not yet over.

At the conclusion of the Games, manager Ossie Merrett pored over the offers his team had received to participate in a number of carnivals. The swimming contingent was particularly sought after. Everyone wanted to see Boy Charlton. Merrett had already accepted an invitation for the entire team to compete in the Tailteann Games in Dublin, along with seventeen other nations. Held immediately after the Olympics, the Tailteann Games were officially restricted to athletes of Irish descent, however in 1924 an exception was made and the entire Australian team was invited. A trip to America for the swim team, as well as gold medallists Dick Eve and Nick Winter, including two days as guests of the Illinois Athletic Club, was also especially inviting. Ossie Merrett was extremely proud of his wonders of the pool. How could he deny them a visit to the famous club, about which they'd heard so much from Frank Beaurepaire, and which was home to Bachrach, Weissmuller and the former great Olympic champion, Norman Ross?

The Olympians left Paris for Brussels by train two days after the Games had finished. During the five-hour trip Ivan Stedman was able to point out many places he remembered from the war, particularly St Quentin, where he had been shot in the back. Dick Eve and Moss Christie were quick to suggest he must have been running away, bringing a wry smile and shake of the head from their older team-mate. Stedman was a scholar with knowledge of Europe and the history of swimming. As such he was a wonderful tourist. The Belgium capital was similar in its charm to Paris though the buildings were more modern. They stayed at the luxurious Scheers Hotel, quite a contrast to the Normandie, as did the American team. On their second day they competed in an international swimming carnival where Charlton won the 500 metres ahead of Frank Beaurepaire and Moss Christie, with three American swimmers behind them.

The 1924 Olympic team was the first to produce three individual gold medallists. Now they were the first Australian team to travel by plane. Manager Ossie Merrett was already a devotee of the new way of travel and had flown across from France to London to supervise Tommy Adrian's treatment prior to the Games. After the carnival in Belgium he announced they would motor to the airport where three large single engine bi-planes stood by to fly them to England. It was an announcement that came out of the blue. When the party passed a cemetery on the way, Frank Beaurepaire joked that they might soon be back.

Commercial air travel was in its infancy and there were many anxious faces when each person was weighed and assigned to a particular aircraft, one of which was deployed purely to carry luggage. The five swimmers, diver Dick Eve, boxer Charlie Jardine, New Zealand swimmer Gwyther Shand and Merrett posed for photographs with other hardy souls before taking off in the first plane. Few had flown before so for them it was an exciting, if somewhat nerve-racking experience. Ossie Merrett had real fun observing the reactions of his group. It rained for much of the trip and a degree of turbulence added significantly to the occasion as the planes crossed cities and farms before the English Channel, often flying a few hundred feet above the water. There were involuntary gasps each time the plane dropped into an air pocket and lost altitude. What was to become commonplace was a very novel experience. The three and a half hour flight was yet another highlight of an extraordinary adventure.

Upon their arrival in England the team settled into the Bristol Hotel in Earls Court and the next day went to dinner at Australia House as guests of the Australian High Commissioner, Sir Joseph Cook. Boy Charlton was seated at the head table and listened as the High Commissioner praised the efforts of the team, particularly his own and those of Nick Winter, Dick Eve and Frank Beaurepaire. The speakers that followed assured the team they were doing more to promote Australia than any politician or even the Wembley Exhibition, where Commonwealth countries were exhibiting their wares in large halls. In his reply Ossie Merrett also made particular mention of the medal winners including Beaurepaire, to whom he referred as Father Neptune. He lamented the poor luck of Slip Carr and sympathised with the rowing eight who had trained so hard but to no avail. He added the team came away from Paris with more than medals; an honoured name in the sporting world. He also lambasted critics who doubted the worth of the Games, citing the amity between Australia and the US, as well as the Commonwealth countries, that had been attained by sporting competition. That afternoon different groups were taken to see the famous attractions of London. The traffic in Piccadilly was even thicker than that of Paris but at least people were driving on the 'correct side' of the road. Team members found it most enjoyable sitting on the top of a double-decker bus and watching by how little they missed other vehicles.

On Saturday, July 26, two days after their arrival, the Australians took part in the British Empire versus America carnival held in the 55-yard pool at Harrow School, which was filled with extremely cold water on an equally cold night. America won the contest 70 points to 50 but not before Charlton and Beaurepaire had finished first and second in the 440 yards. Ernie Henry, though beaten by Weissmuller in the 100 yards, beat Duke Kahanamoku into third place.

The Australians were treated wonderfully in their fortnight stay in London, in private outings and as a team. People could not do enough for them. They were taken to see the sights of the city; the waxworks, the changing of the guard, the tower bridge, Nelson's Column, the houses of parliament, and went to the theatre, swam at the exclusive Automobile Club and were guests at the Wembley Exhibition. They 'paid their way' by sporting appearances but training was up to the individual and results not the main issue.

Boy Charlton and Frank Beaurepaire entered the 500 yards championship of England, at which Ernie Henry won the 100 yards. Following a heat win Charlton came to Beaurepaire and complained of feeling 'a bit crook'. Beaurepaire reacted instantly, insisting two doctors take a good look at him. Australians at home were shocked when a newspaper report came through that Ossie Merrett had cancelled all Charlton's competitive swimming following the race. The doctors advised that the youngster should rest immediately. They believed he should not race again for the rest of the year. Merrett then organised for him to be examined by a Harley Street specialist the following day.

The diagnosis of the high-profile specialist was a 'slight dilation of the heart'. He was adamant the trouble was trans-itory and would clear up with careful attention, diet and a temporary cessation of over-strenuous exercise. In view of this it came as a complete surprise when *The Sun* carried a report from London, just four days later: 'Boy Charlton, who has regained his robust health, will swim an exhibition at Cardiff at the weekend. Dick Eve will accompany him and give a diving exhibition.'

Despite the good news there was still considerable consterna-tion regarding Charlton's future. It seemed unthinkable that the toast of the swim world just a few weeks before should be the centre of so much worry. Charlton was growing quickly, his natural weight was now well over 14 stone (88.5 kilograms) and he had a propensity to put on weight if he was not careful with his meals. He was about to turn seventeen and though he obviously did not consider his heart dilation too serious, and was looking forward to the Tailteann Games, there were some who harboured genuine concern about him.

On August 7, the entire swim team, Dick Eve, Nick Winter and Ossie Merrett, who were to travel home to Australia via America, visited the American Consulate to organise their documents. That evening, their last in London, a large party went to Wembley with passengers from the *Ormonde*. They rode the water chute, the dodgem cars, the scenic railway, visited the mystery house and generally enjoyed the atmosphere of the fair. As Moss Christie admitted, 'We were like a bunch of school kids.' The following day the team left to compete in the Tailteann Games in Ireland. Boy Charlton declared he was looking forward to the meeting and feeling fit enough to swim well.

The Australians left London by train at 8.30 and four hours later were embarking on the *Gambia*, a 2,000-ton vessel, with a captain's bridge fore and aft to save it having to turn around inside the harbours. In the open sea it fairly flew, travelling at 25 knots, crossing the 62 miles of calm blue water of the Irish Channel to Kingston in two and a half hours. It was an exhilarating trip. From Kingston the team made their way by train to Dublin, arriving at 6.30 pm. They motored to St Patrick's College, a training establishment for priests, where they were to stay. Everything augured for a 'jolly' time, with thirty-eight Australians, a Britisher, a South African and a Canadian in one dormitory. Next door were one hundred Americans.

The next day, Ivan Stedman, Moss Christie and New Zealand breaststroker Clarrie Herd went to check out the pool at Phoenix Park. To their amazement the 'pool' turned out to be a lake, part of the Zoological Gardens, and the water extremely cold and as black as pitch because of its extreme depth. The races were to be swum between two pontoons 100 yards apart. Canvas tents on the bank of the lake constituted dressing sheds. With no shelter from prevailing winds it presented a stark contrast to Tourelles and the many pools they had enjoyed since Paris. Because of the cold they did not stay in long but determined to return the next day only to find their trip was in vain as swimming in the lake was not allowed on Sundays.

On Monday all the swimmers travelled to the lake rugged up in overcoats. They shed their warm clothes, donned costumes and had a thorough workout. They had been spoiled by the weather in Paris and were very happy when the sun broke through that afternoon, many deciding to walk to Dublin. Those with a sense of history were interested to see the buildings that had been damaged in the uprisings of 1916 and 1922. The post office and customs house, the scene of the Easter Rebellion, the armed uprising of Irish nationalists against British rule, remained just shells.

The next morning saw the opening day of the first Tailteann Games. The swimmers were pleased to wake in sunshine. By midday a light shower had come and gone and the weather was quite pleasant. Though not in the same form he carried in Paris, Boy was nevertheless in fair shape and won his heat of the 880 yards comfortably from Moss Christie. Frank Beaurepaire was an easy winner in heat two. Charlton also won his heat of the 220 yards, again beating Moss Christie while Ernie Henry beat Ivan Stedman in a second heat. Australia had no specialist backstroker so Ernie Henry, the only one with any ability at the stroke, volunteered to swim. To the amazement of his team-mates he won his heat of the 100 yards in comparatively good time.

Over the next three days the Australians dominated the swimming events. Boy Charlton withdrew from the 1500 metres which was won by Moss Christie, but won the 880, 440 and 220 yards titles. Ernie Henry won the 100 yards, Ivan Stedman the breaststroke then Henry provided the surprise of the carnival by winning the backstroke. Boy was awarded an extra medal for being the outstanding performer. It was a wonderful few days with entertainment each evening and all teams participating in a very sporting manner. The Australians were lauded in the local press, and feted in a way they had become used to. There was no angst caused by the fact that many of them were not of Irish descent, just satisfaction that they had agreed to compete. Boy, though never fully extended, felt well and had no reason to worry about his health.

After ten delightful days in Ireland the team took their luggage to the shipping office and spent the day watching the Gentlemen of Ireland play cricket against the Marylebone Cricket Club. Then followed dinner in town. That evening they left Dublin on the SS *Brier*, a luxurious 605-ton steamer, and went to bed with the *Brier* travelling smoothly on a calm sea and woke next morning beside the jetty in Heysham, Lancashire. There they were met by Mr Woodhouse, secretary of the Bradford Swimming Club, who insisted on shouting breakfast at a local hotel and then drove them in a large Fiat charabanc on a tour of the Lakes District, taking in some of the most picturesque scenery they had ever witnessed including Lakes Windermere, Grassmere, Ullswater and Rydal Waters. A light lunch at Keswick was followed by a trip through the Kirkstone Pass, the highest point in England, arriving back in Bradford just before midday.

They spent the next two days touring in a charabanc as guests of the Bradford Swimming Club first taking in the city of York, where they walked the top of the ancient walls built by the Romans centuries ago, and visited old classic buildings including a church, which they were told was the oldest in the district, built by the Mormons. Then it was on to Hull where they gave exhibitions in the local baths, dined with the mayor, and were presented with Moroccan leather wallets.

The next day's journey to Scarborough took three hours. The weather was cool and the fresh, clear air invigorating. A walk on the beach preceded lunch after which they saw the buildings damaged by German battleships during the war a decade earlier as well as Scottish girls cleaning the fish from the trawlers. The team arrived back in Bradford at 11 pm having enjoyed themselves immensely. They all agreed if any touring team had ever been treated better it must have been a well-kept secret.

Some of the Australians, including Charlton, returned to London briefly before leaving for home. Boy took the chance to buy himself an expensive grey felt hat at one of the West End's most fashionable hatters. He looked very trim, having dieted conscientiously since his heart diagnosis a month earlier. He was among several who enjoyed the English fashions; one of the honorary masseurs appearing regularly in plus fours. Charlton's last meal in London was roast grouse, sent to him by an admirer.

At 7 pm on Saturday, August 23, the contingent bound for America left Liverpool aboard the 20,000-ton luxury Cunard liner *Laconia*. The ship was the second to carry the name, the first having been sunk by a German U-boat off the Irish coast during the First World War. It was a magnificent ship as the Australians were about to discover. Team funds were running a bit low so for the first time Ossie Merrett elected that they should travel second class. This would prove no imposition. So luxurious was the *Laconia* that the second-class cabins, lounge, dining and music room were superior to those in first class on the *Ormonde*. An invitation to tour first class was a real eye-opener. The winter garden, lounge, sports deck and elevator could only be described as opulent. The meals and service proved to be on a par with an expensive restaurant.

With their six-week journey on the *Ormonde* behind them the Olympians now considered themselves experienced seafarers. Boy and Ernie Henry again roomed together while Ivan Stedman and Moss Christie shared a large cabin with the two tennis representatives, Anthony Willard and James Bayley. They had only a week's travel ahead of them to reach New York.

The party soon met up with other passengers and engaged in a series of competitive deck sports that ran over two days. There was a large canvas pool in first class to which they were given access and they made full use of it. The weather was very calm so when a report came though on the ship's wireless that the *Bengaria*, travelling on the same course twenty-four hours ahead, and carrying the Prince Of Wales, had struck a severe storm there was some excitement that the *Laconia* would have to weather it also. This did not eventuate and when the lights of Coney Island appeared at 8 pm on Sunday, August 31, they signalled the end of a very pleasant week.

A doctor from quarantine boarded the *Laconia* at 8 am and after a cursory check of each athlete passed them fit to land. Recovering their baggage and clearing customs proved to be a very slow process and it was mid-afternoon before they reached the Hotel Holley, in Washington Square. Each of them had a private room and was pleased to find it contained a bath. After dinner they took their first walk in the city and, like all others on their first trip to New York, were amazed at the height of the skyscrapers and the number of brightly lit signs. Would Sydney or Melbourne ever look like this? The next day Ernie Henry, Moss Christie, Willard and Bayley went by invitation to see the American champion Bill Tilden win his fifth successive US open tennis title on the famous grass courts at Forest Hills.

From New York the party travelled by train, following the Hudson River for some hours past a number of farming and manufacturing towns including Utica and Syracuse, which proudly called itself the onion capital of America, before arriving in Buffalo, a city much the same size as Sydney. Like New York, it too had many tall buildings and was a blaze of electric lights and neon signs. The next day the group were driven 25 miles to see the Niagra Falls on the border of America and Canada. Accessible only on the Canadian side, the punt trip across the river proved rather more exciting than they had anticipated. The punt travelled at about 6 miles per hour, the rapidly flowing current at 18 miles per hour. In order to cross, the punt crept up the side of the bank, avoiding the current, then turned and made straight for the opposite bank. It was an eerie experience going three times faster sideways than forward.

The team was given a most comprehensive tour of the Falls, travelling down 100 feet in a lift then walking along a tunnel to get a magnificent view of the Canadian Horseshoe, the largest of three spectacular waterfalls, looking through the water as it fell in a mighty torrent into the Niagra River. After lunch they drove on to see the Whirlpool and rode the aero car across the river and back, suspended by a cable, swaying continually 100 feet above the churning water, holding onto a small railing on the side of the car. On the trip back to Buffalo they stopped several times at vantage points to allow the party to take photos. By 9 pm, after a day none would forget, they had been well fed and were on the overnight train bound for Chicago and the famous Illinois Athletic Club.

Situated on the south-western shore of Lake Michigan, Chicago was a bustling city of over two million people. By virtue of its position, en route between the agricultural regions of America's west and the industrial cities of the east and its proximity to the fertile Mississippi basin, it was one of the country's major trading centres and contained a vast network of rail freight and passenger terminals. It was also the centre of much controversy. With prohibition in full swing much of the bootleg liquor flooding the market was produced by the diversion of alcohol sold for industrial purposes and was being transported through Chicago. Not that the Olympians would be affected, nor interested, in Chicago's crime and associated corruption. They simply wanted to see for themselves the facilities and training methods Frank Beaurepaire had rightly declared were the benchmark for nations wanting to compete successfully at international level. They were not disappointed. Arriving at 9 am they were taken to the Lexington Hotel to freshen up then directly to the club. Their arrival had been keenly awaited. Head swim coach Bill Bachrach and Johnny Weissmuller had spoken in glowing terms of their talent, particularly that of the 'boy wonder' Charlton and the sportsmanship of the group generally.

They were greeted by Norman Ross, 1920 Olympic champion, who insisted on taking them to the meet the club president who made them honorary members and gave them a thorough tour, including accommodation rooms, dining rooms, lounges, the gymnasium, above which was a wooden running track, boxing ring and handball courts. In the basement was the 25-yard, tiled pool with a small gutter around the sides just above water level to avoid kick-back. The pool was filled with fresh water that continually passed through a filtration plant. The president told them proudly that more national and Olympic champions had been trained there than any other pool in the country, many of them by Bill Bachrach, a huge man of demanding personality with a reputation as well known as his best performers.

The swimmers had a relaxing session in the pool before lunch, after which the president arranged for Norman Ross (Johnny Weissmuller had not yet returned from the Games) to take the whole party on a tour of the city in one of the club's new coaches. Ross was pleased to able to repay some of the hospitality shown him in Australia three years earlier. Australian swimming authorities had asked Ossie Merrett to invite a champion to tour Australia during the following season. Johnny Weissmuller was the obvious drawcard but his commitments with the Illinois Athletic Club, including the national championships, might well be too heavy to allow him a break at a time to suit the Australian season. Still the invitation was there and the Australian press were already talking about the interest such a tour would create. He would be too fast for the 100 metres opponents but the thought of Charlton and Weissmuller clashing at 400 metres was most exciting. Bachrach had told Merrett in Paris the Americans would be most interested in a visit by Charlton.

That Saturday evening, September 6, Frank Beaurepaire left the team to travel home via Los Angeles. After a walk down Michigan Avenue to do some shopping the team boarded the Pullman train which would take them due west, all the way across the continent to San Francisco on the coast from where they would embark on the last stage of their journey home. The entire Sunday was spent traversing country similar to that seen on the Trans Australian Railway. The Olympians were unimpressed with the Pullman carriages, which they regarded as vastly inferior to similar carriages in Australia, but the boredom of the long trip was lessened by the antics of the porter who continually closed the windows after which they opened them again.

On Monday the train stopped for a few minutes in Salt Lake City, Utah, before crossing the Great Salt Lake. With the line built on trestles a metre above the water it was an unusual experience to look out the windows on both sides of the carriage and see the water dashing past as though they were hydroplaning. By this time their porter had given up on his closing the windows and the breeze was refreshing as the 32 miles of water was negotiated.

Eventually, after two and a half days and three nights aboard the Pullman, they arrived in Oaklands and boarded a ferry that took them across the harbour to San Francisco and the Stewart Hotel. The Stewart was so luxurious they were disinclined to leave it but were immediately taken with how new and clean the city looked, much of it having been rebuilt after the massive earthquake of 1905. The harbour reminded them of Sydney and they were disappointed they would have no time to explore it properly. They took a stroll around the city that evening and enjoyed a swim in the Olympic Club the next morning before setting out for the wharf to board the 9,000-ton *Tahiti*. Several Australians, having read that the team was in town, came down to see them off. There were also a large number of Australian passengers returning to Australia.

The *Tahiti* left San Francisco early in the afternoon and soon passed through the Golden Gate. Again fortune smiled on the Australians. Though now travelling second class because of their limited funds, Ossie Merrett discovered the captain was an old friend and the entire group was afforded the use of first class facilities including the dining room. The *Tahiti* was an older ship with a fair turn of speed and the trip was to be full of fun. Also on board was a large party of film stars from Cosmopolitan Studios, owned by media magnate Randolph Hearst, heading for Tahiti to shoot the film *Never The Twain Shall Meet*. The leading lady, Anita Stewart, and leading man, Bert Lytell, were prolific actors, very well known to most on board, and proved very good company. Soon the Olympians and film stars were getting along famously. Character actor Lionel Belmore, a man well in his sixties, was a large fellow with a boisterous personality and loud voice, honed on Broadway stages. He greeted each day with a loud, 'Everything is going to be – all right'. Soon Belmore would say the first phrase and there would be a chorus of voices from the Australians adding 'all right'.

The trip to Tahiti passed very quickly, thanks in no small way to the company of the film party who joined in the deck sports, the dances, a concert and a fancy dress ball. On one occasion the swimming contingent participated in a 'kangaroo court' in which Anita Stewart was accused of stealing a dill pickle, the property of Bert Lytell. The *Tahiti* ran into one storm only which washed out the deck sports but generally the weather was perfect. Moss Christie celebrated his twenty-third birthday on September 18. Like Boy Charlton, in Dublin, it was his first birthday away from home.

When they reached the beautiful Tahitian port of Papeete at daybreak on September 20, they had been at sea for almost ten days. The *Tahiti* anchored just inside the reef and all had a perfect view of the island, ringed by a coral reef and green with vegetation and coconut trees. Several tall mountains reached high above the township, some of their tops hidden by white cloud. It was an idyllic setting for a motion picture. A doctor came on board and within minutes gave the captain clearance to proceed to the wharf. After breakfast most passengers went ashore and spent a few hours exploring the island. When the ship left that afternoon they were given a rousing send off by the film crew. Passing through the reef those on board gave Lionel Belmore's call of 'Everything is going to be' . . . and the answer came floating back across the water . . . 'all right'. Anita Stewart's mother, who had travelled with her, was ill so Anita could not come down to the wharf to farewell the ship. She sent a message to look out for her as the boat went through the reef. Sure enough she appeared on the beach and waded out to wave goodbye. As the chorus of voices floated across the harbour her faint reply came back. It could have been a scene from the film. The ship was going to seem very quiet for the next few days as passengers adjusted to life without their film friends.

The *Tahiti* was now on its way to New Zealand, stopping for a brief stay at Raratonga, a small island that reminded them much of Papeete. Here the ship anchored a mile off the reef and passengers went ashore on a barge towed by a motor launch. A stroll around The Village was brought to a stop by heavy rain which continued through the night. The *Tahiti* set off again at 4 the next morning with rain still pouring and a large sea started to toss the ship around quite dramatically. Suddenly confident seafarers reverted to being landlubbers again and few came down for meals. Even when the sea abated the decks were too wet for sports so the entire day was spent in the music room and lounges.

When calm seas and sunshine returned the following morning, it brought with it hunger, and there was a dash for breakfast and a flurry to get up on deck once again. On September 28, the *Tahiti* was in sight of the New Zealand coastline and remained so all day. The following morning the ship arrived at Wellington on the southern tip of New Zealand's north island in heavy fog. Clearing customs by 8.30 the team had morning tea then a mayoral reception. Boy Charlton elected not to swim in a carnival that afternoon. Locals were disappointed but he had done no training whatsoever since the Tailteann Games, having heeded doctors' advice, albeit a little late. Moss Christie won the 440 yards scratch race in his absence.

The *Tahiti* left Wellington the next afternoon bound for Sydney, with the Olympians keen to get home and share their experiences. Early the next morning they were awakened with a fierce storm lashing the ship. Mountainous waves flooded the top deck. The porthole above Moss Christie's bed came adrift and he was soaked instantly, much to the amusement of Dick Eve and Ivan Stedman who suffered only a few splashes. Of the entourage only Ivan Stedman and Moss Christie made it to breakfast. In fact, there were only seven passengers in the dining room all told. As they ate they had the strange experience of watching the waves crashing over the forecastle and splashing up against the porthole. When the storm was over there were sheepish grins all around as people slowly appeared on deck. There was excitement and a rush for cameras when, the next day, a number of whales were spotted, one cruising to within 50 yards of the ship.

The *Tahiti*'s arrival in Sydney coincided with perfect weather and calm seas. It was Saturday morning, October 4. The Olympians were up in their pyjamas to see Sydney Lighthouse at 4.30 am then it was off for a shave and a bath and back on deck in preparation for entry through the Heads. At 6 am the *Tahiti* entered Sydney Harbour and anchored off Nielsen Park. It was five months and three days since they had departed on the *Ormonde*. The Manly ferry passed close by and exchanged cock-a-doodle-doos as passengers waved and cheered. Every boat that passed sounded its horn. The quarantine doctor and custom's officer arrived and soon after the *Tahiti* made its way slowly up the harbour to a cacophony of whistles and sirens.

Many sporting teams had arrived home from successful tours in the past but veteran journalists were adamant nothing like this had been seen before. A huge crowd had gathered at No 5 Wharf Darling Harbour to welcome them home. Officials from various swim clubs, relatives, friends and fans craned necks to get a glimpse of their heroes, resplendent in green blazers and cream slacks. An official welcome on the wharf by the NSW Olympic Council preceded collection of baggage from customs. Reporters tried to get interviews as the athletes were bundled into cars and driven to the Town Hall past cheering crowds to a mayoral reception. Boy Charlton was the most eagerly sought. The Town Hall steps were crowded with wellwishers.

The Manly contingent, Charlton, Henry, Winter and Eve, were then driven to Circular Quay where the gaily decorated ferry *Balgowlah* stood by to take them to Manly and more festivities. There was another official welcome on board and when their boat arrived at Manly Wharf at 12.45 they were greeted by a wild cheering from the crowd, which included a large group of councillors, and the sounds of the Manly and Fire Brigade bands. Boy Charlton was then whisked away to officially open the new Queenscliff Surf Club, a modest wooden structure built by volunteer labour, proudly displaying its full measure of equipment, one second-hand reel and line.

The Village, once again bedecked with streamers and bunting, was alive with revellers and stayed so throughout the day and long into the night. At 8 that evening the Manly and Fire Brigade bands were still playing as crowds continued to congregate on The Corso. This was a sample of what Manly had in store for the entire week. It was as though The Village existed just for celebrations. People came from all over Sydney to join in. A number of official functions had been organised by the municipal council in conjunction with the combined district sporting clubs. On Monday the medal winners were guests at a civic dinner at the Manly Pacific Hotel. On Tuesday they attended the Swimming Club dance at Dungowan. On Wednesday they were guests of the Amateur Athletic Club and Bicycle Club at a sports day on Manly Oval. On Thursday it was the Manly Life Saving Club's turn to host them at the 'Serenaders' Palais Theatre. On Friday they were entertained by the Maurice Rosenthal Players at Manly's Rialto Theatre, with half the show's proceeds going to the Manly Cottage Hospital. On Saturday they were guests of the combined football codes at the football jumble at the Agricultural Showground, Moore Park. Between functions The Village simply partied. Boy Charlton was literally besieged at every outing. Stuart Alldritt, a citizen of Manly for much of his life and a man involved in swimming for many years, has clear memories of his mother telling him how she and her girlfriends, then teenagers, travelled from Rose Bay to Manly by ferry just to get a glimpse of him. By the time the medal winners had enjoyed an all-day motor trip to Newport, courtesy of the Manly Rugby Club on Sunday afternoon the group was exhausted. Still, Manly had special reason to celebrate – all three gold medallists being from The Village. Perhaps Boy's Drummoyne team-mate, Moss Christie, summed up the experience for all of them with his final diary entry: 'After the excitement dies down I wonder how I will settle back to work again.'

Boy Charlton's answer came directly. It was like a crack of thunder to sports' fans across Australia. He told the press that, much as he had enjoyed the experience and support of the Australian people, he was finished with competitive swimming. He would return to Hawkesbury Agricultural College to continue to prepare for life as a farmer on the property his grandfather had promised to secure for him.

6

The Jackeroo Meets
Takaishi

ON MONDAY, OCTOBER 20, 1924, Boy Charlton returned to
Hawkesbury Agricultural College and commenced duties in the
blacksmith's shop. For the next three weeks he practised funda-
mental skills commencing with the making of a basic split link
and progressing to more intricate items involved with work as a
farrier. Wal Clout, the resident smithy, was a first-class trades-
man whose enthusiasm was so great he could hardly restrain
himself from finishing the job for his students as they learned the
art of shoeing horses. For Charlton, it was a far cry from lazing
on the deck of a luxury liner waiting for the next meal, or
churning up the last lap of a distance swim cheered on by ten
thousand frenzied fans. Yet he enjoyed it immensely. There was
a tradition at the College where each student burnt his name in
a large, flat board, together with his hometown and date of
birth. When Charlton's turned up many years later on the door

of a fruiterer's garage in Richmond it caused a lot of interest. From the blacksmith's shop he went to the saddlery where he stayed until the end of term in mid-December. When farewelled by his Hawkesbury friends he left a pair of farm boots with smithy Wal Clout who guarded them for years as though they were the crown jewels.

After just two years Boy Charlton's time at Hawkesbury was at an end. His final report detailing his achievements concluded with this observation from the headmaster: 'during his period of residence at the College, he has entered into and taken a prominent part in the various sporting activities at the College. I have pleasure in adding that his conduct has been at all times exemplary.'

During the Christmas break Boy returned to Manly to prepare for the next big adventure in his short life. As he rode the waves in to the beach with his mates at South Steyne and competed in surf carnivals, helping Manly win the inter-club shield for the seventh successive year, plans were settled. His grandfather had arranged for Boy to take up a position as a jackeroo on Kurrumbede Station, Gunnedah, on the black soil plains, 300 miles (500 kilometres) to the north west of Sydney. A jackeroo who could swim like a dolphin, but had never been on horseback, seemed a strange vocation, but something Boy was prepared to do.

Before his departure Boy saw the opening of the long-awaited Spit Bridge, the first pile of which had been driven as Australia's athletes prepared for Paris. Now Manly was accessible to the north shore by road. A toll bridge, which opened for tall masted water traffic, it now carried a steady, almost continuous flow of passengers. In the first four weeks over 60,000 people crossed the bridge, the rates for which were published in the *Manly Daily*:

Passengers on foot . . . free
Bicycles . . . one penny
Motor cycles . . . two pence
Side car . . . three pence
Vehicle drawn by one horse . . . six pence
Each extra horse . . . three pence
Motor car . . . six pence
Motor bus . . . one shilling
Motor lorry up to 3 tons gross . . . six pence
Over 3 tons . . . nine pence
Over 6 tons . . . one shilling.
Trailers . . . six pence
Loose stock, horses and cattle . . . two pence
Sheep or pigs . . . one penny
Ambulance, Police, Emergency vehicles . . . free

Boy's destination, Kurrumbede Station, sat on magnificent farming country, ideal for sheep and produce. Owner Malcolm Mackellar was a wealthy grazier and well-known racehorse owner. He arranged for Gunnedah stock and station agent, Reg Broun, to pick up Charlton and drive him to the station in the first week of 1925. Also in the car were Reg Broun junior, the manager of the station, Richard Dixon, a family friend, and Eric Layh, a Gunnedah bank officer. The party of five, loaded with luggage, set off from Manly on a trip which would take them west, up the steep winding road through the Blue Mountains, down to Lithgow on the far side of the range, through Mudgee and Gulgong then on to Gunnedah. Charlton, shy at any time but particularly so in this company, wore his Australian blazer. It was a long trip in those days and by the time Reg Broun's Australian Six, advertised as 'Australia's own car' though manufactured in England, got to Lithgow it had developed engine trouble. When the party stopped for repairs, local people, young and old, soon recognised Charlton. Though somewhat embarrassed, Boy obliged with autographs as mechanics worked on the car and after some hours the journey was resumed.

They passed through Mudgee without further mishap but 3 kilometres out of Gulgong the gearbox went amiss. To his chagrin Broun found the only gear he could engage was reverse. He had no option but to continue into town backwards. Their unusual entry into Gulgong, along with their famous passenger in his green blazer, now attracted even more attention than they had received in Lithgow, news of their trip having been sent ahead. Charlton was now completely embarrassed. No doubt Reg Broun was as well. Receiving news from the garage proprietor that adequate repairs would take some weeks to complete, the group took a hire car to Coolah, 60 kilometres further on, then caught the mail train, a single rail car, which took them to Gunnedah and the Railway Hotel. Boy, a teetotaller, was too shy to even go in for a lemonade when he found the bar packed with drinkers anxious to welcome him. Even when the publican, Andrew Abernathy, told Boy he had a pool 'out the back' the youngster declined to see if it was true or not. He had come to Gunnedah to be a jackeroo and as such saw himself as a lesser light among his group and could not wait to get to Kurrumbede and out of the spotlight. The trip had been more interesting than anticipated.

Kurrumbede was one of the best-known sheep stations in the district and the larger of two Gunnedah properties owned by the Mackellar family. Malcolm Mackellar's father, Dr Charles Mackellar, bought the property in 1905. Charles's only daughter, Dorothea, now one of Australia's most eminent poets, had lived on the station from the time of its purchase until 1911, when she left to travel overseas. Now living in Sydney, she was a frequent visitor. Kurrumbede had also been the location for *Lure Of The Bush*, a feature film shot in 1917, which starred

Olympian Snowy Baker, who left soon after to continue his career in Hollywood. The homestead was a magnificent, large bungalow with verandahs on three sides, a large living room, several bedrooms, two fireplaces, continually alight during the winter months, and a large windmill that pumped water from the Namoi River.

Boy Charlton was warmly welcomed and treated very well at Kurrumbede. His modesty and reluctance to talk about his triumphs was well accepted by his superiors and staff. He was more interested in hearing about their bush life than recalling his own deeds as he set to work with another jackeroo, two station hands and a horse strapper. The station hands and strapper had grown up in the country and were all competent horsemen who took time to teach Boy to ride. Feeling very much at home with his new colleagues, Boy decided immediately that he was suited to country life. His workmates were very happy to work with the strapping youth with fair hair and bright blue eyes who had been to places they could only dream about.

The swimming club at Gunnedah received a tremendous boost with Boy's arrival. When time permitted he swam in the Namoi River at Cohen's Bridge, where crude starting board facilities had been installed and carnivals were held, and further upstream at 'the dip' where the current flowed quite strongly. Though he was reluctant to perform, he sometimes swam exhibitions in aid of country clubs and a large crowd always attended. Many a youngster would dive in and swim a few strokes before being left in his wake just so they could go home and say they had swum with Boy Charlton. Six weeks after his arrival at Gunnedah, Boy appeared with Dick Eve in a carnival in Tamworth to raise money for the local club. Invitations to swim exhibitions in the city as well as country towns now came thick and fast but Charlton was determined to keep away from the sport as much as he could to concentrate on his new career.

At Kurrumbede he learned the basic skills of drenching, crutching and dipping sheep and, as his riding skills improved, he took his turn at droving. The farm had plenty of soil under cultivation so he was also kept busy with ploughing, sowing, harvesting and maintaining machinery. The youngster was getting a wonderful grounding for the time when he owned his own property. During the summer months the temperatures reached the hundred mark and the dust swirled up and caked on his sweating brow. There was a severe drought the year Charlton arrived and he joined a group of stockmen who drove a large mob of sheep to agistment many miles away. It was during this trip, when he boiled the billy under a eucalypt or took shelter from the burning sun under a willow on the river's edge, then slept under the stars at night with his saddle for a pillow, that he really felt the joy of the bush.

Charlton had been at Kurrumbede just three months when Ossie Merrett passed away suddenly in Manly. He was only forty-one and had no idea that he had cancer while in Paris. His death came as a shock to all who knew him. He had done a wonderful job as manager and tributes came from athletes, sporting organisations and business associates from all over Australia. New Zealand swimmer Gwyther Shand joined fellow Olympians Moss Christie, Ernie Henry, Nick Winter, Charlie Jardine and Slip Carr as the long cortege made its way to Manly Cemetery. Ossie Merrett had often been referred to as the father of amateur sport in Manly and in a fitting tribute the sandstone gates to Manly Oval were dedicated to him and are known to this day as the O.G.H. Merrett Memorial Gates.

Also attending the funeral was Tommy Adrian whose family had been able to organise his return to Manly. He still swam at the baths and would continue to do so for some years but was never the same man. Moss Christie saw him having a leisurely swim in the shark proof area by the wharf one day and tried to catch up to him. Adrian sped up, hoisted himself onto a pontoon and said, 'You never could sprint Moss.' At least his sense of humour had not left him. Veteran Manly swimmer Jamie Jenkins recalls swimming at the Manly Baths when a boy and seeing Adrian arrive with a stopwatch, which he would start then dive in and swim two laps before checking his time. As he swam the boys would stop the watch for ten or fifteen seconds then restart it. Tommy would be amazed at his time and repeat the procedure. So did the boys. They had no idea of his condi-iton, nor what had caused it, and years later felt bad about how they had treated him.

As winter approached Boy began to feel unwell. So much so that he sought treatment from a doctor who diagnosed him with 'a strained heart' and ordered him to have three months complete rest. He returned to his family in Manly where he stayed for the next few months while recuperating. During his stay a shop in The Corso displayed his many trophies and medals including those won in Paris and Dublin. After being given a clean bill of health, Charlton returned to Gunnedah in September to resume duties at Kurrumbede.

The roaring twenties continued to roar. Youngsters flocked to surf club dances and end-of-season balls to do the Charleston and the Black Bottom. Sporting crowds had never been larger. Despite Charlton's absence fans still had plenty to cheer about. The Australia XI defeated England four Tests to one to retain the Ashes in 1925 with leg spinner Clarrie Grimmett commencing his international career by taking eleven wickets in the final Test match in Sydney. The outstanding three year old racehorse Manfred won the AJC Derby after losing half a furlong at the start, but another champion, Windbag, relegated him to second place in the Melbourne Cup. A crowd estimated at almost

75,000 saw the opening of the Olympia Speedway at Maroubra with motorcycles and cars sharing the headlines, roaring around the track at breathtaking speed. In Melbourne, Geelong won its first Australian football title after twenty-eight years. South Sydney's rugby league's Rabbitohs won their competition, commencing a sequence that would give them seven titles in eight years. Glebe–Balmain won the rugby union pennant, denying Sydney University a run of six successive premierships. In the southern New South Wales town of Bowral a young cricketer, a year younger than Boy Charlton, scored 234 not out in a day against Wingello but was bowled first ball when the match resumed on the following Saturday, by another young fellow bowling fast leg spin. The batsman was Don Bradman, the bowler Bill O'Reilly. There would be plenty of cheers for them in the next few years as they established themselves as Australia's finest batsman and bowler, respectively.

Charlton's Olympic team-mates continued to churn up the water, though Ernie Henry had landed a good job with the Shell Oil Company and decided to put his swimming career on hold. Moss Christie won the state 440 yards and 880 yards titles in 1925, when lanes were used for the first time, despite doubts from some about their worth, and again in 1926, swimming approximately twenty seconds slower than Charlton's best time in the 440 and forty seconds slower in the 880. A new name appeared when Queenslander Reg Green won the 1925 national 440 yards title. His time too was well outside of Charlton's. Overseas, Weissmuller and Borg continued to dominate with Borg eclipsing some of Weissmuller's record times. Weissmuller, still undefeated in races, was now rarely swimming beyond 200 metres. The only freestyle record not shared by the pair was Charlton's 1500 metres time, set at the Paris Olympics.

Never The Twain Shall Meet screened in Australian cinemas, to the particular enjoyment of those who had travelled with the cast on the *Tahiti*. Three radio stations were broadcasting regularly in Sydney, mainly at night, and occasional sporting broadcasts were attempted with limited success. Electricity was now available throughout Manly and its outer areas. Gaslight was going the way of the horse and cart. Nick Winter was back at the Manly fire station and still competing in the hop, step and jump, an event made more popular by his Paris success. There was no immediate challenger to his standing as Australia's best jumper.

Oswald Charlton married, for a second time, in 1926, to Beatrice Parkyn, the couple settling down in Killara on Sydney's upper north shore while Boy continued to enjoy Kurrumbede. The drought had now broken and the floods came. When the Namoi broke its banks the black soil plains became a quagmire. Stock was moved to higher ground. Debris floated westward down the river towards the neighbouring towns of Boggabri and Narrabri, along with logs and trees that had been uprooted by the tide. Tractors rescued lorries stuck axle-deep in the soggy ground. Vehicles were winched from creek beds that had been as hard as concrete a few weeks before. The pragmatic and resilient farmers took such hardships in their stride.

By the spring of 1926, the Australian Swimming Union had given up on the idea of luring Johnny Weissmuller to tour Australia. Certainly he would have been a drawcard at many swimming carnivals, though without Charlton he would not have been challenged at any distance. Late in 1926 it was announced that Japan's Katsuo Takaishi, who had been a finalist in the 100 and 1500 metres in Paris, and who had improved immeasurably since, would tour Australia in the New Year and compete in the New South Wales championships. Like Borg, he was extremely versatile. He would be accompanied by Japan's backstroke champion, Takahiro Saito.

When the new Manly Baths were completed in October of

1926, Charlton was invited to the gala opening carnival. His presence added considerably to the excitement. Moss Christie and a host of champion swimmers, past and present, joined Australia's first Olympic gold medallist Fred Lane and 1912 gold medallist Harold Hardwick. Charlton swam an exhibition and did a couple of leisurely laps alongside his old mentor Tommy Adrian. Handicap events featuring clubs from all over Sydney entertained a capacity crowd. The baths were now second only to the Domain in their facilities and had room for eight lanes as opposed to the Domain's six. The starting beam could be lifted or lowered to suit the tide in the same manner as at the Domain, though race starts had to be timed so as not to coincide with the arrival of the Manly ferry and the accompanying bow wash. A fortnight later Dick Eve, diving gold medallist, was appointed by Manly council to succeed his father as manager of the baths on a lucrative salary plus accommodation. Eve's intention was to keep diving and competing as an amateur but the Victorian swimming authorities instigated a move to have him declared a professional. A payback for Beaurepaire perhaps?

Charlton's appearance prompted speculation that he might be prepared to race against Takaishi, but Bill Corbett, writing in *The Sun* on November 3, put paid to any such hopes when he stated: 'Charlton may be discarded as a potential opponent for the Japanese stars Takaishi and Saito. He has lost his swimming enthusiasm. At least it is profoundly dormant.' Or was it?

Boy Charlton returned to Kurrumbede having enjoyed seeing his swimming friends again. He had felt no temptation to compete in the two years that had passed since returning from the Games, but now something stirred within him. Part of the feeling was a certain obligation to those who had supported him. The swimming authorities would be thrilled if he decided to make a comeback in the state championships, as would Australian fans. When Malcolm Mackellar realised his famous jackeroo was toying with the idea of racing Takaishi he encouraged him to commence training. Boy began to swim against the tide at 'the dip', that stretch of the Namoi River where a sudden drop in the terrain caused the current to speed up. He had no stopwatch, not that he would have used one anyway. He simply judged his form on how he felt. For reasons that he found difficult to explain, even later in life, Boy Charlton elected to return to Manly and do some training with Harry Hay. He made no statement to indicate a permanent return to championship swimming, just to compete in the state titles.

Early in December, 1926, he arrived back at Manly for the Christmas break and headed straight for the surf. There was nothing unusual about that. His priorities had not changed. News spread quickly that he was back and in good trim. He displayed a superb physique. Now just a little over 6 feet tall (1.8 metres) with his barrel chest and solid thighs he weighed almost 15 stone (94 kilograms) Looking at him, it was easy to forget how young he was. Might he race Takaishi? The headline in *The Sun* said it all:

TO SWIM. Andrew Charlton Back. Will Meet Japanese.

The swim world was agog. Had the two-year absence from competition lessened Boy's ability? Could he reproduce, or even better, his times of 1924? He was extremely confident that he could; after all he had just recently turned nineteen. Swimming in the surf for Manly and in handicap races at the pool was an ideal starting point. His first competitive swim, a 440 yards handicap event, was taken very easily but he was soon showing signs that he would not take long to reach winning form. Training was not his forte, competing was. Once he had an opponent in his sights he put in the effort as a matter of course. There were five weeks until the state championships; ample time in his opinion.

Japan was a fledgling nation as far as swimming was concerned. Takaishi was the finest of several talented young freestyle swimmers and their first Olympic finalist. His profile was a big factor in the increasing interest in the sport in Japan, a country determined to reach the top. The Japanese did not yet have coaching plans in place like the Americans but read everything they could on the sport and copied international champions. Takahiro Saito was also a very fine swimmer whose style was quite different to the top Australian backstrokers. Their tour, which began in Queensland, took in Townsville, Bundaberg and Warwick before Brisbane. They then gave exhibitions at Wellington and Newcastle in New South Wales prior to their arrival in Sydney. Their appearances had created tremendous interest and both were unbeaten in Australia. Large crowds had seen them set new records at many pools.

When the pair were welcomed at Sydney's Hotel Carlton a host of famous swimmers and other sportsmen attended including Freddie Lane, Harold Hardwick, Moss Christie, cricketer Arthur Mailey and E.S. Marks who, in proposing a toast, championed the idea of regular Pan Pacific Games that would include America, Hawaii, Japan, the Philippines, Australia and New Zealand.

The Japanese immediately proved very popular, being very cheerful and modest to the extreme. In response to an official welcome by the president of the Australian Olympic Federation, John Taylor, Saito read his reply in a manner described by *The Referee* as being 'as nervous as a maiden'. Saito declared that they were looking forward to the competition but above all keen to show they were ambassadors for their country as much as sporting representatives and that it was fitting that sport should play its part in bringing peace to the world.

Under the supervision of Harry Hay, Charlton was soon showing excellent form, lapping fluently in the new Manly

Baths, where the 220 yards championship on the third of the three-day day state carnival would be staged. Boy announced that he did not intend to swim in the 220 but Manly fans, in particular, were hoping he might change his mind. By the New Year it was clear Charlton was as good as ever. At the annual Melbourne and Manly club carnival he swam his best time ever for 110 yards in the relay and won the Northern Suburbs 220 yards championship in record time. Having trained with the 440 and 880 yards in mind his sprinting was quite remarkable. Last of seven after the first lap of the 220 yards he moved up to second after two laps and sprinted away to defeat the very promising Manly newcomer, Victor Moore.

In striking contrast to Charlton, at 5 feet 6 inches (1.6 metres) and 10 stone (64 kilograms) Takaishi was short and slightly built. Saito was of similar physique. Takaishi had been tired on arrival in Sydney but soon recovered and his swims were watched with great interest. He appeared with Saito each day at the Domain, training at his own discretion and sunbaking between swims. Takaishi's trials were also proving most impressive. His powerful six beat kick was a feature of his style and helped produce the ease with which his trim body glided through the water. Most experts thought Takaishi would be too sharp for Charlton in the 220 yards, and would lead the Australian in the early part of the 440 yards but might struggle to hold him off in the latter stages. However, his best time at 440 was three seconds faster than Charlton's. Few saw Charlton's colours being lowered in the 880 yards although Takaishi also swam the distance strongly.

Despite that it was almost two and a half years since his last competitive swim in Ireland, fans had the utmost confidence in their man. The press carried stories of the championships each day. Not since Charlton's clashes with Borg in 1924 had such interest been shown in the state titles. *The Referee* teased fans with:

Paris had seen the high lights in the swimming world at the last Olympic Games. Are we to see something approaching those Homeric contests now that Andrew Charlton and Katsuo Takaishi are ready to test their speed through the water? The young Japanese comes to Australia with the reputation of being second only to Arne Borg as the finest all-round swimmer in the world. We shall soon know if he is the master swimmer in this continent right now. Charlton is ready and on his trials has answered every question.

If the press were excited about the challenge so too were the fans. A heavy demand for reserved seating prompted authorities to open the gates to the Domain Baths at 11 am, two hours before the first preliminary event. Many arrived early and over six thousand spectators crammed into the arena. A pool that held three times that number might well have been inadequate. Small boys who clambered onto the roofs of the dressing sheds were soon followed by a number of agile adults. When the diving exhibition was over, the tower with its six platforms, proved a very popular vantage point, though only the brave reached the top. So too did the roofs of adjacent boatsheds. One young woman brought a cheer when she leapt from the poolside to a pontoon some feet below where she remained to enjoy an uninterrupted view all afternoon. Sailors on the masts of yachts cruising past were reminiscent of the time when Charlton had clashed with Borg.

A very exciting water polo game preceded the main race, the 880 yards title. When the contestants were introduced the reception for Charlton was deafening. Boy's comeback was the one thing all swim fans had hoped for since Paris. After photographs were taken the swimmers made their way onto the starting beam. Takaishi was in lane 1, with Owen Griffiths next to him in 2, Charlton in 3, McNally from East Sydney in 4 and John Kelly from Balmoral in 5, closest to the shore. Starter Percy Russell called the swimmers – 'Face the water . . . GO!'

Charlton hit the water first with Takaishi last away. The Japanese swimmer soon made up the leeway and drew level with the field after 30 yards. The crowd was already cheering loudly as he continued to improve and narrowly led Charlton at the first turn. Charlton, breathing to Takaishi's side during the second lap, drew level as they approached the turn. Though not as fast on the turns he kept abreast of the Japanese champion all the way down the third lap. The roar of the crowd increased markedly as Takaishi again took a narrow lead at the 300 yard mark. The race was on in earnest in lap four. Both swimmers lifted their pace and forged well clear of the others. Slowly Charlton took the lead and drew almost a body length in front. His fans knew what to expect. He simply ploughed through the water, inexorably increasing his lead with every stroke. Takaishi struggled on gamely but the race had become a procession. Takaishi, like Borg three years earlier, was left in his wake as the relentless pressure continued until Charlton had half a lap to spare over his rival. Sprinting over the last half lap he went on to win by more than sixty yards. Lifting the battered brass megaphone to his lips, Joe Morgan announced a world record time of 10 minutes 32 seconds. Boy had taken over five seconds off the previous world record, set by Arne Borg twelve months after the Paris Olympics. The huge crowd continued to cheer wildly in appreciation of what they had just witnessed.

An estimated 7,000 people flocked to Manly wharf to welcome home their conquering hero but when the ferry arrived he was not on it. Boy, as shy as ever, had returned to Manly by car. The swimmers were back in the water on Monday for heats of the 440 yards with the final scheduled for Wednesday evening. Moss Christie, who had only been married the previous week, qualified but withdrew. The four finalists were Charlton, Takaishi, Summergreene from Sydney and Kelly from Balmoral. Charlton drew lane 1, on the harbour side, and Takaishi lane 4.

As Charlton breathed to his left Takaishi would be on his blind side during the final lap, which would be to the visitor's advantage in a close finish. After Boy's amazing victory in the 880 yards it was difficult not to imagine a similar result, though Takaishi was much better suited to the shorter course.

Again the pool was packed as fans took up every vantage spot. Percy Russell sent the swimmers away to a perfect start and the crowd instantly began to cheer. To their surprise Charlton broke the water first and immediately went to the lead. Halfway down the first of four laps, Takaishi, his leg drive churning the water, attempted to draw level but Charlton held him off and made the first turn slightly ahead. Spectators, surprised at Charlton's early speed, were already setting up a din.

Down the second lap, Takaishi had 'the look' on Charlton who was keeping a very straight course. To another mighty cheer Boy turned almost two body lengths ahead in 2 minutes 24 seconds, a fraction of a second outside his own Australian 220 yards record set against Arne Borg. Down the third lap Takaishi clung to Charlton 'like a limpet' but Boy's pace was such that Takaishi could not gain so much as a stroke. When Charlton turned five yards ahead at the final turn the sound of the crowd was at fever pitch. All the way down that long last lap they cheered him on. Charlton responded, stroking power-fully and accelerating away in the last half lap to win by twelve yards. The crowd, their throats burnt hoarse, applauded both swimmers as they shook hands then waited for the time. Joe Morgan again lifted the megaphone to his lips and announced that Charlton had swum 4 minutes 59.8 seconds, breaking his own Australian record by twelve seconds.

Charlton's time, the first sub five-minute quarter mile over a long course, was six seconds better than he had swum in Paris when third behind Weissmuller and Borg, and seven seconds outside Arne Borg's new world record set in a 25-yard pool in

Stockholm. Borg had the advantage of making seventeen turns to Charlton's three. Experts estimated Charlton's time in a short course pool would have been better than Borg's by about ten seconds. This did not really interest Boy who always concentrated on swimming against his opponents rather than the clock. He was just happy to have performed so well and to have rewarded the thousands of fans who had come to support him.

There was one race to go, at his own Manly pool. Everyone was delighted when he reversed his earlier decision and elected to swim the 220 yards event. Takaishi would be favourite, but Boy had surprised Borg at the distance in his epic swim at the Domain in 1924. Furthermore he felt he owed it to the public and to Takaishi to race him at his pet distance. The Manly Baths, capable of accommodating three thousand people in comfort, found room for another six hundred to witness the third clash between Charlton and his diminutive Japanese rival. Alongside the pool the SS *Narrabeen* provided a vantage point for five hundred others, including many well-dressed women carrying brightly coloured parasols. The roofs of nearby boatsheds were also crowded, along with the balcony of the bathhouse 50 yards away.

In the 100 metres backstroke final Takaishi's stable mate, Saito, had an exciting win. His victory brought prolonged cheering as he smiled broadly and bowed to the crowd several times. A large contingent of Japanese spectators saw it as an omen for their freestyler. The 220 yards championship, with a field of six, was expected to be a match race between Takaishi and Charlton. After photographs had been taken the swimmers lowered themselves onto the starting beam. The Australian, who had drawn lane 6, would have the advantage of looking at Takaishi, in lane 3, during the second and fourth laps. Charlton jumped first but Takaishi gathered him in after 30 yards and was slightly ahead at the first turn. It was clear Charlton had decided to stick close to his rival early and try to come home over the top of him. But down the second lap, Takaishi, now swimming his favourite distance, increased his lead to almost a body length. Despite Charlton's best efforts, and the encouragement of the crowd, he could not stay with his rival who made the final turn four yards ahead and came away in the last lap to win by seven yards in 2 minutes 17 seconds, the fastest swim ever in a 55-yard pool and just two seconds outside Johnny Weissmuller's world record. It was a magnificent effort. Manly's nineteen year old Victor Moore, a rising champion, finished third.

Charlton, who had suffered his first loss in Australia, congratulated Takaishi enthusiastically, then took the megaphone and called for three cheers for the victor. The crowd, realising they had seen a very special swim, responded vociferously. Though Charlton was recognised as the state champion, being the first local to finish, there was no doubt the Japanese visitor was the star of the day, a man justly rated in the same class as Weissmuller and Borg. Later in the day Charlton, joined by his pal Ernie Henry, helped Manly to an easy victory over Bondi in the clubs' teams' race.

The series had been all that fans could have imagined. Their champion had come back better than ever, swimming his fastest times over all three distances, emphasising that he really was an extraordinary swimmer. The championships were a bonanza for the New South Wales Swimming Association. More than 14,000 spectators had paid over 1,600 pounds to watch the races, of which about half was clear profit. Boy had done his part. As the New South Wales swimmers, including Ernie Henry, and Takaishi and Saito left for the southern states and the national championships, Boy had a few weeks left of his holiday break. He needed no one to help him decide how to spend it. On the very next weekend he won the belt race and open surf race at the Freshwater carnival and on the subsequent weekend won two of three races at Manly. His old friend Fitz Lough, who partnered him in the two-man teams' race, left him just a little too much water to make up to complete the treble. Charlton was extremely disappointed when the next carnival, scheduled for North Bondi, was washed out by heavy storms.

Ernie Henry made a comeback to top competition and went to Melbourne for the national championships along with Takaishi and Saito. Despite a very limited preparation, Henry finished second to Takaishi in the 100 and 200 yards titles and as the local swimmer took the Australian titles. Takaishi invited Charlton and Henry to go to Tokyo to compete in the Pan Pacific Games but Charlton declined and suggested Ernie Henry do likewise. If they were to continue it seemed a better idea to hold off for a year and go to the 1928 Olympics. Henry reasoned that while Charlton would be certain of selection for Amsterdam if he decided to go, he was not and so Henry accepted the invitation to tour Japan.

The public and sporting press were now talking of Boy going to the Olympics in Amsterdam, still eighteen months away. Ernie Henry was quite right. Obviously he would be picked if available and in reasonable condition. Boy was making no declarations of his intentions. He had achieved enough for now and was due back at Kurrumbede to resume his duties as a jackeroo while his father and grandfather sorted out his future on the land. All fans could do was hope he would find time to do both.

7

Amsterdam 1928

WHILE BOY CHARLTON RETURNED to work in Gunnedah, Arne Borg continued to sweep all before him in Europe. The irrepressible, flamboyant Swede, who was very keen on dancing, was a constant visitor to nightspots, invariably in the company of beautiful women, nattily dressed and smoking the most expensive Havana cigars. His appreciation of beautiful women did not affect his form in the pool. He won the European 400 metres and 1500 metres titles in 1926 and continued to improve in 1927. He was at his peak physically, devoted to his swimming and determined to win the distance double at the 1928 Games in Amsterdam. With this in mind he had been swimming continually since the 1924 Games and had spent some time at the Illinois Athletic Club under the care of Bill Bachrach. Borg had worked out what times he believed he needed to swim in order to be successful and trained accordingly. He was reported to be using a mechanical device that moved up and down the side of the pool and which he had to match to achieve his goal.

America, still leading the way in coaching and indoor year-round facilities, continued to produce many fine young swimmers. Johnny Weissmuller retained his place as their outstanding sprinter but what races he would contest at the 1928 Games, apart from the 100 metres, were up in the air. Japan was slowly emerging as the potential challenger to America's supremacy in the water.

The group of talented young French tennis players who emerged at the Paris Olympics had gone on to become known as the Four Musketeers. Forced to play second fiddle to the Americans in the 1924 Games, soon after they came out on top, France becoming the leading tennis nation in the world. Between them they had won four successive Wimbledon singles titles, beginning in 1924, and in 1927 were the first European nation to win the Davis Cup. This would prove to be the first of six successive victories. At least two had announced their intention of playing in the national championships in Sydney in the New Year and were reported to be keen to see the young 'wonder swimmer' who had taken Paris by storm. They would not be competitors in Amsterdam, where the French would have been warm favourites to win all the men's tennis medals, as the sport had been dropped from the programme due to concerns about professionalism.

In September of 1927, Arne Borg, swimming at the European Championships in Bologna, Italy, set a world record for the 1500 metres of 19 minutes 7.2 seconds, taking almost a minute off Boy's Olympic record set in 1924. As sensational as the time was, the circumstances of the swim were almost unbelievable. Having helped Sweden into the final of the 4×200 metres team's race, Borg lost four teeth when he was kicked in the mouth in a water polo game against France. Unable to eat prior to the final that same day, he admitted to drinking a bottle of red wine before his epic distance swim. At the same carnival Borg won the 400 and 100 metres freestyle championships.

By the time Boy came down for his Christmas break, Borg's record, swum in a 50-metre pool, had been officially recognised by the international governing body. It would obviously take a great swimmer, at his very best, to beat him. No one but Charlton had done anything to suggest he might get down to that time. Boy had not yet committed to the Games and was happy to swim and row in the surf and take part in some handicap races with the Manly Club. On January 4, 1928, he was afforded a marvellous reception prior to an exhibition swim over 220 yards, which he followed by breaking thirty seconds for 55 yards when swimming last for the successful South of The Corso team in the annual club relay.

While Sydney sports' fans thrilled to the superb artistry and powerful tennis skills of Jean Borotra, 'the Bounding Basque', who won the national singles title and the doubles title with another of the 'Musketeers', Jacques Brugnon, Boy Charlton returned on the overnight train to Gunnedah. The twenty year old left with swim fans hoping he would be back in March to secure a place in the Olympic team.

Selection trials for the 1928 Amsterdam Games began in earnest in mid-January. Among several trials were the Australian Games held at Manly Oval, predominantly involving New South Wales representatives. The week-long carnival raised approximately 200 pounds for the Olympic fund and was conducted in a manner closely resembling the Olympics, beginning with Nick Winter taking the athletes' oath. Winter, who had left the Fire Brigade the previous year, was, surprisingly, beaten in the hop, step and jump. Jim Carlton, a product of Sydney's St Josephs College, running with the Botany Harriers, had assumed the mantle previously held by Slip Carr as

Australia's finest sprinter. A new middle distance star had also emerged in the shape of Charles Stuart. In the same week cyclists showed their form at the Sydney Sports Ground and a week later Queensland's hopefuls were in action in Brisbane with backstroker Tom Boast, also a wonderful surfer, and Doris Thompson in outstanding form.

In a decision that caused much conjecture females had been included in Olympic track and field events for the first time and runner Edith Robinson staked an immediate claim for inclusion. But the performer creating the most interest, apart from Charlton, was teenage backstroker Philomena 'Bonnie' Mealing. Already hailed as Australia's best female swimmer since Fanny Durack, the fifteen year old's outstanding times saw her being tipped as a possible gold medallist. In fact, efforts by female swimmers were causing more optimism than those of the men. Doris Thompson had emerged as the nation's leading breast-stroker and Edna Davey, who held every freestyle record beyond 100 yards, announced her availability for Amsterdam.

Australia had produced a very promising young distance swimmer in sixteen year old Noel Ryan, also from Manly, but generally had not kept pace with the improvements of the overseas swimmers. Boy Charlton stood alone as the only likely male medallist. Whether he would even go to the Games was still not known. Malcolm Mackellar would not discourage him but his priorities were still clearly with the land and his own family's wishes. His father and grandfather, who had been very vocal about his going to Paris, were making no public statements this time.

Dick Eve, still Australia's top-ranked diver, had been barred from Olympic competition because of his job at the Manly Baths but was hopeful an appeal, to be heard on February 28, would lead to his reinstatement.

When the Olympic team of eighteen athletes was announced

it was considerably smaller than first planned, due to fiscal restraints. Opinion continued to strengthen that an Olympic team needed coaches, but they were still considered a luxury. The team was financed by the Olympic Fund, public subscription and government subsidy and was chosen in two groups. The top ten, who were assured of participating, included Olympic champions Charlton and Winter, outstanding sculler Bobby Pearce and runner Jim Carlton. Charlton's selection had been a foregone conclusion. His trip simply depended on whether he made himself available and his fitness. The grading of Bonnie Mealing at number eleven caused plenty of comment. Many sports writers and correspondents to the press thought she had deserved a place in the top ten. The next eight were selected in order of merit and added as funds to finance their trip became available. An association or community that could find the full cost for a competitor among this group ensured their inclusion. The New South Wales country town of Goulburn made sure their cycling hero Edgar 'Dunc' Gray had no cause for worry, raising the required sum in a matter of days.

As only two male swimmers were selected, Charlton and Queensland backstroker Tom Boast, Australia, for the first time since 1908, would not be represented in the men's team's race. Their record in this event was second only to the Americans. Boast was an excellent freestyler but the addition of two more swimmers could not be justified. Australia's chances of beating America or Japan were remote and a bronze medal would have been their only hope.

Boy Charlton arrived in Sydney from Kurrumbede on March 8 and immediately announced his intention to go to Amsterdam. His resolve could not be faulted, Charlton going straight from Central Station's country platform to Manly Baths. The very next morning he covered 440 yards in 5 minutes 30 seconds and later that afternoon swam strongly over

1000 yards. On Saturday he joined his Manly Surf Club friends to welcome famous airman, Bert Hinkler, to The Village. The Queensland flier had landed the previous day from his epic solo flight from England to Sydney. At a function at the surf club, held in Hinkler's honour, Charlton announced he would even forsake his appetite for the surf as he prepared for the state championships in three weeks' time. A week later he outpaced the exciting junior champion Noel 'Tiger' Ryan over 440 yards in a training swim then shook off four other swimmers who tried to stay with him over the succeeding 110 yards. He had his first competitive race in the Manly Club's 1500 metres handicap. Starting from the scratch mark he took things easily early but powered home in great style. His time was one minute and twenty seconds outside his Olympic record but he was well satisfied. Harry Hay, assisting with his preparation, was confident he would be swimming record times within a few weeks. Onlookers had no doubt the big man was back.

With his preparation limited to just a few weeks, Charlton entered only one event at the state titles, the 440 yards championship. His appearance boosted interest enormously and helped lift gate takings at the carnival, the profits of which went to the Olympic fund. A packed house attended the 440 final at the Domain in which Charlton was once more opposed to his Olympic team-mate Moss Christie. Boy was not quite at his peak and took his position with a slightly strained back and a sprained ankle, which was painted with iodine, both injuries having been sustained while playing water polo at Manly during the week. However, they gave no cause for worry.

Covering the first lap almost a second faster than when he accounted for Takaishi twelve months earlier, Charlton continually increased his lead. He was twenty yards in front at the 330-yard mark, and powered away in the last lap to win from Moss Christie by thirty yards in a time of 5 minutes

3.6 seconds. This was five and a half seconds slower overall than his time against Takaishi but the ease with which he covered the distance was apparent to all. The wildly cheering crowd could see more Olympic medals coming his way. Later that day Boy anchored Manly's successful 4×220 yards team's race, his time being the fastest of any swimmer.

A feature of the carnival was the magnificent diving of twelve year old Arthur O'Connor, the young boy who had given Arne Borg such pleasure four years before with his fearless diving from the 60-foot tower. The youngster defeated the Australian champion Clive Barrass in the high board fancy diving. Thanks largely to the big crowd who had come to see Charlton the carnival made a profit of 150 pounds.

With money still needed for the Olympic campaign, the Victorian swimming association began promoting a fundraising carnival to be held at Melbourne's City Baths on April 21. Charlton was invited. He had never competed in Melbourne and his appearance would ensure a handsome profit. To the Victorians' delight he accepted. *The Referee* described his acceptance as 'a gracious act'. Boy had no real idea just how much his appearance would mean to Melbourne's sporting public, though Frank Beaurepaire assured them they would see the greatest distance swimmer of all time.

Charlton travelled to Melbourne by train, staying overnight at Albury, courtesy of the Albury Swimming Club, one of the strongest swimming clubs outside any capital city. Rail travellers between Sydney and Melbourne were forced to change trains at the border because of the different rail gauge, an inconvenience that took at least an hour as all luggage was moved from one train to another. The Albury Club invariably took advantage of this by putting up the stars in the best hotel and offering typical country hospitality in exchange for an exhibition swim. They were not going to miss the chance of seeing Charlton.

Boy Charlton's reception in Melbourne was overwhelming, as described by *The Referee*:

Crowds poured into the City Baths on Saturday to see Australia's wonder swimmer, Andrew 'Boy' Charlton, in his first appearance in that city. Seating accommodation had been booked out early and spectators crammed every corner. The visitor was accorded a stirring reception, the like of which has never been equalled in the memory of the baths.

The *Melbourne Herald* was in complete agreement:

For nearly five minutes on Saturday night Boy Charlton, the Manly swimmer, stood with his head bowed on the starting platform at the City Baths, while Melbourne greeted him with a tumultuous outburst of applause. Never in the history of this state has an athlete received such an overwhelming reception. When at last the applause subsided the young swimming giant . . . raised his head, unfolded an immense pair of bronze-like arms and whispered, rather than said, 'I thank you'.

Charlton did not let his Victorian supporters down. After a strong exhibition swim over 300 yards he competed in a special 200 yards handicap against Victoria's 100 yards champion Doug Walter, 200 yards champion J. Wilson, and the Victorian junior champion H.W. Farley. Charlton gave Walter and Wilson a three-second start and Farley ten. Farley made good use of his handicap, maintaining his ten second lead at the end of the first, 33-yard lap. Charlton, swimming easily, was still eight yards away in last place after 100 yards but then made up the deficit in little over a lap and came away to win by seven yards. Charlton had given the appreciative Victorian crowd a sample of his brilliance and received another tremendous ovation as he finished and again when presented the winner's trophy at poolside. The carnival netted approximately 200 pounds for the Olympic coffers.

All eight athletes in the second group were funded well before the Olympic team was due to depart. The touring party consisted of seven track and field athletes, five swimmers, two cyclists, three wrestlers, one sculler, the manager and a chaperone. Australia's three boxers had been outclassed in Paris so it was not surprising that three wrestlers were chosen instead. Dick Eve had failed in his appeal against being a professional, mainly because of the intransigence of the Victorian Swimming Association, so Victorian all-rounder Harry Morris had the distinction of replacing him in the diving and also representing Australia in the wrestling. Apart from Charlton, the outstanding performer was sculler Bobby Pearce who was on the threshold of a brilliant career. Four women were included – runner Edith Robinson and swimmers Bonnie Mealing, Edna Davey and Doris Thompson.

On May 1, 1928, the New South Wales and Queensland competitors, except Bobby Pearce, assembled at the P&O wharf, Woolloomooloo Bay, to board the 16,000-ton liner, RMS *Naldera*, bound for Plymouth. Pearce, about to compete in the national championship regatta on the Nepean River, was due to join the team in Melbourne where Victoria's representatives would also embark. A number of farewell functions for the team and individual members had taken place during the week, the last of which was held at the Town Hall and featured an inspiring speech by Gordon Shaw, manager of the recently returned Waratahs rugby team, whose tour of the British Isles, Ireland, France and Canada had been a resounding success.

A huge crowd had come to farewell the athletes who were

immaculately dressed for the momentous occasion. The men wore green blazers with gold piping on pockets and sleeves, green baggy caps, green and gold striped ties over cream shirts, cream slacks and two-tone brown and cream leather shoes. The four female members wore identical green blazers and two-tone shoes with knee length cream uniforms and cream hats typical of the Charleston era. Manager, Les Duff, and chaperone, Mabel Springfield, assembled the group for press photographs prior to boarding the *Naldera*. It was to be a very difficult trip for Duff who was uneasy about having men and women travelling in the one team, though his concern was not noted until after the Games.

Harry Hay, champion Manly surfer and silver medallist from the 1920 Olympics, who had stepped into the breach after Tommy Adrian's breakdown in 1924, again paid his own fare to travel on the *Naldera*. Hay was now the NSW swimming coach but not an official Olympic team member, so was not part of team functions. He would, however, be paid to coach Charlton and Boast once the team arrived in London. Barring mishaps, such as those that had struck the *Ormonde*, the RMS *Naldera* would berth in England with enough time to give the team a month of excellent training before going on to the Dutch capital. They were to stay at Brighton-On-Sea and train at the famous Stamford Bridge ground where cinder tracks ran down each side and around its perimeter. Stamford Bridge had been home to the London Athletic Club for fifty years, and from 1905 the equally famous Chelsea Football Club. With the football season finished well before their arrival, the athletes would have exclusive use of the arena.

There was a near disaster just minutes before the liner slipped away from the wharf. With streamers and bunting thick in the air, Jim Carlton was walking across the deck when a heavy iron block on a large winch came rattling down and struck him on the forearm. Onlookers were sure his arm had been broken as the young sprinter was in severe pain and felt quite ill for some minutes but he recovered in time to take his place stoically by the ship's railing to say a final farewell. The four females were given huge bouquets and decanters of eau-de-cologne as a parting gift. The ship left punctually at noon with Boy Charlton waving a huge flag carrying *The Sun* newspaper insignia and the crowd singing 'Auld Lang Syne'.

The large three-funnelled liner made its way from the bay, past the Domain Baths, through a flotilla of smaller craft hooting and whistling their own goodbyes. It took almost an hour to clear the Heads and drop their pilot. Now team members settled back, two in each cabin, to contemplate the trip ahead. Boy's companion was the young sprinter Jim Carlton, whose injury had been an inauspicious start to the tour but nothing compared to what was to follow. The *Naldera* struck a severe storm just a few hours out of port and all but four of the touring party had their first bout of seasickness. Boy considered himself an experienced sailor, in contrast to the youngster who had sailed on the *Ormonde* four years before, but he too was ill.

At six that evening, manager Les Duff had a conversation with Captain Dayas who expressed his delight at having the Olympians aboard. Passengers were always excited at having celebrities travel with them. One hour later the captain had a sudden heart attack and died. On the following morning the second in command, Captain Hartley, presided over his funeral service and assumed control of the ship for the remainder of the journey. The team, in full uniform, attended the funeral and burial at sea. The captain's death cast a feeling of sombreness over the entire ship that took several days to abate. As the spirits of the crew lifted, passengers got to know each other with the Olympians immediately proving very popular.

Meanwhile at Penrith, in Sydney's west, on a perfect summer's day, motorcars and trains brought spectators from all over Sydney for the national rowing championships. A massive crowd saw Western Australia win the King's Cup, narrowly defeating the Queensland eight. Sculler Bobby Pearce won the President's Cup, the single sculls title, by twenty-five lengths. Competitors had the advantage of a slight following breeze and Pearce, who had also won the previous year, recorded the fastest time ever by an amateur sculler over the famous Nepean River course. News of his magnificent win reached the *Naldera* as she approached Melbourne, where she was to remain for almost a week.

The teams' stay in Melbourne was an eventful and pleasant one, a mixture of official functions and casual outings organised by various sporting bodies. All athletes were able to do some training and were in good health. Jim Carlton's arm was now quite all right and he joined the others at the track. Charlton and Boast were accompanied by Harry Hay as they trained with the pick of Melbourne's swimmers, including the redoubtable Frank Beaurepaire who, at thirty-seven years, was still the best distance man in Victoria.

Not unexpectedly, the *Naldera* struck rough seas and a number of storms after leaving Melbourne, particularly crossing the Great Australian Bight. Short stopovers at Adelaide and Fremantle gave respite from the weather but no time for any significant training. Most had got their 'sea legs' and only very big seas now worried them. A canvas pool had again been erected on deck and had proven useless in rough conditions but Charlton was not too concerned. Harry Hay kept a good eye on his diet knowing he would get to form quickly enough provided he did not have too much weight to lose. Les Duff was especially keen to ensure all kept their weight down during the long journey.

The longest leg of trip from Fremantle to Colombo was punctuated by deck sports in which the Olympians were regular participants with Nick Winter the most regular winner. Passengers were always pleased when they got the better of team members. The Olympians also joined in evening entertainment with gusto and added considerably to the enjoyment of fellow passengers. As the heat steadily increased approaching the tropics the pool became more and more popular though of moderate use as a training facility. Daily callisthenics helped keep most of the team in good trim as well as spirits. Again the cyclists were the least disadvantaged, being able to use the rollers on board just as well as on land and also able to take a spin on the road at most stopovers throughout the voyage.

Mr Foenander, who had shown such hospitality to the previous team, again met the Australian party at Colombo and they spent most of the day riding in rickshaws and buying eastern wares. With no boxers on the squad the wrestlers engaged in exhibitions but Bobby Pearce, a very good scrapper, was too strong for the local heavyweight champion in a willing spar. The misfortune that had followed the *Naldera* continued when one of the ship's engineers had to be left behind in Colombo due to acute appendicitis and Captain Hartley received word that his wife was dangerously ill. The Olympians had dodged the bad luck so far.

From Colombo the *Naldera* sailed for Bombay on India's west coast where a number of maharajahs and high-ranking public servants joined the journey. They turned out to be India's representatives at a Peace Conference to be held in Egypt and where they were to stay for a week before continuing to London. The Indian party included the Maharajah of Kashmir, travelling to Europe for the first time since being involved in a famous blackmail case, and Rajah Singhi, a nephew of the famous English test cricketer Ranji Singhi. The Australians were as fascinated with the opulent Indian party as the noblemen were with them, the Rajah of Palenpur inviting the team to dine with him in London. The team gave an exhibition of training methods, including one by Charlton in the canvas pool, then had photographs taken in uniform with the maharajahs, ship's officers and selected passengers.

The *Naldera* reached Aden after three weeks of sailing and following a very brief stay headed towards the Suez Canal. Seventy-two year old Reverend Mother St Guy, who was travelling to a conference in France, had also boarded in Bombay. The Australians were amazed to discover she had spent thirty years in a remote area of the Seychelles Islands in the Indian Ocean and had not even been aware of the Great War until she arrived in Bombay after peace had been declared. Sadly she passed away in the obsessive heat and was buried soon after the liner entered the fabled Red Sea.

A headwind arrived making the rest of the trip across the Red Sea much more pleasant and the crew ensured first-time travellers stood by the ship's rail for a good view when the entrance to the Suez Canal was reached. At Port Said shopping was again an exciting diversion for the ladies, some of whom arrived back at the ship with so many purchases Les Duff had to advance them expenses to pay the shopkeepers who accompanied them. Silk scarves and dresses had proven irresistible. When the *Naldera* reached the beautiful Mediterranean Sea and its deep blue water the hardest part of the trip was behind them. The tourist attractions on the Italian coast led them to Marseilles where French fashion lightened female wallets once more and perfect weather was experienced on the Bay of Biscay. Boy Charlton enjoyed sea travel immensely. In fact in later years he confided that had he not been a farmer he would have enjoyed being captain of a liner.

Despite the ill fortune that had befallen the crew and other passengers on their six-week adventure, the team could hardly have had a happier trip. When they arrived, on time, in Plymouth they were met by an excited crowd and a host of pressmen who remarked, just as they had four years earlier, on how fit and healthy the suntanned Australians looked. They were not really fit, just not too fat and wonderfully relaxed. From Plymouth the party travelled by train to London where another large crowd gathered at St Pancras Station to welcome the tourists who were quickly donning overcoats and pulling up collars. This time it was Nick Winter's turn to hold *The Sun* flag. Several in the crowd shouted, 'Where's Charlton, Where's Boy?' and rushed to shake hands. Nick Winter and Bobby Pearce were also sought out by excited onlookers. And so, amid much excitement, the team continued by charabanc to Onslow Court Hotel, South Kensington, where New Zealand's two representatives were also staying. A weekend of sightseeing was planned, including trial trips to training venues, before serious training started on Monday.

The track and field contingent, including Edith Robinson, commenced conditioning work at Battersea Park, prior to being introduced to the cinder tracks at Stamford Lane. Former English champion Harold Abrahams had lunch with the team and advised them on training methods particularly suitable for synthetic tracks, something new to the Australian team. The cyclists went on to Herne Hill to find an excellent banked cement track, which was ideal as both riders were track specialists. Harry Hay took his two charges, Charlton and Boast, to the tepid water at Hammersmith Baths in order to slowly acclimatise them to colder water. Bobby Pearce's skiff had arrived on the *Orama* and he began training on the Thames at Putney with former professional champion Bossy Phelps. Pearce's father, Harry, a champion sculler who had rowed on the Thames twenty years earlier, arrived to supervise his fitness and training regime. While there were no coaches officially assigned to the team there were plenty of willing, experienced hands keen to ensure the team performed as well possible.

Bobby Pearce was extremely disappointed he had not been entered for the Diamond Sculls at Henley, apparently an error by the Australian rowing authorities who believed he was ineligible to compete. By the time his nomination was sent it was too late. Judged by his form at the Games, it was later thought he would have won with ease. Boy Charlton, in a break from swimming in the Baths at Hammersmith, had a long swim in the Thames. He was much trimmer than when he had landed in Paris in 1924 and happy with his preparation.

The Australians appreciated the month spent in London. The Onslow Court Hotel menu had been supplemented with steak, chops, milk puddings and stewed fruit. Though there was a certain fascination with being in a foreign land, the convenience of understanding the language, food and currency was an advantage when the emphasis was on training. There were also opportunities to perform in various carnivals.

On July 16, 1928, a fortnight before the Games were due to commence, and three weeks before the swimming, the Australians moved into the beautiful Hotel Velserbeek on the outskirts of Amsterdam. It was a charming, two-storey, country mansion only a few minutes walk from the sea and an hour's drive to the Olympic Stadium. With the exception of a couple of rooms, the team had the hotel to themselves and the exclusive use of a twenty-four seat charabanc to take them to training, competition and pleasure trips. Away from the distractions and noise of the city, the setting seemed ideal; a perfect place for athletes to relax and concentrate on their preparation.

Despite its idyllic setting and abundant charm the Velserbeek did not work out as well as hoped. With heavy traffic and diversions in place, the Australians found they were spending ninety minutes each way in the charabanc going to and from the city just to drop off and pick up the competitors at different training venues. After struggling with these difficulties for over a week, manager Les Duff arranged for the bulk of the team to relocate to the Lloyd Hotel in Amsterdam, the British team's management's headquarters, which was also being shared by South African and New Zealand competitors.

Duff also approached the Dutch authorities hoping to organise swimming training at the Olympic pool but was told that this was not possible as it was undergoing its finishing touches. No one would be allowed to use the pool until the Games had actually begun. The athletics track was also not finished. When the Americans heard that there was general consternation with inadequate training facilities in Amsterdam they decided to leave their arrival as late as possible. Though the Olympic velodrome was available and the Australian cyclists were very comfortable on it, Australia's plans to get to Amsterdam early had clearly misfired.

Charlton was forced to train between two pontoons in an unenclosed, saltwater canal at Marinewerf, the harbour's naval base. His change room was one of the prison cells at the base. The canal gave him plenty of room for distance training but its hygiene was doubtful. Boy had arrived from London with a cold and sore throat. He wasn't overly concerned at first but was finding it hard to shake off. The cold got worse to the point that he became worried that his condition was not improving at the desired rate. It was a new experience for him to approach a major carnival lacking full confidence. The extremely cold water was not helping nor was his lack of competition at training. His archrival Borg was reported to be in top form.

News from the American camp was that Weissmuller was an unlikely starter in the 400 metres and would contest the 100 metres, 4×200 metres relay and play water polo. The 400 metres would see the appearance of two new American stars in Young Ruddy and Clarence 'Buster' Crabbe. If they could keep Weissmuller out they would have to be very special indeed.

Opportunities to compete against Olympic rivals were rarely passed up. Good competition was considered more important than keeping form a secret. When Boy Charlton was invited to Paris for a carnival featuring the French and Japanese swimmers just one week before the Games began, he jumped at the chance despite still having a slight cold. He could not have been more impressive in winning the 400 metres event in a time only two seconds slower than he had swum in 1924.

Australian sports fans, keen to know the latest news on the Olympic team, were delighted to be able to listen to a special hour-long radio broadcast emanating from Amsterdam at 6 pm Greenwich meantime on Thursday, July 26 (6 am Eastern Australian time) and heard on radio station 2BL in Sydney.

Les Duff began the broadcast with 'Hello good old Aussie: it's great to speak to you all again'. He explained the difficulties the team had faced after their arrival in Holland, that the German team had returned post haste to Berlin once they had seen the training shortcomings and the Japanese had decided to remain in Paris for as long as possible. 'Everyone is straining every sinew to be in top form but you in Australia cannot realise the immense disadvantage with which the team has had to contend.' Duff went on to say the team was in excellent spirits nevertheless and described Nick Winter as a 'sure winner'. Bobby Pearce was also expected to be too good for his opposition and Charlton was as good as ever.

A radio journalist then described in detail Charlton's appearance in Paris the previous Saturday, July 21:

Charlton is immensely popular. He was cheered when he arrived in Paris, and when he went to the stadium on Saturday night and was introduced to an assembly of 8,000 people he was cheered to the echo again.

Charlton was quite shy: he didn't know what to do in the face of the storm of cheering. In fact he blushed, although the blush could hardly be seen, so brown has he become — much browner, even than the Manly sun has ever made him.

It was the same at the banquet on Saturday night — every time his name was mentioned he was cheered to the echo.

Amsterdam, a city of waterways and canals, was a blaze of colour on Saturday, July 28, 1928. The majority of the 347 bridges that spanned the canals featured flags carrying the Olympic colours amid evergreen plants. Avenues of lime trees that bordered the canals were illuminated with thousands of coloured lights and brilliantly coloured bunting. National flags flew above the cobblestoned city squares.

Extremely hot sunny weather gave way to overcast skies, showers and oppressive humidity but could not detract from the spectacle of the opening ceremony as almost 3,000 athletes from forty-seven nations marched into the arena. As reigning Olympic champions, Nick Winter carried the Australian flag and Boy Charlton the placard. For the first time, athletes witnessed the lighting of the Olympic flame.

With the official opening a resounding success, competition began the following day. The first week of the Games was devoted to athletics and the rowing heats. Heavy showers fell over the first two days. Though this made little difference to performances on the cinder track it did affect Nick Winter's approach to the board during the hop, step and jump in which he failed to qualify for the final, jumping more than a metre short of his best. Jim Carlton ran well in the sprints but, like Slip Carr before him, was eliminated when he came in fourth in the quarterfinals. Australia's only finalist was William 'Tickle' Whyte who finished down the track in the 1500 metres. Bobby Pearce, however, was an easy winner of his single sculls heat late in the week.

Boy Charlton's cold had returned as the Games began and he was kept out of the water for two days but swam so well over 1200 metres as soon as he came back he told the press: 'I wish I had been racing today.' When the swimmers were at last allowed to practice in the open-air Olympic pool a heavy storm forced them from the water.

As the crowd arrived on Saturday morning for the opening heats of the 1500 metres there were still conflicting reports about Charlton's fitness and his chances were difficult to predict. The many Australian fans who had travelled to watch him were buoyed by the fact that he had never let them down and had always had the edge on Arne Borg over the longer course despite Borg's amazing times.

Charlton had drawn Borg and one of the two young American sensations, Buster Crabbe, in the first heat, which was swum in heavy rain. Borg went to the lead immediately and set his usual solid pace. Charlton and Crabbe were content to swim side by side in his wake. After 600 metres Borg led by ten metres, a lead he retained for several laps. With three laps to go Charlton and Crabbe increased their tempo and began to take ground from Borg. Charlton had the better sprint and got to within five metres of the Swedish champion at the finish with Crabbe a metre behind in third place. All three went through to Sunday's semifinals and it was not easy to get a guide on whose swim was more impressive. One thing was certain – Borg was in very good form and extremely confident.

In Sunday's semifinal Charlton again clashed with Buster Crabbe as well as America's other budding champion Young Ruddy. It seemed the Americans were determined to test Charlton's stamina as Ruddy went out hard early and led by three metres from Crabbe with a metre to Charlton. After six laps the pace increased but Charlton seemed unperturbed, swimming smoothly and staying in touch. At 1000 metres Ruddy began to feel the pinch and dropped five metres behind Crabbe with Charlton at the latter's feet. Over the next three laps Crabbe attempted to get away from the Australian several times but to no avail. When Crabbe touched a metre ahead it seemed Charlton had done things very easily. Still Charlton's admirers felt some apprehension. They were used to him winning.

Boy was also apprehensive. He felt well and was no longer worried by his cold but knew that he lacked that characteristic stamina that allowed him to dominate the final stages of his races. He made an observation to Harry Hay that the water was cold and the 'heavy' atmosphere made it difficult to breathe. It was as if those giant lungs, which had so impressed the physiologists in Paris, just could not get enough oxygen to operate at their peak. Interestingly, the Americans too were reported to have complained of a similar lack of lung power at the finish of their races. Borg was experiencing no such problems, winning his semifinal by almost a lap from Argentina's Alberto Zorilla, who trained at the New York Athletic Club, and swimming fifteen seconds faster than Charlton. He was certainly the man to beat.

The 1500 metre finalists were Charlton, Borg, Crabbe, Ruddy, Zorilla and Gamet Ault from Canada. The race appeared to be a match between Charlton and Borg with Buster Crabbe the possible surprise packet. The arena was packed for the race, swum in dry, humid conditions. Despite his aversion to Amsterdam's humidity Charlton was hopeful of a bold showing. Borg had drawn lane 2, with Charlton and Crabbe, who shook hands before the start, alongside each other in lanes 5 and 6.

At the sound of the pistol Charlton was first to hit the water but Borg soon headed him and led by a metre after the first lap with Crabbe just behind Charlton. So quickly did Borg accelerate that he led by five metres at the end of the second lap from Charlton who was stroking very smoothly. After 200 metres

Borg had increased his lead to eight metres with Crabbe still slightly behind Charlton. Borg's lead continued to grow as he kept up the pressure. At the 500-metre mark he led by twelve metres with Crabbe struggling to stay in touch with Charlton who continued to swim evenly.

Halfway through the race Borg had maintained his lead but now began to swim erratically whereas Charlton kept a straight course. Though this was not obvious to Charlton, it was to his fans who rose to cheer him on. Despite fouling the lanes on two occasions Borg kept up his tremendous pace. His erratic course could not slow him down. As Crabbe slowly dropped back the American fans joined the Australian chorus. At 1200 metres Charlton, fifteen metres in arrears, attempted to bridge the gap but Borg was equal to the challenge. Despite his best efforts Charlton could only make up a minimum of ground and Borg, his arms flailing with the same intensity as in the first lap, hit the wall with twelve metres to spare and Crabbe a further thirty metres behind.

Borg's time of 19 minutes 51.8 seconds was a new Olympic record, beating Boy Charlton's time in Paris by almost fifteen seconds. Charlton had bettered his own time by four seconds. In the circumstances he could not have done much better and offered no excuses: 'I am perfectly satisfied. I broke my own record. I couldn't have done better. I tried to close with Borg early in the race but it was not possible. Unquestionably the better man won.' Borg, who finished the race looking remarkably fresh, had achieved the first of his two goals.

The next morning the swimmers arrived for the heats of the 400 metres. Borg's sensational 1500 metres victory made him the logical favourite. He was adamant he would win and told Charlton so, predicting that Boy would beat everyone else. The two Americans, Crabbe and Ruddy, had shown good early speed in the longer race and had excellent times to their credit. They might well be better off over the shorter course. There was no fresh man, as Weissmuller had been in 1924, though Takaishi had missed the final. What effect the longer race had made on the field would be an important factor but again it seemed Borg and Charlton were likely to dominate.

Charlton, admitting to feeling tired after his second place in the 1500 metres final, met his old foe Katsuo Takaishi in his heat and was content to qualify for the semifinal. Among the crowd that day was a group of Charlton supporters who had come from the Manly Surf Club, including two late arrivals, Sandy McAlister and Tommy Farrell. They had saved every penny to travel tourist class on the liner *Jervis Bay* with just one purpose: to see their close friend win the 1500 metres. When a stowaway caused the *Jervis Bay* to be delayed they transferred to another vessel, but further problems occurred in London and they missed the race. Having gone forty-eight hours without sleep they arrived at the pool while Charlton's 400 metres heat was being swum. McAlister, a champion board rider, talked his way on to the starting boards and saw the rest of the races from a prime position. Takaishi was fresh, having been eliminated in the 1500 metres semifinal, and determined to win he led all the way for a narrow victory. Only when Italian swimmer Custoli threatened for second placing did Charlton speed up. Borg was the fastest heat winner, beating Ruddy by twenty-five metres.

The following morning Charlton, still not completely recovered from his 1500 metres swim, met a semifinal field that included Ruddy and Alberto Zorilla, who trained at the New York Athletic Club. He had been a finalist in the 1500 metres in 1924 and had finished fifth in the previous day's 1500 metres final, but seemed more suited to the 400 metres, having swum very fast times back in America. Charlton was keen to have another easy race and supporters were not concerned when he was one of four swimmers almost in line at the end of the second lap. Not so Arne Borg who rushed to poolside to cheer him on. As Borg shouted, 'Come on Boy, come on Boy!' officials ordered Borg back to the reserve enclosure while the Swede protested vehemently. By the end of the third lap Zorilla had a clear lead but Charlton had shaken off the others. Zorilla won by a little over two metres with Ruddy ten metres away in third. All three qualified for the final. Borg won his semifinal narrowly from Crabbe and another American Austin Clapp. All three swam five seconds faster than Zorilla had done. Takaishi failed to qualify.

It was not easy to assess the form of the semifinalists, but Borg was strongly favoured to win with Charlton regarded as his only possible danger. Another capacity crowd were there to watch the final at three the following afternoon as the swimmers took their places on the starting board. The starter's gun sounded and Borg, as usual, went straight to the lead. Charlton, Crabbe and Clapp, in adjacent lanes, were level with Zorilla who was in the extreme right-hand lane. At the 100 metres mark Borg led by three metres. After 200 metres he was six metres ahead of the field with Charlton in fourth place. After 250 metres Borg suddenly began to falter, his course becoming erratic. The field picked up two metres on him in the sixth lap and again in the seventh. As the swimmers turned for the last lap the lightly framed Zorilla, swimming with the typical six-beat American crawl, drew level on the far side of the pool. The cheering was tremendous as fans realised any of four could win. Charlton was finishing hard as Borg tried desperately to hang on. Zorilla was on Borg's blind side and Charlton could not see him because of Borg. Zorilla was now in front. Charlton got the better of Borg with twenty-five metres to go but Zorilla hung on grimly to win by a body length from Charlton with Borg a metre away in third pace. The result was a boilover. Charlton, who finished much the freshest of the trio, helped Zorilla and Borg out of the pool. Borg had swum heats that morning of the relay race and was absolutely exhausted. He could barely lift his arms. Zorilla too had given his all.

Charlton congratulated Zorilla on a wonderful tactical race. He told the press: 'I was unable to see him over Borg's head, owing to the backwash from the side of the bath, but I swam all out from start to finish and could not have done an inch better. I was delighted to turn the tables on Borg. This was my best time.' Boy had, in fact, swum his fastest ever 400 metres in 5 minutes 3.6 seconds, three seconds faster than when third in Paris.

Alberto Zorilla's comments made interested reading: 'I hoped at least to get a place but never thought I could win. When the last lap came I shut my eyes and swam blindly . . . until my hand touched at the finish. I never saw Charlton throughout.' So much for his tactics. There were plenty of post mortems after the event. Johnny Weissmuller, who won the 100 metres from Katsuo Takaishi, lamented that he had not started in the 400 metres as he believed he would have won. Borg had attempted too much, said Weissmuller, by swimming relay heats in the morning. He was probably right but Borg loved to compete. Carefully picking his races was not in his make up. Charlton was not one for post mortems. Though slightly below his best he had enjoyed the challenge and had finished second. Both Borg, in the 1500 metres, and Zorilla, in the 400 metres, had swum Olympic records to beat him.

The Australians saw Bobby Pearce win the single sculls in the Sloten Canal in brilliant fashion the following day. He had proven to be in a class of his own, leaving the famous, previously undefeated American champion Kenneth Myers, thirty-five metres in arrears. His time of 7 minutes 11 seconds was not bettered until the Munich Olympics, forty-four years later. Australia's other medallist was cyclist Dunc Gray who finished third in the 1000 metres time trial. Bonnie Mealing had been eliminated in the backstroke semifinal, a disappointment for those who had predicted success, but at fifteen years of age she had time on her side.

Boy Charlton turned twenty-one as the Olympics ended and enjoyed a party with his team-mates. He announced he was now all but finished with competitive swimming. While in Paris, just before the Games, he had been invited to appear in the French Championships at Tourelles, scene of his Olympic triumph. His receptions in Paris had been so wonderful he found it impossible to say no. On August 16, 1928, a week after his last swim in Amsterdam, he arrived in the French capital and, though fatigued from the journey, won the 400 metres by five metres from Canadian Gamet Ault. For his effort he received a special presentation from French president Doumergue. His friend Katsuo Takaishi won the 100 metres.

8

Defying the Doctors

IN THE MONTH THAT FOLLOWED the Olympics some team members again represented the Commonwealth against America in London and others competed in the Tailteann Games in Ireland, where Nick Winter returned to form and won the hop, step and jump. There were countless social engagements for the team and individuals including dinner for Charlton and Bobby Pearce with Scotch whisky magnate Lord Dewar who was an avid sports lover, particularly keen on sculling. It was to have a profound effect on Pearce's career. The Olympians left London, bound for home on September 7 aboard the 15,000-ton, P&O liner *Chitral*. When they steamed into Sydney Harbour six weeks later they received a wonderful welcome. There was no criticism of their efforts but plenty for Olympic authorities, particularly from *The Referee* under the headline, 'Australian Council Must Stir Itself Or Get Out':

The Australian Olympic Council has been deaf, dumb and blind to the needs of Amateur sport in Australia. The majority who sit on it have not shown the faintest knowledge of what modern sport demands, and, consequently, Australian athletes are paying the penalty in international contests. Australia cannot afford to continue to allow its prestige to perish simply because a few gentlemen with fossilised ideas of developing sport refuse to open their eyes to what is required. Something must be done — and done immediately.

The scathing article went on to show the difference between the preparation of Australia's representatives and those of other nations. Particular attention was given to the disadvantages that had faced Boy Charlton:

Contrast the preparation made available for Charlton during the last four years with that enjoyed by Borg. What was Charlton allowed to do? He went to the back-blocks of Australia, where, true enough, he breathed in deeply of God's own air from Australia's open spaces; but training had he none; swimming had he none; save for the beetling splashes a neighbourly pool provided him. Borg . . . he spent four years of hard, stern discipline, specialising . . . specialising. Result? He turned the tables on our wonderful swimmer at the very distance he had been claimed a marvel.

In Boy Charlton's case the criticism was as unfair as it was melodramatic. After all it was not the authorities' decision that Boy quit swimming for a career on the land. Nevertheless it was a fact that the successful overseas athletes were being coached and trained in a most proficient manner. Professional coaching and management were making amateur champions. In Australia it was only the freakish performers like Charlton and Pearce who could succeed against such odds. America had shown the way and other nations were following suit. The back-up staff of the stronger nations at the Games was way beyond what Australia was able to provide. In a press interview, manager Les Duff told how, on arrival in Amsterdam, he had spent three hours personally handling sixty cases of luggage in the early hours of the morning so the athletes could get a good night's sleep. He was not only manager but gear steward and as *The Referee* noted, 'chief cook and bottle washer'. Les Duff's recommendations for future tours would echo those of previous managers. Whether they too fell on deaf ears remained to be seen. Even if they did not, where would finances come from to build facilities comparable to those of opulent athletics clubs in the USA?

For all that, the team had won one gold, two silvers and a bronze medal. With a party of just eighteen, outnumbered twenty to one by the larger nations, it was a very respectable effort. At a welcome home ball at Dungowan in Manly, attended by five hundred dancers, Les Duff, Boy Charlton, Bobby Pearce and Edna Davey were special guests. Duff declared:. 'Charlton was the hero of the 1924 Olympics, Pearce the hero of the 1928 Olympics. Charlton was also a hero of 1928.'

Bobby Pearce was somewhat nervous as he spoke: 'It is a great pleasure to be here, I once lived at the Spit and I must state I have always had a liking for Manly. Boy Charlton and I have been great friends and I thank you very much for bringing me here tonight.' Pearce blushed at the reception his words brought.

When Charlton spoke, people were surprised at his newfound confidence. He was more than happy to share the limelight with his team-mate and able to have some fun with him and the audience. 'Bob tried to souvenir a grandfather clock, but it would not fit in the bus and he tried to get run in for taking the King of Belgium's spurs,' he said, to much laughter. He concluded with: 'There is no place like Manly and I look forward once more to getting back to the beach.' He did the very next morning.

While it was known that Boy Charlton might well be finished with his competitive swimming career he certainly wasn't finished with the surf. His popularity had not been diminished in the slightest by his failure to win gold at Amsterdam. Though his modesty would remain forever, he was outgoing with his surfing mates and loved nothing more than to don a pair of boxing gloves and have a spar in the cock loft, an open area above the surf club. While he waited to return to Kurrumbede he spent every spare moment at the beach. Reunited with the likes of Fitz Lough, Ernie Henry, Sandy McAlister and Tom Farrell who had followed him to Paris, as well as the Davies brothers, the oldest of whom was now studying pharmacy, he took every opportunity to grab an oar in the surfboat or take some instruction from Sandy on the art of board riding. He was an expert surfer, extremely difficult to beat in flat surf, but, due to his bulk, was rather clumsy and slower than the smaller men in the runs into the water and up the beach at the end of a race.

Back in Europe the irrepressible Arne Borg had decided to settle down and became engaged to Elsie Lindberg from Falun, a picturesque village 50 kilometres north-west of Stockholm. Late in 1928 the couple travelled by train across Siberia to Tokyo where they were married, their witnesses none other than Johnny Weissmuller and America's Olympic diving champion Helen Meany. Any differences Borg and Weissmuller might have had at the 1924 Games had obviously been settled and the pair became good friends. After a honeymoon in the holy temple city of Nara the newlyweds set sail for Australia.

By virtue of the Great Depression, 1929 was destined to bring some measure of unhappiness to most people and great financial difficulties to many. For Boy Charlton it was to be the worst year of his young life. During Boy's absence at the Amsterdam Games his father, Oswald, was diagnosed with a carcinoma of the oesophagus, commonly known as cancer of the throat. It was a terrible, debilitating illness, which generally meant the sufferer had about six months to live. Whether he was made aware of his father's illness while overseas is not known. Certainly there was no mention of it in any newspaper reports. Oswald's condition deteriorated rapidly and his death, early in January was a blessing, despite its prematurity. Boy had lost his mother at thirteen years and now his father at twenty-one. Oswald Charlton was buried at Waverley Cemetery.

As Charlton contemplated his future during a perfect Manly summer, his great foe, Arne Borg, arrived for a second tour of Australia with his new wife. The now bespectacled Borg had found the perfect way to pay for an extended honeymoon. From Australia he intended to travel to America, retire at the end of the season and apply for American citizenship. Without Charlton there was no one to seriously threaten his supremacy in Australia unless his mind was not really on swimming. And after all he was on his honeymoon!

With Boy off the scene once more, Manly's new young distance star, Noel 'Tiger' Ryan, though not yet at his peak, was shaping up as Australia's best. Some critics believed that if Borg was below top form Ryan might well cause an upset, or at least push the champion to his limit. In his first swim at Tattersall's Club, the Swede put paid to suggestions that he was half-hearted about his swimming with a record-breaking 440 yards over the short, 20-yard course, which set the tone for his tour.

Boy Charlton was a spectator at the Domain when Borg beat Ryan in the state 440 yards championship by twenty yards, and a week later the 880 yards by twice that margin, breaking Charlton's record by five seconds. On the following Monday, before a packed baths at Manly, Borg took a full eighty-seven seconds off his own mile record and reappeared to play water polo ten minutes later. Whatever his expenses he gave great value for money and the standing ovation said so. Borg went on to swim in Melbourne and Adelaide where he lowered the world 880 yards time even further. Appearances at Brisbane, Lismore, Bangalow, Tamworth and Newcastle followed. In Tamworth he was accompanied by Ernie Henry, who stayed with the carnival promoter, Dr Piper. Borg, upon seeing a vast crowd turn up to the carnival, negotiated an extra fifty pounds expenses 'to put on a really entertaining show', which included a lifesaving demonstration. The good doctor had no real option but to pay him.

Borg remained unbeaten and left with his bride for the United States, his reputation as the world's greatest and most versatile swimmer in no doubt. Australians could only lament the fact that Charlton had been unavailable to compete against him. Soon after Borg arrived in America he was disqualified from the amateur ranks and immediately set up a professional circuit with Weissmuller, beginning in Hawaii and continuing in the US, Japan and Europe, their slogan 'A world record or your money back'. Borg did not settle in America, as he had contemplated, but became a swimming instructor in several countries including Norway, Switzerland, Belgium, Estonia, Latvia and Sweden. With his earnings he bought a cigar shop in Stockholm where he was able to enjoy his favourite vice at cost price.

It was widely known that Boy Charlton was offered a considerable amount of money to turn professional. If there was any stage of his life where he might have considered the move, surely this must have been it. His son, Murray, believes the offer probably occurred about this time. There were professional swim clubs operating in Australia and around the world but the expenses paid by these organisations were a pittance compared to the type of offer made to Charlton. He confided this to his wife Jessie, many years after his retirement. Exactly when the offer was made and by whom, was never made public, but it was

verified in a hand-written summary of his career composed by
Jessie and kept in a family album.

Had he been approached to compete with Borg and Weissmuller? The possibility of a viable, professional swimming
troupe was easy to imagine. The largest venues were invariably
packed when national championships and international events
were staged. On special occasions, such as Charlton's clashes
with Borg, as many were turned away as gained admittance.
Amateur champions were making vast sums of money for
swimming associations around the world, why not for themselves? Johnny Weissmuller had turned his back on the sport
after Amsterdam, at the age of twenty-four and, in his own
words, 'became a beach bum'. Weissmuller was at a loose end,
giving exhibitions and swimming lessons in luxury Florida
hotels, often in return for accommodation. He then signed a
contract to model swimming costumes at US$500 a week, a
fortune at that time. Eventually a Hollywood film career materi-
alised. The trio were among the most famous swimmers of all
time and would have drawn huge crowds all over the world.

Charlton was vague about the exact amount of money offered
him, but son Murray believed it was several thousand pounds, to
be earned over a few seasons. Such an amount of money would
have been enough to buy a magnificent sheep property on the very
best grazing land in the state. To own such a property and be free
of debt would have been any farmer's dream. This would certainly
have been feasible for Charlton. Endorsements for all types of
products, by popular sportsmen, were widely seen and would
have complemented earnings in the pool. Over a decade earlier
Australia's boxing idol, Les Darcy, appeared in press advertise-
ments for suits, fitness tonics and even Osram light globes, posing
with a large globe as a speedball. Snowy Baker advertised health
tonics and liniment. Charlton had already done press advertise-
ments for Bonds swimming costumes without infringing his

amateur status and was about to attract the attention of Jantzen, the makers of a new range of American swimwear. However Charlton could not be tempted to professionalism. His response to an offer made later in life became part of Australian sporting folklore: 'The Australian public would never forgive me. I am not in the sport for what I can get out of it.'

Charlton's problems did not end with his father's death. As he prepared to return to the land, fate stepped in, causing him and his remaining family and friends severe worry. Having suffered intermittently with a sore throat for some weeks, Boy became quite ill. He complained of aching joints and developed a high fever. His doctor diagnosed rheumatic fever and sent him immediately to Royal North Shore Hospital.

Rheumatic fever was a very serious condition, invariably associated with inflammation of the heart and prone to recurrence. It was most prevalent in children up to fourteen years of age, but was not uncommon in people some years older. While it was not likely to be fatal, it was common for the muscles around the heart and heart valve to be damaged and cause sudden heart failure in middle age. With antibiotics and drugs many years off, the only treatment was bed rest and a strictly controlled diet. Neither suited him but he remained in hospital for some months. Even after recovering sufficiently to wander around the hospital grounds he was told that he would be a semi-invalid for several more months. He was not a man to take orders that restricted his activities, as he had shown when defying advice not to swim in Britain immediately after the 1924 Olympics, but he had little choice this time. Cardiologists generally believed that a healthy heart could not be damaged by excessive effort but a heart that had been affected by illness certainly could. Charlton was almost resigned to the fact that his competitive swimming days were over.

Though Charlton's name had naturally been an omission from the sporting pages during that time, his progress was closely monitored in some quarters. The Hawkesbury Agricultural College *Journal* reported in September 1929: 'A.M. Charlton (1924–25) has been in the Royal North Shore Hospital suffering from rheumatic fever. The *Journal* sympathises with him and wishes him a speedy recovery.'

For a decade the Western world had been in a party mood. It was not just the flappers and Charleston dancers who saw no end to prosperity and fun. People borrowed and spent as if there was no settling day. When their world came crashing around them with the New York Stock Market crash on October 29, wealthy men became paupers overnight. Businesses and investors were bankrupt and destitute across the globe. Millions were soon out of work in America and Europe and a third of Australian workers lost their jobs. Dole queues stretched out of sight and rationing became commonplace. People were forced to do manual labour to be rewarded with government subsidies. The Great Depression spared no one and it took America, England and their trading partners a decade to recover.

By summer Charlton was well enough to leave hospital and return to Manly, but forced to take things very quietly, spending much time lazing on the beach as he did each year after coming down from Kurrumbede. As usual he met up with mates from the surf and swimming clubs, enjoyed their company and regularly visited the local picture shows. Andrew Murray Charlton was known throughout the sporting world as 'Boy', but at the surf club he was more often called 'Apple'. The origin of this second, seemingly less romantic sobriquet is somewhat vague. In later years his close friend John Davies declared it had come about because of a rather pronounced Adam's apple. This may well have been true but many of the young women who enjoyed his company at the beach had a slightly different version. On the back of one of several photographs in which the handsome young champion posed with four very attractive girls in new

Jantzen costumes, one of the quartet, Marie Gelling, has referred to him as Apple Charlotte. She explained that this was the name of a particularly scrumptious dessert! He was also known to be a keen dancer who had no difficulty finding dance partners. Which nickname came first nobody knows.

In view of his health and how easily he was taking things it came as a surprise to most when a second report in the *Journal* stated:

> *Andrew (Boy) Charlton (1924–25) intends to seek selection in the team to represent Australia at the Olympic games of Los Angeles of 1932. He has recovered from his recent illness, and returned to Gunnedah in the middle of January. Charlton will not compete in swimming events this summer, but will again take part next season, with a view to representing Australia for the third time.*

Boy felt extremely well as he returned to Gunnedah by train. He was driven straight to Kurrumbede where Reg Broun and his staff were delighted to see him and pleased to be assured that he was in fine fettle. It was hot and dry, just as he remembered it, and the flies were as thick as ever. Rural life had already been hit hard by the Depression as wool prices tumbled, but at least he had a job, a roof over his head and stoic friends around him. Charlton had become more than just a jackeroo at Kurrumbede. His desire to become a farmer was still his most burning passion and he worked diligently and without complaint as the months came and went, bringing with them the lambing and shearing seasons, the unrelenting summer heat and heavy rains that turned the black soil plains to a bog, with just the occasional swim in the Namoi River at the end of a long day.

Never were Australia's sporting heroes to be more important to the public than during the Depression years. A Test match century, the sight of an outstanding racehorse defying the handi-capper or an exciting football or tennis match were occasions of relief for people devoid of answers to the crippling problems of the Depression. Don Bradman, the boy from the bush now playing in Sydney, thrilled crowds as he blazed his way to century after century. His 334 against England at Leeds set a record for Test cricket. The big New Zealand bred chestnut colt Phar Lap was also on his way to sporting immortality. Race-goers adored him. Fourteen successive victories, including the Melbourne Cup when carrying a huge weight, was reason enough but Phar Lap had extra appeal. He was a cheap buy, trained by a battling trainer, beating high-priced horses owned by wealthy men, and Australia loved the underdog.

While a cricketer and a racehorse were the most famous sporting heroes of the Depression years, there were many others. In Europe and back home in Australia Hubert Opperman had proven himself one of the world's finest professional road cyclists. His victory in the Paris–Brest–Paris bike race was justi-fiably regarded as one of the greatest sporting achievements Europe had seen.

Charlton went about his duties on the land as the first British Empire Games (later known as the Commonwealth Games) were held in Ontario, Canada, in 1930. Tiger Ryan won the 440 yards and 1500 yards freestyle. Bobby Pearce, who had lost his job during the Depression and was given work in Canada by Lord Dewar, easily won the single sculls title. A year later he would go on to win the Diamond Sculls at Henley. Ironically his vocational misfortune allowed his entry to the event. As a whisky salesman he was accepted; as a carpenter, though skilled, he was regarded as a manual worker and would have been precluded in previous years!

Though never totally giving up on the idea of a comeback to competitive swimming it was not until Charlton again came down to Manly for the Christmas break in 1930 that he made any real effort in this regard. Even then it was more by chance than design. Towards the end of his holiday he stepped into the pool with the idea of doing a few easy laps. As he hit the water Harry Hay, who was on the boards, automatically started his stop-watch. He could not help but notice how effortlessly Charlton was travelling and summoned some swimmers to join in to see what effect they might have on the lone swimmer. Charlton enjoyed their company and swam twelve laps – 660 yards. When he stepped from the water Hay told him he had covered the 440 yards in five and a half minutes. He felt well and was surprised at his time, considering he had not been in the pool for twelve months and had done no training. Harry Hay was also impressed and said so. When Charlton returned soon after to Kurrumbede, the possibility of a comeback was in the back of his mind.

At the end of the 1930/31 swimming season, Boy wrote to Harry Hay from Kurrumbede Station in May asking his ideas about a return to competitive racing. Hay responded with a detailed letter quoting from his vast experience as a swimmer and a coach. He was of the opinion that, provided doctors' examinations of his heart were positive, Charlton's best days might well be ahead of him not behind him. Most great swimmers had continued to improve through their mid-twenties; Arne Borg being a prime example. Charlton's confidence was boosted by the letter and he decided that he would have tests carried out on his heart and if they proved satisfactory he would aim for Los Angeles in 1932.

Doctor Keith Kirkland, 1920 Olympian, who had raced against Charlton several times, agreed to do a series of tests on Boy if he decided to come to Sydney and train. When Charlton asked permission of Malcolm Mackellar to go to the city early so that he could prepare gradually, he was told he could go whenever he wished and that there would always be a job waiting for him whenever he returned. Charlton wisely decided that a long, slow preparation would be the most efficient way to prove if his heart would stand the strain and also whether he could retain his old form and enthusiasm.

Boy arrived at Manly in early October to prepare for the 1931/32 swimming season. Movietone newsreel cameras filmed interviews with Charlton and his coach, Harry Hay, and within days, cinema goers around the world were aware of his comeback plans. It had been well over three years since he had extended himself in the pool. He went to see Keith Kirkland, whose initial test showed his heart was strong with a regular beat, and did not appear to be unduly affected by exertion. During this period Harry Hay played an enormous part in Charlton's preparation. He kept a close eye on his every move, advising, encouraging and massaging Boy after each swim. Further tests by Keith Kirkland showed his heart was, if anything, improving as his condition hardened. Still there were plenty of times when Boy doubted that he would regain his former glory. Whenever Hay detected the slightest sign that his confidence had dropped he would suggest they relax with a leisurely dip in the surf or go into town to watch a film. Boy loved the cinema almost as much as the surf. It was Hay's way of combining some mental relaxation along with the concentration and effort needed to get Charlton back into the form that had made him so great. The tests on his heart continued right up until the state championships in January.

Charlton was well aware that, for the first time ever, no matter how well he prepared, a local competitor might beat him. Noel 'Tiger' Ryan, his Manly team-mate in the surf and swimming clubs, had continued to improve and was considered a serious threat by all experts. Like Charlton he was a quiet man and a tremendous competitor. Unlike Charlton he was also a great trainer. Ryan was on his way to becoming the greatest surfer Australia had produced. His stature as a still water swimmer was also undeniable. His nickname of Tiger had been well earned.

Aside from his success at the Empire Games, Ryan had won the state 440 yards and 880 yards titles in 1929 and 1931 (though finishing behind the visitor Borg in 1929), the one mile title in 1930 and 1931, as well as both junior and senior surf titles in 1929–30.

Boy's legion of fans were used to his extraordinary comebacks but even they felt some apprehension. Just how much had his illness affected him remained to be seen. He did, however, have one advantage; he was not working and was able to train exactly as he wished while Ryan was only able to train at the end of his working day at the Government Bank. As team-mates the pair often swam together and were reported to be clocking very similar times with similar effort.

There was almost unprecedented interest for a regular club meeting when they raced in separate heats of the Manly Club's 880 yards handicap in the first week of January 1932. Charlton swam strongly from the back mark for the first half of his race but pulled out after 440 yards, much to the concern of spectators. They were relieved to discover his problem was not serious. He explained he had simply eaten too many plums at a picnic at Mona Vale on New Year's Day. Ryan completed his race very strongly, having swum almost identical time as Charlton for the first half of the race.

In the week leading up to the state titles, Charlton swam a trial at Manly that showed he would still be a force to contend with despite his lay-off and battle with fever. Paced by four of the club's top swimmers, including exciting newcomer Sam Herford, he broke ten and three quarter minutes for 880 yards, stroking flawlessly. That evening Tiger Ryan was just as impressive. The impending clash between the 'old' champ and the new brought tremendous excitement to the state titles. Close friends as they were, the rivalry was intense. With the Depression having left the swimming union virtually bereft of funds, only a small team would be chosen for Los Angeles so there was no certainty two distance swimmers would be selected.

On January 16, 1932, five thousand fans arrived at the Domain to see the 880 yards state title, the first of two races between Ryan and Charlton. There were several other attractions that Saturday afternoon, including the clash of Australia's finest tennis player Jack Crawford and the Japanese champion, Jiro Satoh, at the nearby White City courts, so it was a sizeable crowd, and as many as the baths held comfortably. The large contingent of pressmen, as well as three Movietone cameramen, gave an indication of how the sports events of the day were ranked. The field was a strong one with two budding champions, Arthur Besomo of Bondi and Sam Herford of Manly, also expected to perform very well. 'Trudgeon', writing for *The Referee*, described the scene as the swimmers appeared:

Sartorially they made an extraordinary pair as they came on to the platform. Giant Charlton, his bronzedness accentuated by a weird white dressing gown cum split skirt and a football Guernsey: and Ryan in a weird array of pullovers, sox, shoes and an improvised towel skirt. Ryan was dwarfed but his torso would delight an artist. You dismiss him as being small because of his tiny, serious face. It is, as a French writer said of Opperman, who is similarly featured, a 'grandmother's face.' But as was also said of 'Oppy', Ryan too is a 'little iron man.'

The two favourites drew adjacent lanes and Charlton towered over his opponent as they shook hands before the race. Conditions were ideal – a warm, still day and the incoming tide providing flat water. Ryan who had excellent early speed was expected to lead but 880 yards was considered to be Charlton's pet distance and he invariably had planned his race perfectly.

The crowd was quiet as they intently awaited the starter's call. 'Face the water . . . GO!' The field of five hit the water as one for the first of eight gruelling laps. As expected Ryan began very fast, but it took him forty yards to lead clearly, and then only narrowly. At the first turn he had a half second lead from Charlton but was unable to increase it in the second lap at the end of which Charlton drew level. Spectators were surprised when Charlton took a narrow lead soon after as Ryan bungled the second turn slightly. Halfway down the third lap Charlton led by over a yard. The crowd were already urging on the two leaders as the gap widened to the other three swimmers. Had Charlton gone too hard or was he swimming within himself? The next two laps told the story. Stroking with the power and precision that was his hallmark, he slowly increased his lead until it was obvious no one could trouble him. Despite Ryan's courage and skill Charlton came away to lead by over twenty yards with a lap and a half to go. Sprinting through the last 50 yards he won by almost forty yards. It was a mighty effort, beyond the expectations of even his most avid admirers. Patrons had seen the Charlton of old. As the pair shook hands in the water the crowd turned their attention to the fluctuating struggle that saw Besomo touch Herford out of third place.

Race times were of tremendous interest and a huge roar went up as they were announced. At 10 minutes 22 seconds, Boy Charlton had swum the fastest 880 yards of his life. Ryan's time was 10 minutes 45.2 seconds, and Besomo just one second over 11 minutes. Charlton's effort was four and a half seconds better than Arne Borg's record set at the Manly Baths in 1929 and only a second and half slower than the world record set by Clarence 'Buster' Crabbe in a 55-yard pool in America. There was no way to describe the effort other than incredible. Those who had theorised about the way the race would be swum and the magnitude of the task that faced Charlton had been shown once more that truly great champions defy logic, they simply achieve where others cannot.

Charlton had booked his passage to America with his triumph. Now Noel Ryan had one more chance to do the same. Their second meeting was scheduled to take place a week later, over 440 yards, a distance believed to be more favourable to Ryan. Though outclassed in the 880, Ryan had also swum a good time and had every reason to look forward to the encounter. He admitted to being a little short on condition and had no doubt he would be better off for the experience. At the Manly Baths the following Monday night, Ryan equalled Charlton's best 220 yards when he won a heat of the state titles and lowered that time with a brilliant victory in the final on Wednesday night.

Again a huge, vocal crowd packed the Domain Baths for the 440 yards state titles final. Charlton fans were convinced their man would win again but conceded it would be a much more difficult task over the shorter course. Ryan's supporters were equally confident he could set up a handy lead and hold off Charlton when they sprinted over the last half lap. All were hoping that, irrespective of the result, Ryan could produce a performance to guarantee him a spot alongside Charlton in Los Angeles.

They were not to be disappointed as the pair matched strokes from the start. The crowd immediately set up a din, one that did not to lessen for a moment during the next five minutes. As the pair went stroke for stroke down the first lap, Charlton's surprise tactics became clear. He intended to stay with Ryan throughout the race rather than trail him and sprint home. At the end of the first lap Ryan held a slender margin but Charlton drew level soon after. Down the pool they raced each striving for the lead. It seemed Charlton might have been a fraction ahead at the 220 yards mark but Ryan turned the better and again they were level. Still there was nothing between the pair as they turned after 330 yards for the last lap. With the capacity crowd cheering them on each gave his all. No more than ten yards from the finish Charlton lifted and drove to the wall to win by a touch in 4 minutes 55.4 seconds. It was the fastest quarter mile swim anywhere in the world during the previous six months. Tiger Ryan was both disappointed and delighted. He didn't quite win but he was bound for Los Angeles with Charlton and both would be highly competitive.

Movietone's newsreel crew had filmed both races and Australian cinemas were able to screen them within a few days. Charlton's wins were seen by some critics as virtually assuring that his dominance of distance swimming would be resumed, but Gustav Froelich, a former German backstroke champion, now living in Melbourne, warned that this might not be the case. While believing that Charlton seemed certain to regain his very best form it still might not be good enough to hold off the vastly improved Jean Taris of France nor the rising Japanese champion, Shozo Makino, one of several Japanese swimmers who had outperformed the Americans in a meeting between the two countries held in Tokyo the previous year.

Swimming had proven to be Australia's strongest Olympic sport. Charlton and Ryan were now certain selections but so too was Bonnie Mealing, about whom too much was expected in 1928, but who had continued to improve and was now accepted, not only in Australia but across the globe, as one of the world's best swimmers. She was the world record holder for 200 metres backstroke and she too was at the top of her form.

While the heats of the 220 yards titles were being held at Manly on the previous Monday evening, sixteen year old Claire Dennis made an attempt on the world record for the 100 metres breaststroke. In a modified pool at the Domain Baths, under official supervision and using the specified 25-yard laps, she returned a time of 3 minutes 8.4 seconds, beating English woman Marie Hinton's best by almost two seconds. She too had booked her trip to Los Angeles.

Following the New South Wales titles, a three-day carnival, part of the 'National Games', was held in Melbourne to give other swimmers a chance to gain selection for Los Angeles. A highlight of the carnival was the performance of a young Victorian girl, just out of high school, Frances Bult, who won the final of the 100 metres freestyle in brilliant fashion. She became the fifth swimmer named in the team of twelve for the 1932 Olympics. Sadly her preparation for the Games would be hindered by shameless prejudice. There was only one heated pool suitable for training in Melbourne in the winter months, the City Baths, and Frances, like all other females, was barred from using it. Nevertheless she was ecstatic at her selection and determined to make the most of it.

Rumours surfaced during the Melbourne carnival that Charlton would turn professional when he returned from Los Angeles. Two invitations arrived for him in the southern capital. One offer came from a South Australian baths proprietor who asked him to appear at a carnival in Adelaide for which he would be paid twenty-five pounds, the other from the Sydney League Swimming Club, the strongest Australian professional troupe, the letter intimating that Johnny Weissmuller had been signed to appear in Australia. Charlton was upset by the rumours and cabled the Adelaide proprietor: 'consider your offer a gratuitous insult.' He then asked *The Referee*'s swimming writer to state on his behalf: 'I specially desire *The Referee* to let the Australian public know that I have no intention, now or at any future time, of turning professional. My intentions are, after returning from the Games, to get married and settle down on a property of my own.'

Bobby Pearce, Olympic champion and winner of the Diamond Sculls at Henley, was the one rowing representative and Edgar 'Dunc' Gray the sole cyclist. Missing was Australia's finest sprinter, Jim Carlton, who had quit athletics to join the priesthood just days after running a world record on grass at the Sydney Cricket Ground. What time he might have run on the faster synthetic track in Los Angeles would never be known. In his absence selectors chose four runners, the best of whom appeared to be George Golding, who specialised at 400 metres on the flat and over the hurdles. Eddie Scarf, a young butcher and member of the Dee Why Surf Club, was the only wrestler chosen. Completing the party was the manager, chaperone and two masseurs. Though the team was small it had some extremely talented performers. Charlton and Bobby Pearce were already Olympic champions and Dunc Gray was an Olympic placegetter. Though Pearce would not travel with the team, as he was still residing in Canada, Charlton had good mates in Tiger Ryan and Eddie Scarf who swam the belt and often wrestled on a mat on the beach at surf carnivals.

Following selection, Charlton participated in several carnivals across the eastern states but not before one last test on his heart. He was disappointed that Harry Hay was not one of the two masseurs chosen to accompany the team but once again Hay intended paying his own way and would be on hand when Charlton needed him. Returning from Victoria, where he showed surprising speed to win a 60-yards handicap race in Bendigo, Boy undertook a week-long tour of Queensland, which caused a great deal of controversy when clubs complained that they had expected him to perform flat-out rather than swim in exhibitions and handicap events. Asking the best swimmer in the land to perform in Maryborough, Gympie, Nambour, Ipswich, Toowoomba and Warwick in the space of seven days hardly made much sense and he was glad when it was all over. A proposed trip to New Zealand was cancelled when he declared he needed a rest, which he was granted, but he returned for exhibitions in carnivals at Manly and Coogee to celebrate the opening of the Sydney Harbour Bridge, a project first mooted over a hundred years earlier and commenced in 1924. The carnival at Coogee was run on the official opening day of the bridge, March 19, 1932.

There was some controversy when it was announced that the Olympians would sail to the US on the American Matson liner *Mariposa*, rather than a British vessel. So strong were Australia's ties with the British Empire that one New South Wales official sent an official protest to the Olympic committee, but in such difficult financial times the decision was a sound one based solely on cost and practicality. There were not likely to be any complaints from the team. The American shipping companies dominated South Pacific travel and the *Mariposa*, launched only a few months earlier, was the ultimate in modern luxury liners. Much the same size as the Orient and P&O liners, which had carried previous teams to Europe, the *Mariposa* was one of three new ships which would ensure the Matson line remained the foremost passenger carrier across the Pacific for forty years. In keeping with travel through the spectacularly beautiful islands of the Pacific, the big white liner's decor was less formal than the British ships but every bit as inviting. The trip from Sydney to San Francisco, via New Zealand, Fiji, Samoa and Hawaii was to take just under three weeks. This was a big advantage for athletes who previously spent six weeks on board.

Charlton's reappearance as an Olympian naturally caused tremendous interest in many, so when Charlie Messenger, a noted big-game fisherman, decided to measure Charlton's strength in the water, a curious crowd turned up to see how this was to be done. Messenger, a close friend of Harry Hay, had very simple plan. He attached a 1,500-pound breaking strain line to a belt around Charlton's waist, took the large fishing rod in his hand, sat back in a chair that had been fixed to the end of the pool and told Charlton to swim away. When the line broke there was a cheer from the crowd and Messenger told the *Manly Daily* reporter: 'He is stronger than any shark I have ever caught.'

As the swimming season drew to a close, Boy and Tiger Ryan appeared in several carnivals, generally in exhibition swims. They also competed in several surf carnivals, culminating in the national titles in Sydney. Whereas Charlton had invariably held the edge over Tiger Ryan in the pool, the reverse was true in the open sea. Ryan was too good for a strong field in the open surf race but Charlton joined him in the team's race together with Sam Herford and Ryan's brother Owen. They were successful, giving Boy his first national surfing title. The pair were on very good terms when they set sail for America.

9

Los Angeles 1932

AMERICA HAD BEEN VYING for an opportunity to stage the Olympics for some years. The fiasco of the 1904 Games in St Louis had been difficult for them to overcome. Now, twenty-eight years later, they had been given their chance. The 1932 Games were planned in times of economic prosperity but the Great Depression had changed things all around the world. Nevertheless the American government was determined to do all it could to help make the games a success and a magnificent stadium, capable of holding more than 100,000 spectators, was built in Los Angeles, California.

For the first time an Olympic village capable of housing all the athletes was built and costs for overseas teams were to be cut to an absolute minimum. A new velodrome was also built at Pasadena's Rose Bowl, just fifteen minutes from the centre of town at the foot of the San Gabriel Mountains. The 50-metre swimming pool, part of the Olympic complex and situated close to the main stadium, was 20 metres in width, graduated from 16 feet to 5 feet in depth, and included a scum gutter inset into the walls, which made turning speedy and simple. It also included the innovation of a wire that ran above the centre of each lane for the benefit of backstroke swimmers. The fresh clear water was taken from the same source as the Los Angeles drinking supply. Automatic electronic timing was introduced in track events, along with the photo-finish camera.

Convenience and technology was given equal importance. Concessions on public transport were negotiated for all participants and America's prohibition laws were relaxed to allow countries to import and drink wine in line with their normal habits. To further promote support from abroad America even subsidised fares on their shipping lines. This had been an important consideration when Australia chose to sail on the *Mariposa*. Thirty-seven counties participated, only nine less than in Amsterdam, and though there were less than half the number of competitors, quality not quantity was the order of the day. Many world and Olympic records were to be broken. The event was scheduled for sixteen days, a mere fraction of the duration of previous Olympics and a forerunner to future events.

The Australian team arrived in Los Angeles on June 21, 1932. For the first time since 1920, the team sought no government, nor public, financial support, but found a trump card awaiting them in America in the form of Reginald 'Snowy' Baker, without doubt Australia's most gifted, versatile sportsman. Apart from representing Australia at three different sports at the London Games, Snowy was an international rugby player, expert water polo player, horseman and fencer. Soon after retiring from competitive sport he had become manager of Sydney's Rushcutter's Bay Stadium, which he proudly called 'Baker's Stadium'. Together with Victorian businessman John Wren he virtually ran

Australian boxing. Here was an entrepreneur with ambition and ego to match his sporting prowess.

Snowy starred in feature films in Australia then headed for Hollywood immediately after the First World War. He fitted the flamboyant Hollywood film scene perfectly, starring in two action features, in which he did all his own stunts (a remarkable effort, some said, in view of his failing military call-up in Sydney due to a chronic back injury), then became director of the exclusive Riviera Country Club in Santa Monica, a centre for film stars and producers alike. Here he introduced polo to the Hollywood set and was a friend and riding instructor to many of the biggest names in Hollywood, including the late Rudolph Valentino, Douglas Fairbanks and new star Spencer Tracy. He took the Australians to the Riviera Club, dressed in riding breeches and knee-length leather boots and hosted the entire team at his cottage, which he called 'Gunyah'.

Australia's Olympic authorities installed Baker as the team's liaison officer and *The Referee* hired him to cover the games as chief reporter. No better choice could have been made for either position. Baker met the team in Los Angeles together with Bobby Pearce, who had motored almost 5,000 miles from Canada in a coupé, his skiff strapped to the top. A second skiff arrived with the team from Australia. From the time of their arrival news of the Australian Olympians appeared in the local press and also came back to Australia. No team ever had better contacts, nor received so much publicity. Their popularity was virtually assured. Baker was in his element as he personally took the team on tours of the film studios. Later they were entertained at the homes of the stars and lunched with the Hollywood social set. The whole adventure was almost unbelievable, especially to the younger members of the team. Sprinter Eileen Wearne was interviewed on a nationwide broadcast by the famous actress Mary Pickford, wife of Douglas Fairbanks, both of whom expressed a desire to visit Australia. On a trip to MGM studios the ladies met Jim Thorpe, the famous American Indian athlete, as well as California's Governor Rolph who had sailed on the *Tahiti* to Australia some years earlier and was keen to talk about his visit. Autograph hunting soon became a favourite diversion from training.

The men, particularly Charlton and the tall, elegant George Golding, both bachelors, were photographed with famous stars, always immaculately attired in their green and gold blazers, cream slacks and two-tone shoes. Their appearance gave no indication of a team short of money. Baker's wealthy and generous contacts were a considerable help to competitors existing on a few shillings a day. The most popular of the comedians at the time, Harold Lloyd, had a mansion with a large pool and took a shine to the Australians, whom he invited regularly to his home. Their popularity blossomed, particularly because of their modest ways and easygoing nature. The women athletes were, according to Baker, 'about the politest foursome of young ladies one would meet in many a moon. They are as far removed, both in manners and appearance, from their pert, snappy American flapper rivals as kangaroos are from a Mississippi mule.' One assumes this was for the Australian press only.

In such opulent and exciting surroundings, and being the centre of so much attention, it would have been easy to lose focus on the task at hand but this was never likely. Manager James Eve was more at home with a team of mixed gender than his predecessor Les Duff and had a good grip on things immediately. Chaperone, Mrs Mary Chambers, was very strict with her ladies who were seldom apart from the group. The female athletes were accommodated in the luxury Chapman Park Hotel that had a dining room capable of seating two hundred people. It was situated close to the Olympic stadium and within easy walking distance of the famous Brown Derby restaurant, known to the Australians through the stories of Damon Runyon.

The men, with the exception of Bobby Pearce, stayed in the huge Olympic village, overlooking the Pacific Ocean, just a few minutes from the main stadium. The village was made up of five hundred and fifty prefabricated cottages each of which housed two men. It stood on 330 acres and had its own electricity supply, fire department, hospital, post office and amphitheatre. There were forty separate kitchens and dining rooms, enough for each team. The Australians elected to share their dining room with the small New Zealand contingent who brought their own cook and shared his expense.

Accommodation had been provided for athletes in previous Games, however many team managers preferred to have athletes stay in alternate venues. This was the first time the Olympic village was used extensively by all visiting nations. Bobby Pearce was given permission to stay at Long Beach near the rowing course, 20 miles from the city. Having made his own way to Los Angeles, thereby saving his fare on the *Mariposa*, he was given an allowance that allowed him to train with a professional champion just as he had done in Holland before the 1928 Games. He and his wife shared a cottage with Major Goodsell who was preparing to race for the world's professional championship against England's Ted Phelps, Pearce's training partner prior to the Games in Amsterdam. Again Pearce's father Harry paid his way to supervise his training. Baker reported that Pearce was in wonderful condition, describing him as 'the beau ideal of an athlete, well set up and full of zip', and that it would take an exceptional performance if he were to be beaten. After one gruelling session Major Goodsell was quoted as saying: 'He will have to capsize to lose.'

The Australians were among the first overseas teams to begin their preparation. The *Mariposa*, despite being so well appointed, proved inadequate from a training point of view. The pool was no better than those on previous vessels but with a mere eighteen days spent at sea and over five weeks before the competition would start, confidence was high. Charlton and Ryan checked out the Olympic pool just a day after arrival and were very pleased with it and also that it was available to them. Charlton immediately impressed Snowy Baker whom he described as 'a gigantic man alongside some of the others'. According to Baker his every move was watched with great interest by the Americans who regarded him as the man to beat. Baker reported that Boy swam within four seconds of his best Olympic time for 1500 metres just a week into his preparation. He renewed acquaintances with Johnny Weissmuller, now an actor shooting his first motion picture, *Tarzan The Ape Man*, and the redoubtable Duke Kahanamoku, who, just a month short of his forty-second birthday, was on standby as a reserve for America's water polo team.

Australia's swimmers had been in training for over three weeks when the American Olympic trials were held. Clarence 'Buster' Crabbe, third behind Borg and Charlton in Amsterdam, won the 1500 metres from fourteen year old Ralph Flanagan. No time was given, which seemed to indicate it was nothing flash, as America was not known for hiding good performances. Crabbe also won the 400 metres in a time of a tick over 4 minutes 56 seconds, which was a little slower than Charlton and Ryan had swum in Sydney. It seemed to augur well for the Manly team-mates who were training twice a day, though little had been seen of the Japanese who unsuccessfully requested a special time at the pool be kept exclusively for them. Albert Zorilla, Argentina's surprise winner of the 400 metres in Amsterdam, was also reported to be in good form having come via the New York Athletic Club. Frank Beaurepaire arrived to lend a hand at the Australian camp and the entire swimming squad was apparently in excellent form despite a report that Noel Ryan had beaten Charlton by forty yards over 800 metres.

A fortnight before the opening ceremony, both cyclist Dunc Gray and Charlton came down with influenza. Gray, a teetotaller, was convinced by manager, Jim Eve, to forget his aversion to alcohol and take the old-fashioned remedy of a stiff drink of brandy, a glass of hot water and lemon juice, an aspirin and a warm bed. Two days and nights sweating under heavy blankets did wonders for him. Charlton had more time to recover so stayed out of the pool for a few days and made sure he kept warm. He was worried that if the flu worsened it could bring on another bout of fever, though he made no mention of this to anyone at the time.

By the day of the opening ceremony he was reported to be in quite good order and ready to return to the water. Suggestions had been made that Charlton might be withdrawn from the 400 metres to allow him more time to recover from the flu and to concentrate on the 1500 metres. It had also been mooted that Ryan might be withdrawn from the 1500 to concentrate on the 400. Neither was likely to happen. On the eve of the Games, Tiger Ryan wrote back to Australia saying how well the swimmers had trained. The conditions suited them perfectly with hot days and cool nights making it easy to get a good sleep.

Los Angeles was agog with excitement for the first day of the Olympics, 105,000 people turning up for the opening ceremony in which Boy Charlton carried the flag for Australia. The fourteen strong contingent was convinced each of the athletes were potential finalists with the possible exception of the distance runners. All four female swimmers had produced outstanding times.

As usual track events dominated the first week's proceedings while Eddie Scarf and Dunc Gray also began their quest for medals. Gray had two assignments at the velodrome, the sprint followed by the 1000 metre time trial. He was narrowly and controversially beaten in the semifinal of the sprint by Louis Chaillot of France. Though confident he could win the bronze medal he was given permission to withdraw from the race to concentrate on the very arduous time trial to be held later that night. Waiting to ride eighth of nine competitors in the solo event, he watched the time gradually come down to one that was better than he had ever ridden. When he took four tenths of a second off the best time he was assured of second placing. The last rider, Holland's Jacobus van Egmond, who had beaten Chaillot in the final of the sprint, tore around the track with all eyes glued on him. His time of 1 minute 10.3 seconds was three tenths slower than Gray and the Goulburn carpenter became Australia's first ever cycling gold medallist.

Eddie Scarf, a very fast and clever wrestler, who had not conceded a fall in practice, also gave a wonderful display. Narrowly beaten in his semifinal he took the light heavyweight bronze medal to become Australia's most successful wrestling Olympian. On the track George Golding made the final of the 400 metres but was eliminated when he came in fourth in the semifinal of the 400 metres hurdles. Bill Barwick was run out in his heat of the 1500 metres as was Eileen Wearne when she came fourth in her heat of the 100 metres, but Alex Hillhouse made the final of the 5000 metres. So Australia's first six competitors had made three finals and collected a gold and bronze medal.

Swimming began on Saturday, August 6, a day before Boy Charlton's twenty-fifth birthday, with the women's 200 metres breaststroke and 100 metres freestyle. Clare Dennis won her heat of the backstroke, breaking the Olympic record in the process, and progressed to the final to be held later in the week. Frances Bult was third in her freestyle heat and improved markedly, coming in second in the semifinal the following day. On Monday she finished fifth in the final where all swimmers broke the previous Olympic record. The young Melbourne girl could have done no better as she swam two seconds faster than her previous best.

Monday also brought the first appearance of Boy Charlton and Noel Ryan in the 400 metres. There was tremendous interest in Charlton's effort. Harry Hay, writing for *The Sun*, expressed the view that he was feeling better but not nearly himself when he faced the water. It was not a difficult heat and he won quite easily in a little under five minutes. Charlton said he felt only a little tired in the arms but 'otherwise, not bad'. Hay said he expected Charlton to get down to around 4 minutes 53 seconds for the final which would make him very competitive even if he was still a little below his best. Tiger Ryan also won his heat, in slightly slower time, but was happy with his performance. On an interesting day, the 1928 champion Alberto Zorilla withdrew with injury, Jean Taris was fastest heat winner by several seconds, Buster Crabbe won his heat in an identical time to Charlton and three of the strong Japanese contingent also qualified. Obviously there were plenty of chances and the 8,000 capacity crowd looked forward to the next day's semifinals.

Charlton had one aim and that was to make the final while taking as little out of himself as possible. He was hoping that each swim would help get him back to form for the 1500 metres event and faced a field of five needing only third place to make the final. Buster Crabbe led all the way swimming 4 minutes 52.7 seconds. Noboru Sugimoto was second in 4 minutes 59 seconds and Charlton third in 5 minutes 2.1 seconds. This was a little over two seconds slower than he had done in his heat. Tiger Ryan struck a very strong field with Jean Taris and two Japanese competitors, both of whom who were rated above Sugimoto. Taris set a sizzling pace but could not hold off Yokoyama with Oyokota third. Ryan could do no better than fifth, and though he swam almost two seconds faster than Charlton he missed the final. His had been the fastest heat. At the end of the day the qualifiers were Jean Taris, Buster Crabbe, Charlton and three Japanese swimmers, Oyokota, Yokoyama and Sugimoto.

The Japanese men's team had quickly made its mark. Of the three finals already decided they had finished first, second and fifth in the men's 100 metres freestyle, first, second and third in the 100 metres backstroke and first, second and sixth in the 200 metres breaststroke. Now they had half the field in the 400 metres final. Katsuo Takaishi and Takahiro Saito, who had inspired the new breed to such heights, watched from the stands, their impassive faces screening what must have been extreme satisfaction.

Immediately after the men's semifinals came the heats of the 100 metres women's backstroke, in which Bonnie Mealing made her first appearance, and the final of the 200 metres breaststroke in which Clare Dennis, easily the fastest qualifier, was equal favourite with world record holder Else Jacobsen of Denmark and Japan's Hideko Maehata. Bonnie Mealing, from whom so much had been expected at Amsterdam, was quite nervous but swam well to be second in her heat and qualified for the final. Clare Dennis, the sixteen year old Sydney girl was determined to lead all the way in her final in an effort to demoralise her opposition. Though never able to get far in front of Jacobsen she did lead at every turn. Coming down the fourth and final lap she refused to surrender the lead and as Jacobsen tired slightly, Dennis held off the fast finishing Japanese girl Maehata to win by a tenth of a second with the Danish champion a close third. It was a wonderful win in one of the most fiercely contested races of the meeting and had the crowd cheering wildly all the way. Her time of 1 minute 6.3 seconds was a new Olympic record.

The men's 400 metres semifinals had been held at ten in the morning. The final, to be held at 3 o'clock the following day, was the highlight. At his absolute peak Charlton would certainly have been a genuine chance. After all, he had swum 4 minutes 55 seconds for the 440 yards in Australia, which was three yards longer than 400 metres. But realistically he knew he was not likely to pick up the ten seconds he needed to figure in the finish. Yokoyama had set Olympic records in his heat and the semifinal but it was Jean Taris and Buster Crabbe who dictated tactics in the final. Taris led from the start but Crabbe was never more than two lengths behind him. At 300 metres there was just a body length between them. Halfway down the last lap Crabbe drew level and with a desperate drive won by a touch, much to the delight of the American crowd. His time of 4 minutes 48.4 seconds was one and a half seconds outside Taris's world record. Boy Charlton finished sixth behind the three Japanese swimmers. He had broken 5 minutes but not by much. He made no excuses but knew he faced an uphill battle in the 1500 metres even though that distance was more to his liking. Only time would tell if his plan to swim the 400 metres had been a wise one or not.

The heats of the 1500 metres the next day preceded the final of the 100 metres backstroke, for which Bonnie Mealing had qualified. Was there hope for Charlton and Ryan after the disappointment of the 400 metres? Perhaps. Frenchman Jean Taris was definitely better suited to the shorter event and some suspected Crabbe might be as well even though he had finished third in 1928. Charlton chased American James Cristy throughout his heat but was never going like a winner. Cristy won in just under 20 minutes while Boy struggled to dead heat with Japan's Sunad Ishiharada in 20 minutes 9.5 seconds. Noel Ryan swam well in his heat to finish second. Though his time was a fraction slower than Charlton's he did it with less effort. Both qualified for the next day's semifinals and there were no surprises among the placegetters.

Bonnie Mealing looked far more relaxed before her final than she had done in the heats and was responsible for a magnificent effort. She faced America's world record holder Eleanor Holm, who so far was one of the outstanding performers of the Games, and was determined to stick with her from the outset. Though losing ground soon after the 50 metre turn she attacked all the way down the second lap and at one stage looked likely to overtake her rival. She was unable to do so but finished a gallant second to give Australia their fourth medal of the Games.

The semifinals of the men's 1500 metres coincided with the final of the single sculls. Charlton and Ryan contested the same semifinal, which was won in a very fast time of 19 minutes 38.7 seconds. Ryan battled on courageously to finish third and make the final but Charlton, never able to challenge the leaders, finished eight seconds behind his team-mate in last place. It was the first time in seven Olympic events he had failed to qualify for the final. The reason for Charlton's failure was difficult to fathom. There were many theories. Perhaps his illness was worse than he had admitted. Yet he had said that even before his illness he knew he was not going as well as he should. Some believed he needed a spell and that he had trained too hard after his illness. His wife Jessie wrote, many years later: '. . . because he did not want to tax himself he did not do well.' In his big mate's absence, Tiger Ryan swam a magnificent race in the final of the 1500 metres, his time of 19 minutes 45.1 seconds the fastest ever swum by an Australian. He finished a gallant fourth behind fourteen year old Japanese Kusuo Kitamura, who defeated his team-mate Shozo Makino and American James Cristy.

At a function in Manly for Charlton and Ryan, held on their return from the Games, Charlton underplayed his problems, saying: 'I have no kick coming for being beaten by better men, but when I fell by the wayside, Noel Ryan took my place and there was no one prouder than me at the wonderful race he put up.' Tiger Ryan later told the audience: 'It's all very well for "Charlo" to say he fell down, but only a man with his heart could have done what he did.'

One thing about which there was no doubt was that there was a new order in men's swimming. The young, fit, well-trained Japanese had swept all before them, winning all but one of the six events. The manner of their victory in the 4×200 metres relay summed up just where they stood in relation to the other nations. They took almost forty seconds off the world record and lapped second placegetters, America. The only gold medallist not from Japan was the handsome, suntanned Buster Crabbe, whose spectacular 400 metres victory immediately brought him to the attention of Hollywood's filmmakers. Famous swimmers, male and female, were especially attractive to talent scouts. Duke Kahanamoku, Johnny Weissmuller, along with Eleanor Holm, Helena Madison, Josephine McKim and many more found parts on the silver screen. When Boy Charlton was asked to audition he politely declined. Somehow the green rolling pastures and eucalypts on an outback sheep station held more attraction than a stream in Mexico, paper maché rocks and a Hollywood tree house.

Bobby Pearce, sculler nonpareil, who won his heat easily, was regarded as a near certainty for the final against four rivals and so it proved, Pearce becoming the first Australian to win gold at two successive Olympics. Though his margin was only three quarters of a length he was always in control of the race. Pearce paid his runner-up, America's William Miller, the compliment of rating him as the best sculler he had faced.

The Los Angeles Olympics had been a resounding success. Ninety thousand people attended the closing ceremony and, for the first time, the Games returned a handsome financial profit.

The Australian team's performance was outstanding. Three gold medals, a silver, a bronze and four other finalists was better than anyone could have hoped for from a team of twelve. Jim Eve had managed his charges admirably. Chaperone Mary Chambers had been very strict on the women but the worry of mixed teams had been largely put to rest.

Boy Charlton knew his Olympic days were past him. Not only had the Japanese lifted distance swimming to a new level, but youngsters were taking over. When he won in Paris in 1924, as a sixteen year old, such a feat was a rarity. Now the 1500 metres champion was fourteen and the runner-up seventeen. Holland's runner up in the women's 100 metres was also fourteen and Clare Dennis was an Olympic champion at sixteen. Suddenly swimming was a teenager's sport. It was time for Andrew Murray Charlton to concentrate on a career. Despite his failure in Los Angeles it would be almost thirty years before Murray Rose would top his score of five Olympic medals. Charlton's retirement from Olympic competition coincided with that of his brilliant team-mate Bobby Pearce, who turned professional soon after the Games and remained undefeated until his retirement from sculling in 1948.

10

One More Swim

WHEN BOY'S GRANDFATHER, Andrew Howard Moore, promised to set him up on the land back in 1924, the youngster had no reason to doubt that this would eventuate. After all, he was a man of considerable means, one of the country's most prominent businessmen and had always been very close to Boy and his sisters, particularly after the death of their mother Ada. However, his grandfather's situation dramatically changed in 1926 and with it his immediate priorities. That year Andrew Moore's wife, Rachel, some years older than he, died. The couple had been married since 1873. Within three months, the seventy-five year old married Rose Ethel Welsmen in Katoomba. Few knew that Rose, who was thirty-eight, had borne him a son, known as Howard Moore, ten years earlier. The pair moved from Kilrea to a new home in Mosman with their young son.

Four years later, in January 1930, Andrew Moore died of

natural causes. His large funeral was attended by some family, members of the business community, local politicians and public servants. His will included generous grants to various institutions including Prince Alfred, Camperdown and Crown Street Hospitals, as well as Randwick Home for Infants. He also left a sixth share of his estate to each of his three grandchildren, another sixth to his young son, Stuart Howard, now thirteen, and a third to his older son, Andrew de Horne Moore. The grandchildren each received 6,000 pounds.

When twenty-five year old Andrew returned to Kurrumbede Station after the 1932 Olympics it was the start of his eighth year at the property. The desire to strike out on his own as a farmer was still uppermost in his mind. The sizeable sum left by his grandfather would be a big help but was not enough on its own to buy a good sized property. Then came a phone call from his boyhood surfing mate, John Davies, who had just set up Canberra's first pharmacy at Kingston. When offered a chance to work with him in the pharmacy, Boy saw it as a possible step towards becoming independent.

Murray Charlton always believed that his father invested money in the pharmacy but Boy's godson, Andrew Davies, John Davies' nephew, and his mother Eleanor did not. Certainly he would have been in a position to do so. In any case, Boy decided to join his long-time surfing friend. He knew nothing at all about pharmacy but trusted his mate and reasoned that if the enterprise went well he should be able to accumulate some money to add to the deposit on a property of his own.

Now the proud owner of a small car, Boy set off from Kurrumbede, with the best wishes of Malcolm Mackellar, headed for the national capital and a new career. His long car trip provided nothing of the drama, nor embarrassment, of that which originally took him to Kurrumbede and he arrived safely in Canberra to help set up the practice. He and John Davies, who Charlton referred to as Jack, shared accommodation behind the pharmacy.

Determined to do all he could to settle in to his new surroundings and make his new venture a success, he joined the Canberra Swimming Club, for which he swam and played water polo, and was made club captain. He also joined the Royal Canberra Golf Club, where he took lessons from the well-known professional, Jim Patterson, and played tennis regularly. The excellent baths at Manuka, together with his new lifestyle and regular working hours, saw his interest in swimming regain momentum. The pool was not heated so swimming was out of the question in the cold winter months but it was an excellent facility. The icy waters of the Molonglo River were no more inviting. As the warmer weather arrived he became a constant visitor to the pool. The Hawkesbury Agricultural College *Journal* reported he had settled down well and was enjoying his new lifestyle.

If the move to Canberra was a good one for Charlton, so it was for John Davies. The chemist shop traded very well immediately. The modest big fellow who served in the pharmacy was very popular with customers, as John had predicted, and business soon boomed. Much to Boy's embarrassment his friend even put a sign in the window inviting sports fans to come in and shake hands with the champion and stating that young ladies who bought their cosmetics at the store qualified for a kiss from Australia's most famous swimmer and eligible bachelor.

Boy Charlton had been given honorary membership to the Manly Surf Club and drove to Sydney on weekends during the swimming season where he stayed at the Davies' family home in Osborne Street. He also spent Christmas holidays at Manly and would ring Frank Davies, now club captain, to say when he was arriving, telling him 'enter me in everything' at the next carnival. The *Manly Daily* always found Charlton's arrival in The Village newsworthy. An article regarding his attendance at the Punchinello Revue at the Manly Amusement Pier, which appeared under the headline 'All Girls Love Apple', was typical.

When Boy surfed he represented the Manly Club, in the pool he swam for Canberra. The Manly Surf Club continued to provide as much enjoyment as ever. In November their enthusiastic committee organised an impromptu carnival featuring the three Manly clubs, South Steyne, North Steyne and Queenscliff, for the visiting American tennis team led by their then United States and Wimbledon singles champion, Ellsworth Vines. The Americans, dressed in blazers and cream slacks, sat in deck-chairs enjoying a series of events, including surfboat races, the likes of which they had never seen before.

The ever innovative committee were disappointed when a proposal to feature a parade of attractive young ladies in pyjamas during their major, annual carnival in January of 1933 was rejected by surfing authorities. The rejection prompted an amusing verse published in *The Bulletin* which began:

> *There'll be stunts by the score to applaud and encore*
> *With the usual éclat and emotion*
> *As the lifesavers urge their craft through the surge*
> *For feats on the edge of the ocean.*
> *There'll be carnival high to enrapture the eye*
> *With glowing and rich panoramas*
> *But a ban has been laid on a beauty parade*
> *Of girls in alluring pyjamas.*

There was no impediment to a Saturday night farewell dinner at the Steyne Hotel for three Manly Surf Club members, Bob Louden, Geoff Bland and Aub Hodson, who were due to sail on the *Ulysses* with the Wallabies on their first ever tour of South Africa.

Though harbouring no desire to again chase international stardom, Boy decided, prior to the summer of 1934/35, to contest the state titles in the pool and the surf, once more. Considerable interest had been generated by his arrival in Canberra. That now grew when he spoke to Cinesound at Manuka Baths in early December 1934: 'I'm happy to be here in Canberra with my old friend John Davies and also to have the advantage of the Canberra Swimming Pool. I intend to do training here and try and reproduce some of my old form and then go on to Sydney under the guidance of my old coach Harry Hay.'

Swimming authorities had invited several international stars to Australia, including the French distance champion Jean Taris, and they were naturally anxious to have Charlton compete along with Tiger Ryan. With the addition of young Sam Herford, Manly's latest distance find, the races were certain to provide plenty of excitement. Noel Ryan had continued on his winning way in Charlton's absence, annexing the state 440 and 880 yards titles in 1933 and 1934, the national 440 and 880 yards and mile titles in 1933, and the distance double for the second time at the Empire Games in London in 1934. For Charlton it would be a chance to show his Los Angeles form was an aberration. His 880 yards time of 10 minutes 22 seconds, recorded three years earlier, was still the fastest 880 swim in Australia. Whether he could repeat that was questionable, but, in racing parlance, he was a great first-up performer.

Following his tenth-of-a-second defeat by Buster Crabbe in Los Angeles, twenty-five year old Jean Taris, France's greatest ever swimmer, had been as dominant in Europe as Tiger Ryan had been in Australia. Though his best distance was 400 metres, he had broken world records, from 300 to 1000 metres, claimed more than thirty national titles and had won the European titles at 400 and 1500 metres in 1934 by comfortable margins. Taris had agreed to swim in carnivals in Melbourne before coming to Sydney so he would be well prepared by the time he got to the Domain Baths.

Charlton had kept reasonably fit and trim over the winter months with golf and tennis and began conditioning work at the Canberra pool as soon as the weather allowed. When Harry Hay visited in late November to implement a coaching regime, he returned with positive reports about his former charge saying he expected Charlton to return to something like his 1924 and 1928 form. A few weeks later news filtered through that Charlton was rapidly improving, swimming with a modified stroke that lessened his body roll and round-arm action and also incorporated a continual six-beat kick. Throughout his career Charlton had derived very little benefit from his leg action. Even the scissor kick that Tommy Adrian had introduced when Charlton was a youngster was mainly for balance and stability. He had covered 400 yards in 4 minutes 55 seconds, breaking Sam Herford's record in Canberra, and 440 yards in 5 minutes 20 seconds at Narrandera early in December. Manly swim fans were delighted to read that he had accepted an invitation to appear at their gala carnival on December 29, 1934, and would swim in whatever event was put on for him. Tiger Ryan was sure to be there and was swimming every day after his duties at the bank despite Sydney's worst December weather for many years. When the Duke of Gloucester attended a special surf carnival, held in his honour at Manly in late November, Ryan won the open surf race as he usually did.

The Manly Club decided on a 550 yards handicap event for Charlton's comeback. He received a tremendous ovation as he stepped onto the boards. Spectators got their first look at his new action during the first half of the race but then he went back to his usual round-arm style. He finished fourth in very good time and appeared to recover quickly from the exertion. Tiger Ryan swam 440 yards in better time in his handicap event, and fans had seen enough to whet their appetites.

Charlton returned to Canberra the following day and then came back to Sydney a fortnight later to swim in a 440 yards handicap at the Domain Baths, in which he was asked to give starts ranging from just one second to Sam Herford, fourteen seconds to his former Olympic team-mate Moss Christie and twenty-eight seconds to Frank Griffiths. The race proved to be a very exciting one with Charlton, swimming with his modified stroke, still last as they turned for the fourth and final lap. He quickly overtook Herford, then passed the others in turn. With 25 yards to go he challenged Moss Christie for the lead. Christie fought back and it was not until ten yards from the finish that Charlton took a narrow lead to win by a yard. His time of 5 minutes 11 seconds would need to come down by about ten seconds to worry Taris or Ryan, but he was improving all the time. After the swim he told reporters he was happy with the way he had swum, particularly as it was the first time he had really tested his new stroke. Again he hurried back to Canberra.

When Charlton returned the following weekend he would stay with the Davies family for the next six weeks until his clashes with Taris and Ryan were over. Meanwhile, Jean Taris announced he was not going to swim in the 880 yards, an event he had won narrowly from Sam Herford in the main Melbourne carnival. He was determined to concentrate on the 440 yards, the race he hoped to win in the 1936 Olympics. Charlton was very disappointed, some said even a little angry, as he had put a lot into training after being assured Taris would be a starter. When Taris realised this he sportingly reversed his decision. So the trio would clash twice. Charlton and Ryan kept up their training in handicap races at Manly. Both turned in good 880 yards swims with Charlton swimming faster times but Ryan seemingly achieving his with less effort.

The state championships were run more than a month later than usual so as not to clash with the Melbourne carnivals. A typically large crowd attended the Domain Baths on a perfect Saturday afternoon in late February 1935 to see the battle for the 440 yards title. Evident among the throng was a large French contingent, which had come to see their favourite son, accompanied by their national diving champion, Emile Poussard. The scene was very much like that eleven years earlier when the unproven youngster Charlton clashed with the great Swede, Arne Borg. The Governor and Premier arrived early, along with junior ministers, to attend the programme. The Domain was obviously the place to be. The first highlight was the springboard diving contest featuring the French champion, Poussard, and the state's three leading divers. To the delight of the French contingent, their man won a keenly contested diving title from Harry Tickle and Arthur O'Connor.

The carnival coincided with a falling tide that created shallow water at the northern end of the bath, so a pontoon was placed in position, which meant the 440 yards would be swum over six laps of 73⅓ yards. As the pontoon was being positioned both Taris and Ryan had a dip. All swimmers received a rousing ovation as they were introduced and Charlton, in particular, took the boards to a tremendous reception. In a field of six Charlton had drawn lane 2, Herford 3, Ryan 5 and Taris 6. Ryan and Taris would have a good look at each other but Charlton would have more difficulty planning his race. Percy Russell got the field off to an excellent start and the crowd began cheering immediately. Taris's flotation and strong leg drive were evident as he led Ryan clearly at the first turn with the rest of the swimmers tightly bunched. Down the second lap they came with fans watching to see if any challenge was forthcoming. Approaching the second turn Taris held the lead and Charlton dropped back to fourth behind Herford. It was clear that Taris's intention was to break up the field and he led by two yards at the halfway point from Ryan, with Charlton challenging Herford, but well behind the two leaders.

At the next turn Taris still led but Ryan was determined to stay with him. His nickname of Tiger had been hard earned and he clung to the Frenchman like a leech. At the final turn there was nothing between them and the crowd roared as Ryan surged to take the lead soon after. Charlton was a further ten yards away but finishing strongly. Ryan had surprised Taris with his burst soon after entering the last lap but he now had to keep his advantage for sixty yards.

With the large crowd all on their feet Ryan battled to hold off this rival. Despite a surge by Taris in the last few strokes Ryan held on to win by less than half a yard. Charlton was ten yards away in third place. The race had been a thrilling one. It was a rare defeat for Taris and a magnificent win for Ryan, one of the finest of his career, in the time of 5 minutes 1 second. How did Charlton's swim rate? Experts were divided in their opinions. Certainly he finished well but it seemed unlikely he would turn the tables, despite his liking for the 880 yards course.

Another huge crowd arrived to see the 880 yards title decided the following Tuesday on a warm, still night. Once again, because of the low tide, the pontoon was positioned so the swimmers would negotiate twelve laps of 73⅓ yards. Following his epic win on Saturday afternoon, Tiger Ryan was a warm favourite. Taris seemed less suited than at 440 yards, particularly as he had trained especially for that distance. Charlton was the unknown quantity. In his comebacks of 1927 and 1931 he had been explosive, taking all before him. While he might have misjudged his race in the 440 yards, his time was fifteen seconds from his best. Even his most ardent admirers were more hopeful than confident. On the positive side they knew this was his best distance and he looked as fit as he ever had.

Emile Poussard again got French supporters off to a good start by winning the diving contest. When the finalists were called to the boards for the main race Charlton was in 1, Taris was next to him, young Manly newcomer Jack Drinkwater was in 3, Ryan in 4 and another Manly youngster, Bill Furey, in lane 5. On the starter's call all hit the water together and it was a half lap before Taris took a very narrow lead from Ryan with Charlton close behind. At the first turn there was only a yard separating the trio and halfway down the second lap there was little change. It was obvious Charlton was determined to stay handy to the leaders. Ryan slowly bridged the gap on Taris and the pair were level after 220 yards. There was a roar from the crowd when Charlton drew alongside them going down the fourth lap. His move made for an exciting race. At the 440 yards mark Charlton and Ryan were level with Taris having dropped two yards back, but the French-man's form was still holding well. For the next two laps Ryan and Charlton battled for the lead as Taris dropped away slightly.

In the eighth lap, first Ryan and then Charlton appeared to lead momentarily only to see the other come storming back. During the ninth lap Taris rallied to almost join the two Australians, but it was not for long as the pressure increased. It was in this lap that Charlton gained a lead of almost a body length. As the bell rang to signal two laps to go, the noise of the vast crowd was almost deafening. All the way down lap eleven Charlton held his lead but Ryan was fighting strongly as he always did. As they turned for the last time Ryan was within an arm's length but Charlton again pulled away to lead by a yard with 50 yards to swim. Ryan's challenge was not done yet. Slowly he pegged back the big man until both drove for the wall with Charlton winning by less than half a second. The race had been one of his greatest and fans threw hats and programmes into the air, then stood for minutes roaring their approval for the pair and the gallant Frenchman Taris who had finished third, ten seconds behind them. Though Boy had swum twenty seconds outside his best time, recorded in 1927, it was, all things considered, one of his greatest efforts.

Three weeks later the country's best surfers assembled for the national junior and senior championships at Bondi. No fewer than twenty-four clubs from Sydney, New South Wales Country, Queensland and Western Australia competed. Charlton was to swim in the open surf race and the four-man team's race in which he represented Manly. What better way could there be to finish his career than with a national surfing title.

A crowd of 10,000 turned out on a very warm March day to watch the championships. Conditions were ideal with good waves rolling in and the 200 yards swim to the buoys was a true test for the very best surfers. Tiger Ryan was Australia's outstanding surf swimmer but Charlton was no slouch and in a particularly strong field a bit of luck and an opportune wave could make all the difference on the way into the beach. Both won their heats in impressive style.

In the final Charlton, as usual, gave the nippier runners quite a few yards start early but took the lead by the time the field was halfway to the buoys. This is how *The Referee*'s surfing reporter saw the second half of the race:

Charlton had a lead approaching the buoys. Ryan, at this stage, was in the bunch, having been blocked out. Then out of the blue arose a bare-headed swimmer, who was actually disputing the lead with the big Manly man.

The thrash along the width of the buoys gave the onlookers a better view of the race, and much speculation was rife as to who the stranger could be. On the home stretch he was still there, and Ryan was now making a bold bid. Charlton appeared to be caught in a slight northerly sweep and drifted away from the field.

Ryan came through to the front about twenty yards from shore, with a lead of about three yards to the bare-headed swimmer. Starting to wade, Ryan appeared to have the race won and Charlton was still battling in deep channel.

The unknown was handy when a small wave loomed up and Ryan decided to retreat to get it. Meanwhile his closest opponent had caught it and by the greatest mischance Ryan did not get much assistance from it and a slight snowy-thatched youth ran up the beach a winner by about ten yards.

The winner turned out to be a former Manly swimmer, Wally Scott, now a member of the north coast club, Blackhead. Charlton had to settle for third place. In an amusing sequel to the race, Scott was asked why he had not given his mother a kiss after the race as another north coast swimmer, Ritchie Walker, had done when he won the senior belt race. Wally Scott replied: 'I was so tired, I couldn't have kissed Joan Crawford!' Wally Scott had been at Manly until the start of the season when he went to live in Taree.

Later in the day Charlton and Ryan combined to help win the team's race as they had done in the summer of 1931/32. Charlton had his moment of triumph by winning the race with Ryan second and the other two Manly men, Eric Clift and Phil Smith, third and fourth, thereby gaining the best possible score of ten points. After the carnival Boy was adamant there would be no turning back, this time, on his decision to retire from competitive swimming. A fourth Olympics, in Berlin the following year, was out of the question. He would, however, consider a proposed overseas tour with a twenty-six man surfing team if the tour went ahead and if he was selected. This did not eventuate.

Charlton's decision to forget about the 1936 Olympics was a sound one. The highly politicised Berlin Games would not have suited him at all. In stark contrast to their wonderful efforts in Los Angeles, Australia's team to Berlin, though much larger in number, were to win just one bronze medal, in the triple jump. Tiger Ryan did not go and only one of the five swimmers made a final. The era of the talented amateur who regarded sport as a pastime and could still win at international level had gone. Some enthusiasts believed the modern Olympics had lost their way and no longer served the purpose for which they were resumed. One thing was very clear. If Australia was to compete at top level a whole new attitude to sport was needed. It was an attitude that Boy Charlton would never have adopted.

Whether the thought of a kiss from an Olympic champion had any bearing on her shopping habits is highly speculative, but one very attractive young lady did come to buy cosmetics at John Davies Kingston pharmacy. Her name was Jessie Hyles, elder daughter of a well-to-do and highly respected country family, who owned a large property called Uriarra, 20 kilometres west of Canberra. A friendship quickly developed. Jessie's social life was a busy one and Andrew was slowly introduced to a large number of her friends. She was a keen golfer and tennis player who always attended the round of balls and functions associated with rural life and Andrew Charlton became her constant companion. It was ironic that Jessie Hyles, who had seen the endless struggles farmers had to endure to make a living on the land and who had told her friends she would never marry a farmer, had found a city man who was determined to become just that. After a two-year courtship the pair announced their engagement and Andrew left the pharmacy to commence a life on the land. His decision to join John Davies had proved a sound one but here, at last, was a chance to become a sheep farmer.

Andrew invested in a property, putting up a third share of the money. Jessie's father, Ernie, paid a third for Jessie and a third for her brother, Jack. The 12,000-acre farm was part of a larger property on the Braidwood to Goulburn Road and needed a name. Andrew decided to call it Kilrea, after his grandfather's house in Manly, next door to where he had grown up. He and Jessie were destined to spend most of their life together at Kilrea. They were married at St Mark's Church of England, Darling Point, Sydney, on March 20, 1937. Andrew's uncles, Archdeacon W.A. Charlton and Reverend Les Charlton, officiated at the service.

Andrew proved to be an extremely diligent farmer, which was just as well because the land was poor and absolutely infested with rabbits. His first task was to drastically reduce the rabbit population – an Australia-wide menace – before he could even contemplate the need for more stock. In each of the first two years at Kilrea, with the assistance of paid teams, he dealt with a million rabbits and actually sold off 2,000 acres of the worst rabbit country. Success as a sportsman had come from huge natural ability. He had to be encouraged, even cajoled into training, but this was different. He worked from dawn until dusk, and often later, on the property on which he ran some cattle but mostly Merino sheep.

Ernie Hyles was one of the largest sheep dealers in the state who often gambled by buying large numbers of stock then trusting it would rain and the price of sheep would rise. When it didn't Andrew could expect a call informing him he would have an extra three thousand wethers to look after until it rained, as Ernie's other properties, strategically scattered around the country, were stocked to capacity. This would infuriate Andrew who always stocked Kilrea conservatively because of the possibility of drought. Ernie Hyles' gambling nature and Andrew's conservatism could not have been more different. Despite these differences the pair became firm friends and had genuine respect for each other.

As Boy Charlton battled with the elements, his American peers, Duke Kahanamoku, Johnny Weissmuller and Buster Crabbe, were making their living from their fame as swimmers. The Duke, idolised in Hawaii as Charlton was in Australia, served as sheriff of Honolulu for thirty years but found time to play bit parts in over thirty films. Weissmuller modelled swimwear, played the lead in a dozen Tarzan movies and also starred as Jungle Jim. Buster Crabbe followed Weissmuller into the film industry and he too enjoyed a lucrative career, succeeding Weissmuller as Tarzan before starring in cinema serials as Buck Rogers and Flash Gordon. Unknown to Charlton, Weissmuller lived his life after swimming always fearful that his Olympic medals would be stripped from him. He had, in fact, been born in Austria and his grandmother had swapped details on his birth certificate with his younger brother who was born after his family came to America. Johnny Weissmuller lived in fear of shame. Boy Charlton's fears were to do with drought and falling wool prices.

Andrew and Jessie had two children, Patricia Helen, born in October 1940 and Murray Andrew born in August 1943. In between Andrew served in the 7th Regiment Bungendore Light Horse, a reservist unit, going into camp at Wallgrove. He quickly gained promotions to lance corporal, sergeant and eventually lieutenant (probationary) before being discharged in 1943, by which time the likelihood of a Japanese invasion of Australia had passed. He enjoyed army life, being in the company of many country people and good horsemen. He had the satisfaction of doing his duty, even though the irony of possibly fighting for his life against erstwhile opponents in the pool was not lost on him. While Andrew served with the Light Horse in Australia his older sibling Enid, a nursing sister who never married, served overseas with the Australian troops in Egypt. Ada had married an Adelaide businessman with farming interests and Andrew only occasionally saw her.

The battle with his father-in-law's risk taking continued. In 1950 a neighbouring property came up for sale. It had much better soil than Kilrea and Ernie Hyles was determined Andrew should buy it if the price was reasonable. Andrew attended the auction with his father-in-law but was outbid. Obviously disappointed, he told Ernie he could not afford to pay any more, only to be told, 'Yes you can, because the final bid was mine, made on your behalf!' Andrew had no choice but to borrow the money to buy it. It was a purchase that was the making of Kilrea. Work was still tough and Andrew still lived in fear of drought or a drop in wool prices, but the farm was now a much better property.

The family swam in the Shoalhaven River and took surfing holidays at Manly, renting a flat and spending much time with Frank Davies and his wife Elanora, who had also been married in 1937. Andrew Boy Charlton was godfather to their son who was named after him. The men had plenty in common as Frank was a wool broker as well as a keen surfer. Ironically an accident in the Shoalhaven, in which young Murray almost drowned, made him terrified of water. His dad could not teach him to swim but he was eventually bribed, with the promise of a bike, and overcame his fear of water at Manly where he was taught to swim by a swimming instructor. Andrew later taught him to surf.

Andrew and Jessie sent their children to boarding schools in Sydney. Patricia went to Abbotsleigh, where she became a champion swimmer, but was later discouraged by her father from taking up the sport seriously because he thought there were more important things to do and was concerned too much swimming was inclined to make girls too big in the shoulders. Andrew was among a large percentage of the male population that still held the strong conviction that constant, strenuous exercise was not meant for young women. Murray went to Shore where he was a champion rower and a representative footballer.

Andrew kept track of his surfing mates and spent time with them when he holidayed in Manly. Among them was the remarkable Noel Ryan who had continued to swim competitively in the surf and the pool, winning his last New South Wales mile title in 1946 and competing in open surf races at carnivals featuring the state's top surfers well into the 1950s. Each afternoon Charlton spent an hour or two having a few beers with his friends, not at the surf club, but at a favourite rendezvous on The Corso. Though not a heavy drinker, and never one to use hard liquor, he was, however, like so many at that time, a heavy smoker.

In 1956 the Charltons bought a cottage at Rosedale, on the South Coast, some two hours' drive from Kilrea. It became their regular holiday destination, and remained Andrew's favourite spot for the rest of his life. At Rosedale he fished, surfed and walked or lazed on the beach, just watching the surf roll in. Here he taught Murray to ride the waves. Patricia left Kilrea soon after finishing school and married into a farming family at Guyra, north of Armidale.

When Australia staged their first Olympics in Melbourne later that year, Boy Charlton was invited to attend the swimming as a special guest of the Australian Swimming Union. The Games clashed with the shearing season and he declined even though he had competent staff to cover his absence. However, Jessie insisted and eventually he relented and had a wonderful time, meeting up with a host of former Olympians, including

Duke Kahanamoku, and many other sporting celebrities. His modesty and shyness was still very much a part of him and he passed up a chance to be photographed with Murray Rose, who became Australia's second 1500 metres winner, the first since Charlton in Paris thirty-two years earlier, saying it was Rose's moment not his. Sam Herford, a Charlton rival in the 1930s and close friend coached Murray Rose.

Though shunning the limelight he came to Sydney and swum at the Domain Baths with John Konrads, Australia's newest distance sensation, in 1959. Charlton had been invited as a guest of the Union of Old Swimmers, as had Konrads, who had never swum at the Domain. A 'race' of two laps between the pair was arranged and watched by one hundred veteran swimmers. An announcement that, as the pair were amateurs, there was to be no betting on the event drew a hearty laugh from the crowd. They swam stroke for stroke for two laps, Charlton employing his rolling style while Konrads travelled smoothly beside him. A roar went up as Charlton sprinted to 'win' the race by a touch, inflicting Konrads' first 'defeat' of the season. Next year Boy travelled to Townsville to see Australia's distance champions Rose and Konrads prepare for the 400 and 1500 metres events in the 1960 Rome Olympics. With no heated pools available in Sydney the warm water of Northern Queensland was a delightful, if distant, alternative for the Olympic swim team.

The following year he and Jessie holidayed in Tokyo and Charlton was embarrassed at the fuss made over him. His 1927 swims against Katsuo Takaishi were part of swimming folklore in Japan. Mr Takaishi had become a very wealthy businessman, sitting on the boards of several companies, and President of the Japanese Swimming Federation. He also afforded Ernie Henry wonderful hospitality in 1964 when he visited to coincide with Japan's first Olympics. Charlton was invited to return to Japan to coach but his heart was still in Kilrea and he declined.

When Murray finished his schooling he was set to follow his father's footsteps and attend an agricultural college. Everything was set for him to go to college in Wagga Wagga, but he made his own decision to go jackerooing instead to South Australia. When he returned home in 1963, after two years of extremely hard work in the toughest of conditions, he had ideas on how to revitalise Kilrea. He had seen how poor land had been turned into high producing sheep and cattle country. His father had improved the 40-acre horse paddock and another 200 acres for the ewes to lamb but the balance was untouched. Murray's plans involved borrowing a large sum of money over a ten to twelve year period so that the land could be improved to carry four times the stock. But Andrew, who had lived through the Great Depression, was still worried by debt and terrified of bankruptcy. Eventually Murray's persistence won out and together they went to see the bank manager who Murray recalls was as conservative as his father. As it happened the government was encouraging farmers to improve their land, lending money on very attractive terms. They qualified for a loan and so Andrew agreed to borrow money to spend on 8,000 acres. The pasture-improved land was soon running one and a half sheep to the acre as opposed to a half. Even so Murray's ideas invariably ran into trouble due to Andrew's extreme conservatism.

Murray found a true supporter in Jessie who was as positive as Andrew was negative. So father and son, despite their differences, battled on, each as determined as the other to ensure that Kilrea would be a success. Occasionally, on the very toughest day, the older man reflected on his decision not to become a professional swimmer or even a 'film star'. Not that Murray believed his father really regretted this. It was merely a comment on how tough farming was with little rain and poor soil.

The Hawkesbury Agricultural College *Journal* reported in 1966:

In one of the south-east's unseasonably drier pockets much of a grazier's sown pastures are holding up well in the light early winter falls. He is Mr A.M. Charlton, famous from an early age to pre-war generations as 'Boy' Charlton, courageous young Olympic swimmer and national record breaker.

The chief of Kilrea Pastoral Company, he works 8,000 acre Kilrea with the help of his son Murray and staff. The programme, broadly, is to raise Merino numbers progressively both for wool cutters and breeders and cattle count in times of normal rainfall, on light decomposed granite soils. Still suffering the driest 18 months on record, the property has been 30 years under its present ownership.

In 1967 the Sydney City Council determined that the Domain Baths, refurbished at a cost of over half a million dollars, would be named after Andrew 'Boy' Charlton. The following year he came to Sydney for the official opening and swam the first lap of the new pool. It was the first time Murray had seen him swim other than in the surf. He recalls his reaction: 'Dad was a sick man, suffering from emphysema and was sixty years old. He hadn't been in a pool for years. It was the first time I'd ever seen him swim properly. Even then at that age you could see his flotation and style. He looked great.'

Although they took regular Christmas holidays at Jessie's insistence, little else could convince Andrew to leave the farm, even for short periods. The funeral of Manly team-mate Tiger Ryan, who died suddenly from a heart attack after a swim at Manly Baths, was one such occasion.

Andrew and son his Murray worked Kilrea until Jessie convinced Andrew to retire from the land in 1972. By this time the whole of Kilrea had been improved and the purchase of three other properties had seen stock numbers rise from 7,000 to 30,000. Andrew Charlton's dream of being a successful grazier had long since become a reality. He and Jessie returned to

Sydney to live in Avalon on Sydney's northern beaches. That same year he was inducted into America's swimming Hall of Fame in Fort Lauderdale, Florida. Charlton, who smoked heavily all his life, was now suffering badly from emphysema. In August of 1975 he presented his medals and trophies to the Sydney Town Hall and they were eventually displayed at the Olympic swim centre at Homebush. He was one of nine heroes of the pool initially inducted into Australia's swimming Hall of Fame along with early Olympic champions Freddy Lane, Fanny Durack and Dick Eve.

Strangely Charlton had finished his extraordinary swimming career with two national surf titles but none in the pool. The reason was simple: he never competed in a national carnival. During Olympic years, national titles gave way to selection trials and state championships, which he invariably won. He claimed thirteen state titles from fourteen attempts, at distances from 220 yards to a mile, in his unique, frequently interrupted career, between 1923 and 1935.

Andrew Charlton rarely spoke of his swimming career at home, once saying that if he had his time over again he might not swim competitively at all, but simply enjoy the surf. However, he kept in touch with his greatest rival, Arne Borg. They exchanged letters and an occasional photograph.

Boy Charlton died of a sudden heart attack in December 1975, aged sixty-eight, and was cremated at the Northern Suburbs Crematorium. Unlike many surf club members, including his coach Harry Hay whose ashes were scattered in the surf at Manly where he had spent so many happy hours, Andrew Boy Charlton's ashes were scattered, at his own request, on the property at Kilrea. Sam Herford told the Sydney press that with modern training methods no one could have touched him: 'No other male swimmer ever captured the imagination like Boy Charlton. The public loved him. He wouldn't train, he didn't like it. He went through the water so easily he was like a torpedo.'

There are many Boy Charlton anecdotes. Jamie Jenkins still recalls being run over by Charlton when he shifted course in the old Manly pool: 'I was about twelve and Boy was training for the Olympics in Los Angeles. He came right over the top of me and I went straight to the bottom. He was a huge man and I spluttered to the surface a bit annoyed, but when I realised who it was I didn't really mind so much. Not everybody could say they'd been sunk by Boy Charlton.'

Stuart Alldritt, a man who has been involved in swimming all his life, remembers walking, as a boy, on the sand at Fairy Bower, when his father pointed out a big suntanned fellow buying a biscuit from a bare-footed woman. The vendor was a very well-known, eccentric, local identity called 'Sweet Nell', who for many years walked the length of Manly beach, looking for all the world like a gypsy, her skin almost blackened by the sun, selling Brandy snaps from a barrow for a penny. 'See that fellow buying the biscuit from Sweet Nell,' said his father, with great reverence, 'that's Boy Charlton.'

Max Riddington, a national champion in the surf, as his father had been and his son would be, has a similar story: 'I was a junior at the time and decided to start in the open surf race. It was a big carnival at Manly, all the top surfers were there, and I was pretty nervous. The balcony on the old club was packed and I was about to get ready to go down for the race when I saw Dad talking to this gentleman right down the end of the balcony. I swung my towel around my neck, ready to go down to the start, and then I saw Dad signal me to come over to him, which I did of course. He said, "I'd like you to meet . . . Andrew Boy Charlton." I was so pumped up I swam one of my best races ever. Some years later I sat next to Boy Charlton at Noel Ryan's funeral, which was very special because Dad had been a really close friend of Andrew and I'd modelled my surfing on Tiger Ryan.'

Ken Knight, four years Charlton's junior, who swam on the same programme as Charlton and Borg in 1924, recalls him arriving one day at the Domain Baths, unexpectedly and without swimming gear: 'He had just come down from the bush and asked if anyone could lend him a towel or a costume. People almost knocked each other over to get him one,' said Knight. 'As it happened I was nearest and so he used mine and I was very excited. He was so popular it was hard to believe.'

Murray Rose, the next of the great Australian distance swimmers and winner of three gold medals at the 1956 and 1960 Olympics, recalls his only meeting with Charlton, which occurred purely by chance, at Manly Beach in the early 1960s:

'I was body surfing and there were some good waves on, which doesn't always happen at Manly. I was out there with a few others and I cracked this wave, a pretty good one, and rode it in all the way to the beach. Then I realised there was one other swimmer who had also ridden it all the way in. We stood up, simultaneously, in the shallow water and looked at each other. He said, "I know you, you're Murray Rose," and I said, "That's right and you're Boy Charlton." I had never met him but had seen lots of photos of him and obviously he was a part of the legacy that I grew up with. So we exchanged a few pleasantries and then he said, "Look the waves are too good, let's get back out there." That was our only meeting.'

Owen Griffiths, who swam in the epic 440 and 880 yards races featuring Charlton and Borg in 1924, was still winning veterans' races when he was in his late sixties. After breaking the world's one-mile record for swimmers over sixty-five he was asked, by *Daily Telegraph* reporter Rod Humphries, had he ever beaten Boy Charlton: 'Oh yes,' he said, 'the first time I raced him and the last. The first was a schoolboy scratch race at the Domain. I was sixteen and he was thirteen. That was the first time he got his picture in the paper. The second time was in 1932 when he was having his last appearance before going to the Olympics in Los Angeles. I beat him in a belt race at North Narrabeen. He was always a good sport. I'll never forget it. I felt a bit embarrassed when I beat him by about ten yards but he came out of the water and sang out, "Good boy, Owie."'

Sir Nicholas Shehadie, famous rugby international and former Lord Mayor of Sydney, recalls meeting Charlton when the latter arrived at Wallgrove to serve with the Light Horse. It was Nick's first job, as a camera assistant with Fox Movietone, and he was part of a crew sent to film an interview with the new recruit: 'It was pretty exciting meeting Boy Charlton in your first week's work,' he says. 'I thought I'd like the job but unfortunately the boss asked me to wash his car the next week on a wet and miserable day so I left and got a job in a biscuit factory. Still I got to meet Boy Charlton.'

Murray continued to work the farm for some years, eventually selling Kilrea and moving to Queensland. He set his mother up in a house in Manly where she lived on into her nineties, always spritely and positive. A fitness fanatic, she refused to take the bus anywhere she could walk and also spent countless hours playing bridge, her favourite pastime. She remained firm friends with Eleanor Davies, another spritely ninety year old, until she moved north with her son Murray. In 1997 Jessie attended the dedication of the new Manly Swimming Centre to her late husband. Mrs Jean Hay, Mayor of Manly, who prompted the naming of the pool, was mindful of the fact that it would have been Boy's ninetieth birthday and that his memory 'could continue to be an inspiration to the young people of the district'. Jessie spent the last two years of her life in a nursing home in Noosa, cared for by her son Murray and his wife Margie.

Andrew Murray Charlton's name does not appear in a list of national champions but it is remembered in the Andrew Boy Charlton Pool at the Domain, which was again refurbished, at a cost of several million dollars, in 2002, in the swim centre at Manly, in the Charlton Bar at the Manly Pacific Hotel as well as Charlton College, Hawkesbury, now part of the Western Sydney University Campus, and at Sportsman's Park in Goulburn. His name also appears in the Path of Legends at the Olympic Pool in Homebush and on the Esplanade at Manly.

Charlton won only one Olympic gold medal. At the conclusion of the 1976 Olympic Games, held less than a year after his death, almost forty individual Australian athletes, the majority of them swimmers, could make the same claim. Some won two golds, a handful won three. He did not die uncrowned champion of the world at twenty-one like the boxer Les Darcy, nor did he die at the peak of his career like Phar Lap. Despite his enormous natural ability he did not stand so far above all comers, before or after him, as Don Bradman, nor the famous billiards player Walter Lindrum. Yet for reasons that are not easy to explain he achieved popularity and status enjoyed only by those regarded as sporting immortals. He was unique. A most reluctant, modest hero in an age where conditions, ethics, and ideals are now difficult, if not impossible, to understand. He offered no excuses for his rare defeats and shunned the glory that came with his many victories. Despite his casual attitude towards training and a reluctance to regard swimming as other than enjoyment, Boy Charlton was a great competitor, a champion by any standards. He was a players' player. The most important breed of player of them all.

BOY CHARLTON

With barrel chest and fine physique
Raw talent that was quite unique
A quiet, handsome, suntanned youth
Who uttered not one phrase uncouth
Whose shyness showed in every word
Made former records look absurd.

In tidal pools with no lanes marked
On megaphone the starter barked,
He swam such times the doubters cried
'He must be swimming with the tide
Torpedos move with lesser speed!'
But suddenly the world paid heed.

For in those famous Paris Games
He matched it with the greatest names
As cruising through that distance swim
He made the others look so grim
Then pulled away with mighty stroke
Three records in that race he broke.

Defeat in metric's quarter mile
Could not reduce the Charlton smile
Weissmuller beat him by a yard
And Tarzan never swam so hard,
They never ever met again
Weissmuller kept to sprinting men.

By now a hero oh so young
Across the world his praises rung
But as his reputation came
He turned his back on fickle fame
Then headed bush to rope and ride
And swim at night on river's tide.

He saw the big names come and go
But inner talents always glow
Each time he came to Sydney town
He beat them to that swimming crown,
For ten long years he held them all
Three times he heard the nation's call.

Come swim with me the water's clear
And later on we'll share a beer
Fear not defeat, fear not disgrace
The fun is there for all who race,
To win or lose is both a joy
The name is Andrew – call me Boy.

Acknowledgements

ONE OF THE JOYS OF WRITING about a much-loved character are the people who come forward to help. First I'd like to thank Andrew Charlton's son, Murray, and his charming wife, Margie, for their hospitality and assistance. Murray openly discussed his life growing up with his erstwhile famous father, then a battling sheep farmer, and supplied wonderful photographs, together with a copy of team-mate Moss Christie's detailed diary from the 1924 Olympics.

Harry Gordon, superb sports historian, shared his considerable knowledge of Charlton's Olympic career and supplied me with a transcript of an interview with another team-mate, Ernie Henry. Stewart Alldritt, an Australian swim selector since 1982, meticulously checked facts on Charlton's career in the pool and supplied information on the changing strokes that led to the Australian crawl.

Thanks to my first contact, the eighty-five-years-young Jamie Jenkins, who still swims daily at the Manly Swimming Club, and to Ray Moran, who devotes countless hours preparing and maintaining records, newspaper clippings and photographs at Manly Surf Club. There I met Max Riddington, whose reminiscences of early Manly surfing days could fill a book. John McRitchie of Manly Library's local history department was always available and helpful.

Tony Merrett, grandson of Ossie Merrett, manager of the 1924 Australian Olympic team, supplied detailed information and Boy Charlton's godson Andrew Davies and his mother, Elanora, had first-hand knowledge of Charlton's association with the Davies family. Special thanks to my Swedish-speaking friend Yvonne Gersbach who gave up much time on a busy trip to Sweden to research Boy's greatest rival Arne Borg, and to Sallie Johnstone, nee Griffiths, for her help with the famous Griffiths brothers.

Swimmer Ken Knight, who swam at the Domain in the 1920s, and Olympic champions Murray Rose and John Konrads had happy memories of meeting Boy, while Christine Gelling gave me wonderful photographs of the young surfer with the dazzling Jantzen girls at Manly in the late 1920s.

Susan Franks at Hawkesbury Agricultural College found every reference to Charlton in the College *Journal* as did Mrs Benedek at Sydney Grammar School. Hawkesbury ex-students George Bennett, Tony Martin and Phil Clements were also most helpful. Shirley Coote of the Gunnedah Historical Society provided me with photos and information of Charlton's time at Kurrumbede.

It would be most remiss of me not to mention my editor, Lydia Papandrea, who was as patient as she was proficient. Last, but certainly not least, sincere thanks to our present superb Olympic champion Grant Hackett, a modest man in the Charlton mould, who very willingly wrote the foreword to the book. I hope it does them all justice.

Bibliography

Clarkson, Alan. *Lanes of Gold: 100 Years of the NSW Amateur Swimming Association*, Paddington, NSW: Lester–Townsend Publishing, 1989.

Dart, R.N. *Hawkesbury Agricultural College 1891–1941*. Sydney, NSW: B.E. Macarthur Press, 1941.

Fenton, Peter. *For the Sake of the Game: 1927/28 Waratahs*. Crows Nest, NSW: Little Hills Press, 1996.

Gordon, Harry. *Australia at the Olympics*, St Lucia, Qld: University of Queensland Press, 1994.

Heads, Ian and Lester, Gary. *200 Years of Australian Sport: A Glorious Obsession*, Sydney, NSW: Lester Townsend Publishing and Angus & Robertson Publishers, 1988.

Lomas, Graham. *The Will to Win: The Story of Sir Frank Beaurepaire*, London: Heinemann, 1960.

Wallechinsky, David. *The Complete Book of the Olympics*. South Yarra, Vic: Hardie Grant Books, 2000.

Weissmuller, Johnny Jr. *Tarzan, My Father*. Toronto, Ontario: ECW Press, 2002.

The newspapers of the day were extremely useful throughout my research for this book, in particular *The Referee* and *The Sydney Morning Herald*, which gave details of Boy's successes in the pools of Australia. Just as important was the diary of Moss Christie, kindly loaned to me by Murray Charlton, which provided a lot of the detail about the 1924 Paris Olympic Games.